D0225370

586267

ORGANIZATIONAL COMMUNICATION

COMMUNICATION AND SOCIAL ORDER

An Aldine de Gruyter Series of Texts and Monographs

Series Editor

David R. Maines, Wayne State University

Advisory Editors

Bruce Gronbeck • Peter K. Manning • William K. Rawlins

David L. Altheide and Robert Snow, **Media Worlds in the Postjournalism Era**

Joseph Bensman and Robert Lilienfeld, **Craft and Consciousness: Occupational Technique and the Development of World Images** (*Second Edition*)

Valerie Malhotra Bentz, **Becoming Mature: Childhood Ghosts and Spirits in Adult Life**

Herbert Blumer, **Industrialization as an Agent of Social Change: A Critical Analysis** (*Edited with an Introduction by David R. Maines and Thomas J. Morrione*)

Dennis Brissett and Charles Edgley (*editors*), **Life as Theater: A Dramaturgical Sourcebook** (*Second Edition*)

Richard Harvey Brown (*editor*), **Writing the Social Text: Poetics and Politics in Social Science Discourse**

Norman K. Denzin, **Hollywood Shot by Shot: Alcoholism in American Cinema**

Irwin Deutscher, Fred P. Pestello, and Frances G. Pestello, **Sentiments and Acts**

Bruce E. Gronbeck, **Rhetoric and Socioculture**

J. T. Hansen, A. Susan Owen, and Michael Patrick Madden, **Parallels: The Soldiers' Knowledge and the Oral History of Contemporary Warfare**

Emmanuel Lazega, **The Micropolitics of Knowledge: Communication and Indirect Control in Workgroups**

David R. Maines (*editor*), **Social Organization and Social Process: Essays in Honor of Anselm Strauss**

David R. Maines, **Time and Social Process: Gender, Life Course, and Social Organization**

Peter K. Manning, **Organizational Communication**

Stjepan G. Meštrović, **Durkheim and Postmodernist Culture**

R. S. Perinbanayagam, **Discursive Acts**

William K. Rawlins, **Friendship Matters: Communication, Dialectics, and the Life Course**

Vladimir Shlapentokh and Dmitry Shlapentokh, **Ideological Trends in Soviet Movies**

Jim Thomas, **Communicating Prison Culture: The Deconstruction of Social Existence**

Jacqueline P. Wiseman, **The Other Half: Wives of Alcoholics and their Social-Psychological Situation**

ORGANIZATIONAL COMMUNICATION

Peter K. Manning

ALDINE DE GRUYTER

New York

About the Author

Peter K. Manning is Professor of Sociology and Psychiatry at Michigan State University and holds a research position in the School of Criminal Justice. He has served as a Visiting Professor at Goldsmiths' College, University of London, the Sloan School, MIT, and SUNY, Albany and was Beto lecturer at Sam Houston State University in 1990. He was a Research Scholar at the Department of Justice, LEAA, Washington, D.C. (1974–75). While at Oxford, he was at one time a Fellow of Balliol and Wolfson Colleges and held a position in the Centre of Socio-Legal Studies. He is author and editor of 12 books and many journal articles. His current research concerns organizational communications, decision-making (with Keith Hawkins) and nuclear safety regulation.

ALDINE DE GRUYTER
A division of Walter de Gruyter, Inc.
200 Saw Mill River Road
Hawthorne, New York 10532

The paper used in this publication meets the minimum requirements of American National Standard for Information Sciences—Permanence of Paper for Printed Library Materials, ANSI Z39.48-1984.

♾

Library of Congress Cataloging-in-Publication Data

Manning, Peter K.
    Organizational communication / Peter K. Manning.
        p.   cm.—(Communication and social order)
    Includes bibliographical references and index.
        ISBN 0-202-30401-9 (alk. paper).—ISBN 0-202-30402-7 (alk. paper)
        1. Communication in organizations. I. Title. II. Series.
    HD30.3.M365   1992
    302.3′5—dc20   91-43555
                                                                                CIP

Manufactured in the United States of America
10 9 8 7 6 5 4 3 2 1

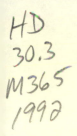

In memory of my sister, Nancie Lou Manning, 1942–1966, and for my brother, James Marshall Manning

Contents

PART III.   INFERENCES AND DIRECTIONS

Acknowledgments

The book is dedicated to my sister and my brother, and as always, is for my parents. This book grew from and was shaped by my friendship with Betsy Cullum-Swan. She helped me imagine its form and content, advised me on matters of style, and read most of it. Later, she encouraged me to finish it. I remain grateful for all that she has done for and with me.

I thank many other supportive colleagues: Steve Barley, John Van Maanen, Linda Putnam, Martha Feldman, and David Maines. They read parts of this and other messy manuscripts and provided comments. Keith Hawkins has more than once wrestled a weak metaphor or a slimy simile to the ground for me. I am very grateful for their patience, and careful unselfish critiques. I also thank my several colleagues in Oxford, and at Michigan State University, SUNY, Albany, and MIT. Glimpses of these ideas flashed in and out of my lectures, research duties, and tutorials in a period that was a wasteland for me—the mid-eighties.

I am grateful for the support and encouragement of Chris Vanderpool, chair of the Department of Sociology, Bob Trojanowicz, former director of the School of Criminal Justice, and Don Williams, M.D., former chair of the Department of Psychiatry, all at Michigan State University. Richard Koffler at Aldine smiled appropriately at some points and was demanding at others, and this is a better book as a result of his efforts.

One is inevitably shaped by lingering and swirling representations, ghosts and spirits (Bentz 1989), and what passes for "mood swings" in the trade publications. I offer a warm thanks to the patient and often brilliant listeners: Michael Hobbs and Barrie Biven. I suspect that there is always more to be said, if not listened to.

Peter K. Manning

I
THEORY

Organizing the Study of Communication

Introduction

The analysis of patterns and processes of organizational communication is a fundamental aspect of the study of social organization. Some scholars consider the communicational unit the essential or defining feature of all forms of social organization (Luhmann 1985). Unfortunately, although this interest in communication is focused conceptually, scholars lack a general framework for studying how communication is organized. For example, with some notable exceptions such as Chester Barnard (1938) and Anthony Giddens (1984), scholars have analyzed structure more than process, and agency or ends more than modes of enstructuration. The social structuring of communication, pattern or process, has received even less attention. The concept of organizational communication remains a rather restrictive gloss for the means by which organizations establish and maintain their boundaries and integrity.

A central concept of this book is organizing. Key to organizational communication, organizing is "a consensually validated grammar for reducing equivocality by means of sensible interlocked behaviors. To organize is to assemble ongoing interdependent actions into sensible sequences that generate sensible outcomes" (Weick 1979:3). Studying organizing means explicating the shared rules, codes, and norms that order sequences of mutually interdependent action, and how continuous marking and affirming of behavior by symbolic repertoires is used by organization members to interpret communication. This means that communication *is both context dependent and has generalizable meanings*. I hope this book will illuminate processes of organizing and the ways in which social actions are ordered by communicational (symbolic) means.

Communication—ambiguous, paradoxical, and equivocal—should be seen as a defining feature of human beings, and an appreciation of its vagaries is a valuable step toward a sensitivity to the diversity and sensibilities of people. We should question the kind of pragmatism that overvalues the role of the "facts" and the "bottom line" in problem-solving and in organizational goal achievement. *Ambiguity, doubt, and uncertainty are the essential and key features of modern life*. This proposition has several implications for the study of organizational communication.

Organizations, which attempt above all else to manage and routinize uncertainty, are constrained by a scarcity of time and resources, memory and concentration, narrow and limited roles, and organizationally sustained conflicts (Feldman 1988a). Focusing on the *outcomes* of organizing obviates the identification of necessary preconditions, the social processing of defining and ordering problems, often done without a clear and known design (Feldman 1988a).

Organizational action is instrumental (goal-oriented) action, but it is also expressive, setting out moral boundaries, reinforcing bonds, naming, and ordering. It is a means of "talking to ourselves" as Merelman (1984) puts it, or "enacting" an environment as Weick (1976, 1979) asserts. It serves to display the boundaries and features of symbolic worlds and to contain the fantastic symbolizing and emotive nature of humans. Such displays of symbols as sending memos, issuing directives, writing formal reports, parades, office parties, greeting and parting rituals, giving gifts, and even everyday events like games and television programs, are occasions for the observation of dramatic or expressive action.

Culture and expressive meanings cannot be isolated from social structure and social relations because they reciprocally mark and sustain morally binding obligations. Culture is a set of strategies, accounts, and rules of thumb, employed to cope with problematic situations (Swidler 1986). A significant facet of culture is the process of making readings of other peoples' readings and our responses to them (Geertz 1973).

The marking of some collective readings, shared and publicly communicated, as "different," is, in semiotic terms, a form of contrast signalling authority and power. Thus, rituals and culture take their meaning from the framing of differences. In line with this argument, while the traditional questions of communication process are discussed, this book focuses on the interpersonal and inter- and intragroup facets of external communication, and the communication of group integration and culture. It provides also a perspective.

The only way to have detailed understanding of organizational communication is to gather and analyze the communications found therein. This requires a systematic frame of reference such as dramaturgy. The organizational context for performing expressive action studied dramaturgically is illustrated here.

Dramaturgy

Dramaturgy requires a brief introduction (more details are provided in Chapter 3). The word *dramaturgy* is derived from the term *drama*, or the selective presentation (either by elevating or suppressing some aspects) of symbols constituting a message. Dramaturgical analysis seeks to understand the process by which communication expresses meaning and how this meaning is structured and orders social relations (Burke 1962, 1965; Gusfield, 1989). Examples of the workings of drama are seen in historical documents and literature, in poetry, and in banal materials like office memos, news clippings, or corporate annual reports.

The dramaturgists make a deceptively simple point: symbols name situations, motivate people, and express and mark social relations. The relevance of this idea in communicational analysis is apparent. Symbolic work (in this case speech) is a reality, a constraint, that exists *sui generis*. Talk is not "merely symbols," unrelated to the abstract structural entities of fundamental interest to social scientists. Symbols are real, effective, and affective, and symbolic action is powerful and constraining (Duncan 1968, 1969, 1985). These features of organizational communication, especially found in organizations issuing authoritative communication (governmental agencies and their surrogates), are of abiding analytic interest. Organizational action is social action, and is therefore one variety of dramaturgy (see Edelman 1964, 1971, 1987; Merelman 1984; Gusfield 1976, 1981). Analysis of dramaturgical action does not presuppose or require a focus on unit acts, selves, or indeed on interpersonal processes at all (Maines 1988; Maines and Charlton 1985). It has been studied as societal and organizational action (Blumer 1990; Edelman 1964, 1972, 1987; Hall 1972, Merelman 1969; Gusfield 1963, 1981; Goffman 1969, 1981, 1983b).

Studies that capture the notion of organizing best are rooted, on the one hand, in phenomenology and pragmatism and, on the other, in traditional social-psychological and social research on social structure, organizational and interpersonal structure, and process (Hall 1987; Hall and Hall 1962). Examples are discussed primarily in Chapter 4. The police and other institutions can be studied dramaturgically [see, for example, Goffman (1962) on the asylum, Blumberg (1967) on courts, and Denzin (1986) on Alcoholics Anonymous].

Dramaturgy studies symbolic action, and conceives of this exercise as a study of expressive meaning. It attaches particular importance to the ways in which *signs* [acts, objects, persons, or gestures that symbolize or represent something else in the mind of someone (Peirce 1931)] communicate aspects of social relations, or selectively reflect social relations within a group. Actions, like signs themselves, give specific signals or cues, but they also suggest, imply, or may be suggestive of other meanings as well. What is of interest is not only what is denoted by a sign, action, word, or display, but what is implied, connoted, or given off. The meanings of communications are often frozen by the capacity of those in power and authority to conceal contrary information, to lie, to dissemble, and to frame media communications. Such communications are found also within and between organizations.

Mechanistic and deterministic themes continue to dominate social thought, even in imaginative approaches to organizational analysis (Rappaport 1968; Hilgartner and Bosk 1988; Meyer and Rowan 1977; Perrow 1986). The notion that information and instrumental action determine the structure and function of organization remains, and is mirrored in the artificial (and perhaps meaningless) distinction made between "instrumental" (purposive, ends-oriented, functional, rational) and "expressive" (symbolization for its own purposes, as seen in ritual and ceremony) action. All social action is interpreted action or *conduct*, and thus always conveys something of the social qualities of the communicator, context, and communication. Social action, on the other hand, is always purposive, "motivated," or determined in some sense. What is central to defining a problem is an identified relationship between forms of action and ambiguity, between what is done and what is said, between behaviors and moral codes.

A first chapter should set the stage for a book, and my own natural history of studying communication may assist in this task. While studying primarily police organizations in the field, I began to recognize the extent to which studying organization is studying organizational communication. I consider my work since 1987 to be on organizational communication.

A Natural History

In several books on the police (Manning 1977, 1980, 1988a), the notion of organizational communication was refined from the study of rather broad propositions about the role of drama in policing and social control, and the resultant dilemmas Anglo-American police attempted to resolve, to a rather closer examination of the role of information. This process traced, in part, the communicationally based process of the *enstructuration* (Giddens 1984) of policing as a differentiated, informationally shaped formal organization.

The general proposition that organized the research and fieldwork carried out in London and in the United States in 1973–75, resulting in the publication of *Police Work* (Manning 1977), was that police communicate their purposes, authority, and societal role through rituals, collective celebrations, rhetoric, strategy, and tactics. This general idea, although valid, was gradually refined.

The differential emphases on aspects of organizational action, the connection of these communicational acts to a traditional form of (policing) organization, and the internal bases for mobilization of such dramatic symbolization was historically documented and linked to current practices. The police celebrate social values, and the links between these social values and the authority of the state are marked in their displays of force and violence. Police authority, granted by the deference of the public audience, produces, processes, amplifies, and suppresses differentially messages about the nature of the social order, and the ranking of groups (including themselves) within it. They reify their central sacred quality in societies with thin materials—few traditions, myths and little history—from which to embellish and renew sacred ties. By managing their mandate, they induce or persuade or make possible the cooperation of their significant audiences in their performances. It was rather easy to "see" how these ideas were associated with policing in England, and how they had less tenacity in America.

Having established that policing was in part dramatic action did not answer to what extent police organizations were information-dependent as opposed to expressively oriented in their actions. The *Narcs' Game* (Manning 1980) explored relationships within specialized police units between levels of information and resources, and between information and measured outputs or "effectiveness."

While the first two books addressed the role of information and ritual in the enstructuration of the police, as well as in communication with the public, *Symbolic Communication* (Manning 1988a) specifically explicated the invisible social machinery that shaped modes of processing calls to the police. This machinery works to define all that is taken to be information: it is a social construction technology. The organization of centralized call processing of messages within two police organizations in the United States and in England and the role of noninformational matters in sense-making were detailed. The pipeline theory of communication and a simple referential semiotics (the idea that words are pictures of extant reality and are more or less accurately descriptive) were challenged. The brief snippets of information conveyed in police calls were not, in and of themselves, sufficient bases for police action.

Police encoded and decoded messages consistent with their own visions
of the nature of problems. They applied their own routine solutions to
what they defined as the problematics of the calls. Information, if it
could be isolated easily within a call, generally little affected the nature
of the police response, since virtually all calls viewed as valid produced
the dispatch of officers in cars.

Since the analytic foci of the three studies changed, the sort of fieldwork undertaken changed as well. The fieldwork in London in 1973
focused primarily upon the internal bases for police cohesion and division, especially the meaning and significance of rules and authority. I
identified sources of the underlying paradoxes of policing that police
tried to obfuscate by impression management. Communication to the
police and processing thereof was deemed important only in regard to
its role in producing various paper representations of police work.

The *Narcs' Game* (Manning 1980) fieldwork, done in two departments
in the same metropolitan area in 1975, took up the nature of organizational constraint on individual action, given a level of information on
drug use and drug dealing within a jurisdiction. This focus meant using
a combination of tracking cases on paper, in meetings, and in raids, and
juxtaposing formal authority and plans with actual practices. Constraints operated to make ironic the formal bureaucratic planning and
authority of the drug police, and officers at all levels faced repeated
failure when plans were compared with outcomes.

In *Symbolic Communication* (Manning 1988a), based on fieldwork in the
American Midwest and in the Midlands of England from 1979 to 1982,
the focus was on police processing of calls. Calls from the public about
complex personal matters were converted into organizational communication that shaped police actions and decisions. Understanding the role
of the police communication system (PCS), which receives, encodes,
and allocates officers to the calls that are the basis for over 90 percent of
all police mobilizations (Reiss 1971), should be a key to understanding
the role of information in mobilizing the police. Fieldwork focused on
the PCS itself, the roles and tasks carried out, the codes used and coding
practices or interpretations made, and the computer-based technology
that enabled centralized call collection and disposal. By close tracking of
the flow of messages within two police organizations in two nations, it
became clear that noninformational matters shaped communicational
processing dramatically.

Symbolic Communication partially opened the black box (a device with
invisible internal mechanism, which—like a computer—was believed to
produce nonproblematic information) of police information-processing.
What sort of communication produces the sorts of messages and jobs
police are obliged to do? The observations and interviews were designed

so that one could ask how meaning sufficient for organizational action is produced from telephone calls ranging in length from a few seconds to a few minutes. Since the amount of information conveyed in such calls is minimal and yet is routinely seen as adequate, matters other than information must be operating to shape message processing.

This brief natural history suggests that conceptual refinement results from research and that research is required to specify many of the key aspects of organizing studied dramaturgically.

Concepts

Organizational communication can be variously defined. For working purposes I prefer to think initially of organizational communication as having two aspects. The first is the processing of information in message form into, through, and out of organizations. However, organizational communication also entails the analysis of all the nonmessage and noninformational matters and the performing of communication that shapes such "processing" of communicational transactions and gives them organizationally valid meaning. Thus, organizational research should explicate the social climate, social context, and formal structure within which organizational communication as performance takes place. Although social climate is a rather vague term, it seems to encompass the mood of social relations as well as cognitive processing of communication (see Poole 1985; Ott 1989). The social context, or what is brought to communication by the participants (Levinson 1983), is a feature of the organizational climate. Contributing to and shaping organizational climate and context are formal organization, the formal communicational systems of organizations, and situated patterns of discourse.

The assumptions that social relations are ordered as is language and that social analysis can draw on this analogy have stimulated some of the most recent important advances in conceptualizing social life (Hawkes 1977). Advancing this proposition brings us directly to the topic of semiotics, or the science of signs, which is the heart of the science of linguistics, the perspective through which organizational communication will be seen in this book.

The workings of signs, or signwork, are powerful bases for social organization. This book is primarily concerned with the interlocking social, cultural, and organizational connections made between a message and other messages, especially within the organizational climate. The redundancy of organizational communications, in part produced by routine ways of responding to a central or core stimulus in a message or

set of messages (Feldman 1988a), and in part by patterns of interpretations made by organization members of potentially discrete messages
from a message flow, permits concerted collective action. Working out
joint activities on the basis of shared meanings is essential for organizational survival. We will peer more deeply into sign work in the following
chapters.

A socioemotional or dramaturgical metaphoric vision of organizations
and organizational communication demands a subtle rendition of the
nature of human beings, and of our central feature, symbolizing, as well
as the nature of the communicational work. It should be recalled that the
study of symbols is, at very least, the study of the means by which
human beings lie. Society, as Simmel (1954) reminded us, is based on
secrecy, deception, and lies. It could not be otherwise. Organizations
thus are predicated on maintaining secrecy by the well-developed rhetorical means by which they produce the fronts, "lines," "scenarios,"
"spins," "tales," and "takes" that convey authenticity and sincerity to
the public and validate the trust on which their legitimacy is built.
Modern life, for most, is organizational life, but this does not deny or
reduce the quintessential sentient and symbolic nature of human communications. Let us look at more precise definitions.

Definitions

Four families of definitions are required to set out the conceptual
territory we traverse in further detail in subsequent chapters: information, organization, communication, and organizational communication.
They are cast within an informed dramaturgical perspective.

Information. From a closed-system perspective, information is anything that reduces uncertainty about the next part of a message. However, units and bits are socially defined, unlike electronic impulses, and
so "data" or what might be seen as stimuli or signals, should be distinguished from information, which is data to which response is made
(Kreps 1990:31). If we move from this to a more socially sensitive definition, such as Bateson's, new vistas open. Gregory Bateson (1972) calls
information a response to data, "a difference that makes a difference."
Social definitions, in part patterned by perception, selective attention,
and habituation, produce *meanings* that organize relationships to data,
people, and other information. Information is created by individuals as a
result of socialization experiences. The particular context of interest
here, formal organization, is a highly refined cognitive environment
where very precise meanings are cultivated, refined, taught, and
learned. Organizational meaning and information become conflated in

practice. They are encoded and decoded to maintain a sense of order and continuity. In this sense then, the idea of information cannot be easily separated from social context and from group relations that define how and what will be taken as valid, as real, and as socially relevant.

Organization (see Manning 1982a:118–25; 1988a:35–35). In a general sense, the word *organization* stands for formal organizations, with defined roles, tasks, hierarchies, and structures of authority (Haas and Drabek 1973:8–13). Organizations are relatively permanent and relatively complex (many norms, values, roles, and tasks guide organizational interaction) interaction systems with characteristic technologies and knowledge bases. Organizations are also social forms within which patterned, highly ritualized, and conventionalized interaction occurs repeatedly. The focus here, on ritualized and symbolic interaction, entails analysis of selected communicational patterns (who interacts, in what roles, how frequently, with whom, about what), internal communicational systems (both formal and informal), the organizational environment (that which is defined as outside the organization, but affecting its action choices), organizational boundaries, and the nature of loyalty and membership. These definitions also facilitate the analysis of communication with those organizations and entities that constitute the external environment.

From a communicational perspective, formal organizations have a number of primary features. Organizations are

1. ecologically delimited and bounded places in which densely configured interactions occur under a mandate or charter (its rationale or purposes) and mission (stated aims and goals as well as strategies and tactics—resource allocation decisions—used to obtain them)
2. filtering modes for screening and taking in information, and encoding, transmitting, and decoding it according to recognized conventions and tacit premises, i.e., social context or knowledgeability
3. sets of named roles and tasks ordered by authority (vertical and horizontal), a characteristic technology, and various rules for procedures
4. characterized by refined internal communication networks (which may be variously shaped or represented by technologies such as electronic bulletin boards, which link members both officially as well as unofficially or informally)
5. extensively communicating with networks of message sources clustered as markets, agents, competitors, and publics of various kinds (e.g., clients, customers, patients, students, general public)
6. means for converting nature into culture and externally generated messages into encoded and routine communicational units

7. political entities that cope with and both reduce and amplify ambiguity and uncertainty in the environment.

Organizational work is both self-referential or expressive and pragmatic, just as the actions of organizationally based actors are both expressive and pragmatic.

Communication from an individual perspective is sending messages with significance for others. From an organizational perspective, it refers to the collective representation of ideas. Messages can be given (directly observed) or given off (inferred). Any sign can communicate: any gesture, posture, word, material object, or arrangement of material objects can communicate to someone about something. This communicating includes gathering, processing, sending, and receiving information that enables organization members to understand the internal and external environment (see Kreps 1990:13). It has many functions: ambiguity-producing as well as -reducing, problem-solving, social differentiation and integration, relational functions (tying people together or separating them), and strategic functions (obtaining an objective, especially within a formal organizational context) (Conrad 1989).

The analysis of communication involves more than studying messages. Communication involves interpretation of actions and thoughts, and even imagined ideas and intentions. As Putnam notes (1986:152), one cannot study *messages* (networks of patterned sets of selectively assembled signs that are marked and conventionalized) without a close examination of *message factors*, or elements of the communication, the *interpretation* of these factors, and the *social context* in which they arise and are acted upon.

Organizational communication from a formal perspective is the processing of data in message form into, through, and out of channels formally designated within defined organizations, including the study of all the noninformational matters that shape messages. However, the study of organizational communication also entails exploring the implications of communication within that system: the rules and procedures governing the communication; the levels, boundaries, and roles and tasks within the organization; the continuous process of creating, affirming, changing, and enacting interlocking behaviors (Putnam 1986; Weick 1979); as well as the impact of patterns of external communication on internal communications.

These analytic distinctions may help to untangle communications logically, but detailed research upon communicational practice is needed because communications and response take place almost simultaneously in an encounter. As one person asks a question, the other is imagining the answer, interpreting the verbal and nonverbal aspects of the question, responding to the possible readings that the questioner may have of his or her response, and even while hearing, taking the role of the questioner or answerer in the next round or exchange. The net result may produce some mutually shared understandings, but certainly organizing is taking place.

Audiences

This book is designed to be used as a text for advanced undergraduates and graduate students in sociology, communications, social work, and criminal justice. It covers the content of organizational communication from the interpretive perspective (see Kreps 1990; Rogers and Rogers 1976; Conrad 1989). Selected themes and theoretical perspectives are articulated. Although it covers a wide range of types of studies, it is not a literature review of the field of organizational communication. The book is empirically based and illustrates ethnographic field research in the dramaturgical tradition. It is as much a book about doing organizational fieldwork as it is about organizational communication.

Although I retain great sympathy for the didactic value of the case method, and rich examples drawn from the "real world," my focus is upon process and organizing, matters that cannot be frozen in retrospective ad hoc summaries. I draw on the works reviewed in Chapter 4 and on my own work on public bureaucracies to illustrate the perspective. Studies of matters interpersonal and social psychological, especially those focused on internal processes, small group studies, and attitudinal studies, play a limited role in this book. This is not to say they are irrelevant to understanding organizations. The focus of this book, however, is on the production and reification of meaning, and this holistic matter cannot be reduced conveniently to properties of roles, individuals, or even offices.

Contents

The following chapters set out a perspective within which organizational communication can be studied. The materials presented illustrate information flow, message transmission, and strategic and instrumental communication in conjunction with analysis of the problematic duplicity and paradox, and descriptions of the often rich emotive tone of communication. The chapters contain detailed descriptions of the organizational contexts within which communication occurs. The book has several

themes: the utility of dramaturgical analysis, the constitutive effects of
language in shaping social relations, the role of paradox and its resolution, and the importance of considering both internal and external
communication. The book takes up two other main points: the utility of
ethnographic and field studies, and studies of organizational communication in a dramaturgical mode.

In brief, this volume aims to present a concise analytical framework
for ethnographic and qualitative analysis of organizational communication. It begins with an overview of types of communication in societal
context, outlines paradigms for the analysis of organizational communication, provides succinct examples of field studies of organizational
communication, and presents research supporting the utility of interpretive paradigms influenced by sociosemiotics.

Chapters 1–4 complete Part I of the book, which sets out theoretical
matters. This chapter sets out the focus of the book, illustrates the
dramaturgical perspective, and provides a few key definitions. Chapter
2 lays out some necessary comparative background on the nature and
function of communication in different types of societies. Postmodernism and the concept of a postmodern society are introduced. Chapter
3 reviews some of the major paradigms in organizational research and
the role of communication within organizations. The primary distinctions drawn are between functionalist and interpretive paradigms
broadly construed, and variations on the interpretive paradigm. The
featured dramaturgical/semiotic perspective that highlights the centrality of discourse and paradoxical messages is outlined here (and further
elaborated in Chapter 6). Chapter 4 includes work on eight styles of field
research: syntactical and semantic analysis, semiotic analysis, textual
analysis, text/record analysis, narrative and folktales analysis, organizational culture analysis, loose-coupling analysis, as well as a field study of
corporate managers. It suggests *orienting questions* that guide the analysis in the remainder of the book. What meanings are to be studied,
where they are to be studied, when they are to be studied, how, why,
and with what methods. The primary focus of this book is on how to
discover, by what specific qualitative methods and techniques, patterns
of organizational communication.

Part II of the book, consisting of Chapters 5–8, is subdivided into two
chapters that focus on internal communication and two that focus on
external communication. Chapter 5 presents two ethnographic field
studies of communication, one in the police and one in an agency
regulating nuclear safety. Chapter 6 is an ethnographically based analysis of communicational paradoxes and their resolution in organizations.
It draws on my study of police communicational systems and uses
message analysis to discuss double binds and paradoxical messages and

their resolutions. The role of organizational culture in framing and resolving the meaning of messages is outlined. The overall role of information in organizational communication is assessed. Chapter 7, the first of two on external communication, outlines the problematics of external communication in crisis and noncrisis circumstances, using examples from the American police responses to the murder of an officer and to changes in urban social structure. In the first example, several Dallas killings and a police funeral are discussed, while the second example covers the underlying bases for and assumptions of the idea of community policing. This analysis of police communication raises a question about the extent to which such communicational or rhetorical strategies resolve the underlying dilemmas of policing. Chapter 8 analyzes the "safety discourse" and various metaphors of safety used by the Nuclear Installations Inspectorate in Britain in its manuals to reassure the public and maintain its political mandate.

The third part of the book contains concluding remarks. Chapter 9 sets out a paradigm including roles in the field, targets for observation, settings for fieldwork in organizational communications, and analytic techniques. Sets of significant variables—personal, relational, structural—that shape messages are illustrated by examples from the message-processing of police. Special attention is given to the paradoxical character of many organizational communications, and modes of responding thereto. A section on the importance of narrative style in writing research reports on communication suggests themes in anthropology and literature that may be expected to continue to shape research debates in the future. Chapter 10 returns to themes in Chapter 2, and presents some of the promising features of postmodern ethnography of communication.

It is a truism to claim that all communication shapes and is shaped by the society in which it takes place. It is necessary to demonstrate how this actually occurs. Although the book is not historical in character, it addresses the differing nature of communication in primitive and modern (and postmodern) societies, as well as the perspectives of contemporary organizational communication analysts.

Organizational Communication in Context

Introduction

Communication is context dependent and draws on many social sources of meaning other than the content of a given message or series of messages. Sources of meaning may include very broad sociopolitical factors, such as the type of society in which it occurs. This chapter reviews the role and function of communication in three broad types of societies: preliterate, modern, and postmodern. Some aspects of postmodernism as a context for communicational analysis are discussed.

Communication in Context

The aim of this section is to compare the quality, function, and consequences of dominant forms of communication in different sociocultural contexts. This outline will provide the reader with a rudimentary understanding of selected similarities and differences found between preliterate, modern, and postmodern societies. Following Schutz and Weber (1947, 1964), the three societies are presented as *ideal types*, or selected, abstracted, idealized versions of societies in which certain features of analytic interest become the basis for the comparisons. The simplest and most basic point to be made is that size brings within it changes in the division of labor, social differentiation, and changes in the frequency, quality, and character of communications. In short, communication changes from face-to-face to some combination of face-to-face and mass communications. In postmodern society, tertiary or media-mediated experiences become the most common and salient. In this sense, the social types presented capture correlates of and changes in the nature of communication.

Changes in Communication in Types of Societies

Preliterate Societies

- Dense and closely articulated social relations.
- Shared symbols and symbolic repertoires.
- Roles are simplex (few sources, role signs) and sign vehicles are known and local.
- Social control is consistent and determined by many institutions.
- Intimate relations, family and kin relations, and ascribed statuses are key to ordering.
- Ecologically bounded and defined.
- Economically self-sufficient.
- Nonindustrial roles predominate.
- Money is absent.
- Communicational channels are shared.
- Networks are known, face-to-face communication is prevalent.
- Mass communications are absent.
- Bureaucracies are absent.
- Authenticity, authority, and the sacred coalesce.
- Sacred canopy of religion defines ultimate truths and dominates.
- Social and moral boundaries are clear and well-understood; moral categories are shared.

Modern Industrial Societies

- Social relations are loosely linked.
- Nonshared symbols and symbolic repertoires exist.
- Roles and sign vehicles are both local and national.
- Social control is narrowly defined and often formally determined.
- Intimate relations are embedded in diffuse and loose networks of acquaintances.
- Class, race, and achieved statuses are key to social ordering.
- Bureaucratic (service-based) work is central.
- Ecological boundaries are diffuse; national boundaries are salient.
- Knowledge production is valued (science, R&D, intelligence).
- Money is the great zero symbol having all possible meanings and none at all.

- Authenticity and authority coalesce.
- Secular knowledge legitimates meanings.
- Moral codes and boundaries are messy, and not well understood; moral categories are vaguely shared.

Postmodern Societies

- Social relations are keyed by media.
- Symbols are shared as media mediated.
- Roles and sign vehicles are massified, visual, distant, and artificial (created).
- Social control is reflected in media and weakly articulated.
- Nonintimate relations rise in centrality in shaping identity and self; family, kin, and other ascribed statuses are less likely to key ordering.
- Media societies are ecologically unbounded, symbolically entail experience of world events as "personal."
- Simulacra (images) are both creators and created of the desirable; the real is that which is capable of reproduction (Baudrillard 1988).
- Economically interdependent (individually and nationally).
- Work and leisure roles are in tension.
- Money is the great zero symbol, signifying all possible meanings and none at all.
- Shared communicational channels and networks are known; both face-to-face and larger, looser sets of mass communication networks key meaning and experience.
- Bureaucracies are work settings for most.
- Authenticity, authority, and the sacred coalesce.
- Secular meanings dominate.
- Moral codes and boundaries are messy, and not well-understood; moral categories are vaguely shared.

Having laid out these types, we are now positioned to ask what sorts of communications are characteristic of the emergent postmodern society, and how this postmodern view of the future differs from an alternative vision of the future, the knowledge society thesis.

The Challenge of Postmodernism

Changes in the nature of social relations clustered into these types of societies have important implications for the nature, functions, and quality of communication. The marking of social relations, the differentiation of groups, the cultural and social ranking and differentiation of individuals within groups, the transmission of information, and expression ("culture") are altered fundamentally (Guiraud 1975). Organizational communication becomes more common, and is the working model for many modes of public communication. These changes are strongly influenced by media logic and the formats of the media that arise to coopt and control information and meaning in the postmodern world (Altheide 1979).

We can scan these ideal types or somewhat exaggerated depictions of societies for relevant implications for the study of communication. To some extent, the focus and examples will inevitably dwell upon present modern, urban, Anglo-American societies, and the nature of communication processes in these societies. This does not imply a linear progression of societies, or a high degree of homogeneity of communicational processes within them. These are empirical matters to be established. However, some of the most important facets of the postmodern ideal type of society can be noted, as can the implications of these facets for communicational analysis. In an important sense, the reader should attend most to the changes in the various dimensions listed, and try to see modern and postmodern societies as variations on earlier patterns.

It is important to recognize that recent developments in social theory have suggested that mass communications are now the principal driving force in social relations and social change (Baudrillard 1988; Lyotard 1984; Denzin 1986). Although it is as much an antitheory as it is a theory, postmodern theory is both a characteristic perspective within and a feature of contemporary society (Denzin 1986). Postmodernism is a reaction to modernism, the nineteenth-century philosophy that saw rational progress through knowledge and science as inevitable (Berman 1988). Postmodernism is a kind of antitheory that rejects metanarratives (even though it is itself a metanarrative!) or totalistic rational explanations. Postmodernism eschews metanarratives such as Marxism, Freudianism, sociology, and scientific reasoning generally. (Metanarratives are story forms that define the nature of reality.) Postmodernism elevates to centrality imagery and appearances, rejects cultures as wholes, seeing them as cacophonies of signs, suffused with pastiche and parody, and reflects a painful reaction to the perceived failure of rationalism and social planning and the exhaustion of social thought (Manning 1990a). Communication in postmodern societies will differ in kind, amount, quality, and location, and organizational studies should take these changes into account.

Postmodernism has connections to French sociology and American pragmatism and symbolic interactionism (Manning 1990c; Clifford 1988). It is quite clear that the social roots of postmodernism—disillusionment with rationality and illusions of progress, and the failure of modern liberalism to cope with overwhelming irrational and surreal forces of change—are also the principal sources of French sociology (Lévi-Strauss 1945; Lemert 1990). Postmodernism also shares many intellectual roots with American symbolic interactionism because it contains an important place for spontaneous, nonrational actions, highly situated and emergent meanings and symbolic bases for thought. Ideas at the center of the postmodern challenge, such as the relevance of pragmatic action within given contexts rather than principled decisions based on dogma or ideology, are consistent with those of the leading American pragmatists (Rorty 1979).

The similarities between postmodernism and symbolic interactionism are important, as symbolic interactionism is the central sociological social psychology. The irrational and semiconscious aspects of symbolic interactionism have an enduring tradition, and share the same origins: the Bergsonian vitalism and Hegelianism craftily assembled with pragmatism by Mead (1934). Symbolic interactionism has an enduring interest in describing in detail symbolic aspects of life. It elevates to centrality the spontaneous interpretive self and the role of the situated and negotiated order, and has shown a passionate resistance to formalization and systematization. Postmodernism is not a systematic theory, but a *perspective*.

Postmodernism as Perspective

Postmodernism studies totalities as collections of images, sets of *simulacra*, profusions and collections of signs. Postmodernism questions, doubts, and distrusts all forms of knowledge, especially those claiming universal and transcendent truth, objective wisdom, or absolutes of any kind. Postmodernists not only doubt and eschew such ideas or systems of thought currently in use in industrialized societies, they reject the notion that such knowledge is even possible. Even if it might be possible to produce such knowledge, it will be of dubious validity.

Writers in the postmodern style seek to reconstitute sociophilosophic analysis after the disillusionment of intellectuals with enlightenment and progress, assembling fragments of meaning now existing in a moving, shifting pastiche. Postmodernism is a critical perspective used to dismiss traditional modes of thinking in natural and social science: it is antiscience and anti–social explanation and asserts as a central feature of postmodern society the emptiness of social thought.

The perspective is critical of the assumptions of rationality made by theorists of modernity, especially Jurgen Habermas (1979, 1984), and sees the decline of literacy, the intellectual culture itself, and the rise of electronic language as all of a piece (Agger 1989). Some postmodernist themes are antirational and surreal (see Schneiderman 1983; Baudrillard 1988:Chs. 5 and 6 on seduction and death).

All writing and speech, even the most precise and clear examples, will contain self-contradictory and obscure meanings (Derrida 1976). Perhaps to point out the rich figurative and metaphoric resources of communication, and its uncertain and volatile aspect, postmodern writers pun bilingually, play with metaphors and tropes, and drift rather easily into allegory and hyperbole. While totalistic generalizations are to be assiduously avoided, abundant and contentious general observations about the nature of capitalism, the media, or politics punctuate postmodernist writings. Postmodernism presumes the inability to understand fully "reality": indeed, distinctions between reality and appearances are false, factious, and misleading. Such distinctions deter an understanding of the arbitrariness of all such distinctions. The postmodern observer sees a myriad of signifier-signified relationships (understood almost tacitly within life worlds), and an abundance of signifiers whose referents are unknown and unknowable. As a result, even the quest to pin down reality leads only to other signifiers referencing yet another set of signifiers, and so on. The vague sense that there is something more to existence than mere images and symbols, the desire to consume even more symbols, maintains both a tension and deters the realization that behind images are still more images, a plague of signs.

Postmodernist writing concerns what things are *not*. It seems to be wary of full confrontation and exploration of the nature of the human situation that results from the absence of order and markers for reality. It rejects positivism, and operational or statistical aggregations that seek cumulative, ordered, comparable editions of the true rendered by accurate successive and cumulative approximations. Power writes that postmodernism "seeks to make visible the fact that there is something which may be thought but cannot in principle itself become visible or represented" (1985:3). In one sense, Power refers to the semiotic axiom that signs take their meaning from difference (that which is not stated, such as the mental distinctions made between the signs a, b, c, d). A sign is fundamentally incomplete without an interpretant, that which makes the links known. Postmodernism shares with its progenitors in French structuralism a preoccupation not with surface manifestations of features of what is taken to be the social, but with identifying the structures or principles that underlie or order these "surface features" (Culler 1975).

Changes in Social Relations and Communication in Postmodern Societies

Let us take up the kinds of social relations and *communicational processes* suggested as typical in contemporary Anglo-American societies by writers in the postmodern tradition (Baudrillard 1988; Lyotard 1984; Deleuze and Guatturi 1976; Denzin 1986; Lyotard and Thébaud 1985). A number of significant changes in communication and in social relations in postmodern or "postmodernlike" societies can be identified. They are given here in no particular order, although some of the points listed above as characteristic of types of societies organize the outline.

Both the degree of intimacy and certainty in communication decline in postmodern society. People share fewer close, intimate relations governed by known and agreed-upon values, standards, and moral codes (or rules for interpretation). In this case, public communication, especially among strangers, is not likely to be embedded in known premises, use shared vocabularies, and manifest similar symbolic repertoires (sets of symbols such as cliches, slang, framing remarks, and rituals that introduce them). Ambiguity and equivocality increase. Ambiguity is reflected and amplified even as variety is reduced. The possibilities for marking social relations unambiguously decrease. Ambiguity and uncertainty in communication are assumed and taken for granted especially in interactions with strangers and mere acquaintances (Wuthnow 1987). These tactics of hedging and "face work," maintaining one's own face, themselves reinforce the sense of ambiguity and chance as salient in interpersonal relations.

The self becomes fragmented, in part because a surfeit of information, an information overload, exists (Klapp 1978). The level of socially unwanted communication, noise, increases as well. Klapp (1986) terms this increase in unwanted communication "bad redundancy." Thus, while vast amounts of information may be available, they are both distrusted and often satiating or anxiety producing.

As the quality of social relations changes, the potential for misrepresentation, lying, deception, and betrayal increases apace. It should be noted that two features of human beings are symbolic and linked: their capacity freely to use symbols (mainly language) and their ability to deceive themselves and others, to lie or mislead (Rappaport 1971).

Images and impressions substitute for personal experience. As a *simulacrum* or image, a signifier or expression without a signified or content (Baudrillard 1988), is widely reproduced and reified, especially by the mass media, it becomes a commodity. An image, especially one produced and reproduced by the media, is no longer tied to experienced reality or the reality of everyday life. It becomes an independent reality unto itself: "the media provides the public with the illusion of reality and actuality" (Denzin 1986:196). The reality to which imagery refers is the reality created by imagery (other images) and the hyperreality (signs about signs taken as objective or universalized opinion or truth) it produces and reproduces. Thus does imagery embed communication. Communication arrives both in abstract and general categories and immediate experiences that may be in contradiction.

The mass media increasingly set out the *formats* within which experience is cast (Altheide 1979) and they dramatize and reify *programs* or plans for action or plans to be organized and consummated at a later time (Perinbanayagam 1985:105). These media influences enhance the reflexivity (self-awareness) of action choices.

As a result of the surfeit of mass-produced images, formats, agendas, and plans, gaps arise between interpersonal meanings and mass-produced, media-mediated meanings. These may grow and become the source of new forms of alienation and distance among group members. Rather than deracination and rootlessness, people in the postmodern period feel various forms of difference and similarities to the imagined feelings of others.

Self and other, group and group, economic dependency and ecological boundaries are blurred by nationalistic ideologies. With the new nationalism and chauvinism come attempts to define truth and produce a hegemony of authoritative definitions of truth, of the right and proper. Authority substitutes its force and violence for interpersonal standards or sacred standards used to construct truth.

No longer the source of truth, science and knowledge are increasingly reflexive. That is, they both make claims to truth and control the standards by which truth is to be determined. Both serve to define the nature of information and produce it as a consummatory good sold as a service. *Truth is determined by authority relations of various kinds.* Scientific language is as vulnerable as any to reinterpretation and distortion, and can no longer represent or correspond to "reality" (Rorty 1979).

In spite of the growing power of science, scientific knowledge, like other attempts to create total or holistic explanations, is discredited. Authority substitutes for truth. Jean-François Lyotard (1984), the French philosopher, argues that these metanarratives are distrusted and are in decline. Only the linkages between state authority and science sustain the overt credibility of scientific research and findings.

Language categories used to establish the correct, suitable, and proper are messy and not well-understood. "Political correctness" substitutes for honesty or integrity. Moral categories and rules are not shared or, if shared in the abstract, are not interpreted in shared ways (see Denzin

1986; Lyotard 1984; Wuthnow 1987). This layering of consensus is a feature of the "crisis in representation" associated with postmodernism.

The twin notions that communication entails, includes, and always involves corrective negative feedback and that "meaning" is established when an intended message is received are untenable. For example, if organizational communication is thought of as "strategic" (Conrad 1989), then the management of the appearance of understanding is as important as clear and ambiguous communication (Jackall 1988). One manipulates the rules. A recent Sunday supplement published a list of rules for office politics and success that included lies, misrepresentations, self-deception, and the management of appearances to avoid appearing too competent, skillful, or ambitious (*Detroit News*, April 1989). Competent management of the appearance of sincerity is sought. As soon as one masters the appearance of sincerity, one has it made in the modern world.

Modern communication is not based entirely on shared social values, and edges along the lines of "working consensus," whereby the appearance of agreement is sought. The organizational preoccupation is more with achieving surface agreement with agreement on basic value premises. Lyotard (1984) has argued, in a theme that parallels Habermas (1984), that language should be merely adequate to situational exigencies, or performatives that guide and outline action choices, rather than a means for communicating absolutes in generalized forms of authoritative communication. Language is only an attempt that will surely and truly fail to represent the layers of untruth, and so can be used merely to play with the "unrepresentable" (Denzin 1986:202) or that which is unsayable.

The real is what appears to be so, or is merely reproducible (Baudrillard 1988). These reproducibles, or signs that stand for something, circulate and are produced and consumed as goods. Signs are desired, valued, and exchanged. Performers sell themselves as persona and use their persona to sell yet other images.

This sketch perhaps makes clear that although preoccupation with communication is generic, and knowledge of communicational processes is fundamental to social order and ordering, communication has changed in nature and function in modern and postmodern societies. Words change in function from achieving coherent expressive and instrumental aims embedded in shared contexts, to shabby instruments. Or as Heidegger says, they become vehicles like streetcars, which anyone can jump on and off. The tools needed to study communication change. Rather than verities, one seeks only differences. It is not surprising that semiotics is the working tool of the postmodernist; as Eco writes, "semiotics is in principle the discipline studying everything which can be used in order to lie" (1979:7). The term *truthful communica-tion*, according to Goffman (1959), indicates nothing more than whatever an audience will accept as true. Communication in modern times is the study of that which completes the sign [which, as Peirce (1931) writes, is "fundamentally incomplete"], and therefore alerts one to the study of the interpretant, context, and the field.

It is not clear that a linear movement to postmodernity has taken place, for many feel that knowledge and rationality have conquered the deep irrationalities of our times. Countertrends exist in modern social thought, and some observers reject the postmodern thesis. Some remain sanguine, even hopeful, and suggest that a "knowledge society" based on science and rational knowledge is now emerging.

A Knowledge Society?

An alternative to the postmodernist thesis is the knowledge society thesis.[1] This thesis sees modern industrial society as increasingly knowl-edge and science driven and patterned by the rational application of knowledge to social problems (see for example, Bell 1973; Bohme and Stehr 1986). The thesis appeals, unlike that of the postmodernists, to the central preoccupation of intellectuals: the notion that salvation will re-sult from knowledge. According to Bell, knowledge is now the central and ever-growing basis for authority and governance in industrialized societies. The argument, in succinct terms, claims that science, a set of procedures for producing meaning, increases and amplifies the authori-ty and relevance of knowledge and the level of self-awareness of society, and it patterns the growth of high technology. Yet science in turn is patterned by structures of meaning. Technology, admittedly, may drive science. However, a third set of factors, such as political power, may shape both. In "a knowledge society with penetration of all its spheres by scientific knowledge" (Bohme and Stehr, 1986:8), it would seem that the feedback loops from science to technology, technology to science, and from both to other structures of meaning are complex.

Several weaknesses in this argument, as persuasive as it is, are impor-tant for their bearing on communication studies. Significant in this argument, and other versions of it that seize on the phenomenology of the production of all forms of scientific knowledge (Latour 1988; Latour and Woolgar 1979; Knorr-Cetina 1981; Ashmore 1987), is the absence of a close analysis of the role of the power and authority of the state in funding, censoring, amplifying, and suppressing differentially all that will be seen as legitimate knowledge. Unquestionably, the state has a superordinate role in the production, control, and dissemination of knowledge as well as the distortion and use for political aims of all that passes for knowledge. In addition, there are variations in the role of the state in participation in such patterns across developed societies, as well as within the developing sector. In addition, internal variation in the meaning and or consequence of "knowledge," and the differential distribution of knowledge in elite, ruling, and scientific groups, are both questions bearing on the validity of this thesis. There are certainly different forms of knowledge with quite different utility functions.

It would appear that a series of issues consistent with the knowledge society thesis are contradicted by a set of disturbing and powerful counterthemes.[2] The postindustrial society thesis overlooks a very significant contra-puntal theme: the growth of "antiknowledge" and anti-intellectual themes in modern industrial societies. Is there a sustaining culture of knowledge, rooted in coherent elites and governmental agents, or are these fragmented and distinctive sectors? Does respect for knowledge and its creation and preservation embed knowledge technology and the techniques by which it is communicated?[3]

These questions are lucidly evoked in postmodernist writings, and the complex relationships between information and culture have long occupied political theorists (Berman 1988; Harvey 1989). The information-based society does not efface the effects of massification and the dedifferentiation of traditional bases of social order. Rationality and science insinuate themselves into and mediate everyday life while serving to erode the validity and perceived utility of folk wisdom (Dr. Ruth and Dr. Spock, "the Frugal Gourmet," and Julia Child now serve as surrogate media-designated "moms" and "dads"). While there may be growing dependence of business, government, and the professions upon scientific knowledge or at least systematic, organized knowledge ["usable knowledge" as Lindblom and Cohen (1979) term it], it is increasingly seen as yet or merely another "tool" for manipulating people, making businesses grow, "reaching" customers, and the like.

Knowledge, technology, and legitimation are uneasy partners, and increasingly law, a knowledge system not much discussed among post-industrial theorists, marks the limits of control and authority. But is law based on consensus and shared social values or is it just a communications-processing structure? The most powerful and original treatment of the role of law in modern societies is found in the work of the German sociologist, Niklas Luhmann, especially in his brilliant comparative theory of law and legal evolution, *Sociology of Law* (1985). In his view, law is a normative means or set of *procedures* for processing conflict that does not rely on societal consensus or patterns of normative agreement to reach decisions. Law works solely on the basis of expectations (tacit agreement to honor the procedure and the outcome) about expectations (the nature of law jobs) shared by those who choose to litigate. Luhmann believes that a kind of minimalist agreement exists among participants in litigation to accept binary, court-produced "outcomes." Matters other than the legitimacy of the procedural structure as a means of generating solutions to conflicts are differentiated and bounded as irrelevant to the work of law in modern society. This suggests that knowledge is less important than images and expectations about procedures and institutions.

The nature of cultural fragmentation and confusion that accompanies the rise and increased power of science destroys the traditional context within which "knowledge," "wisdom," "science," and even "scholarship" grew and flourished. Massification produces a society where knowledge becomes yet another form, the content of which is banal, empty, trivial, and reduced to the common denominator. This is an argument about the inadmissibility of the knowledge society on cultural grounds, and is found in the works of Ortega y Gasset (1932) and Theodor Geiger (1969). These critics of contemporary society explicate with disgust the powerful deracinating effects of homogenization of experience and taste and the destructive consequences of the dedifferentiation and massification of society.

Finally, the disappearance of the self as a bounded, continuous, and sensate locus of being proceeds (Sypher 1963; Lemert 1979a). In this sense, the diffuse sense of responsibility, the failure of nerve and courage, and the reshaping of persons into passive consuming units adds to the amorphous and non-knowledge-based character of modern experience.

These several themes are easily illustrated with reference to everyday observations. Witness the arrogation of knowledge and cultural hegemony over matters medical by private corporations and resultant loss of authority once granted the professions. This new power and authority exists without the structures of accountability once represented by local communities and patterns of informal social control of clientele choices (Starr 1983). Notice how the public face of religion has deteriorated into a series of pruriently "exposed" media-generated spectacles, shabby exploitative commercialism, disingenuous confessions, and "falls from grace." Consider also that other professions are increasingly submerged in commercialism and self-seeking economistic calculations: the "bottom line" and ways to seek and take the main chance shape career choices and practice location. Note also the declining regulation of scientific developments by government, and the "privatization" of science. Even the FDA and other agencies in the health field are granting greater power to the drug companies to market drugs, especially in the cancer and AIDS fields. Science and carefully experimentally controlled testing of drugs is giving way to the more "efficient" market forces. These trends are also immediately obvious after even a brief look at the burgeoning biotechnology field and related computing and high-technology industries (Rogers 1984). Note the erosion and reduction of scholarly traditions and protections such as the abolition of tenure in Britain. Knowledge is distressingly both created and controlled by cynical commercial interests. Even treason has become a commercial venture. See daily the increasing distrust and cynicism directed toward science and scientists, and public exposure of evidence of fraud and plagiarism among academic scientists. Scientific knowledge is reduced to the trivial information gathered in polls, consumer data, advertising surveys, and electronic intrusions into life in the form of tinny voices at the end of the telephone saying, after a long pause, "Hello, I have an important call for you. . ."

These developments suggest that although knowledge in the abstract may be increasing, its symbolic or imagery role is more central than its traditional functions. The growth of knowledge is only one feature of social change.

A major role in altering the context within which knowledge is produced, used, and sold is surely played by media, as Baudrillard (1988) has powerfully and cynically pointed out. Observe the systematic exploitation of ignorance and irrationality by national politicians, amplified and escalated by shallow-minded media reporters and "talking heads." See, in the presentation of routine news, the escalating lust after knowledge for profit. Events fabricated by the media for meretricious purposes become the dominant factor in many lives, and the media reflect back to viewers the media's preoccupation with their own vapid "personalities," hairspray-created bimbos, and overpaid "stars." What is termed "in-depth news" is a flickering sequence of brutal scenes and close confrontations with survivors and families completed by 30-second summaries of the "situation in the Middle East." Reduced to their hairdos and eye shadow, performers, rather than journalists with writing, researching, or judgment skills, are paid millions to pontificate about matters they do not understand, analyze, or care about. Telescoped media events substitute for direct experience. And these collapsed events, keyed by iconic cues and narrative sequences, increasingly are created, amplified, and reflected back at us by advertising people and actor/puppet politicians.

In these media-created pictures, icons of our modernity, the banal is glorified; hymns are sung to soft drinks and to cars; men lust for beer; women crave the right scent; everyone is empty and like any other object, in need of being filled. . .with something. Emptiness and fulfillment are both sold as oscillating and desirable state of being (Barthel 1988).

In summary, this argument overlooks the changes in the meaning and use of knowledge; the hermeneutic process of interpretation stands between "technology," "science," the media, and the protean self. It is not knowledge that drives social relations, but the reflexivity and subjective interpretation of events given meaning in institutional and organizational contexts. Science, increasingly, serves the state and broader commercial interests rather than objective or even pragmatic goals of creating new knowledge.

Implications of Societal Context
for Studying Organizational Communication

Several important implications of the change in the meanings and uses of communication are outlined in the knowledge society and postmodern society notions. They surely affect importantly and should shape the foci and methods employed in field studies. There are at least five important implications of the influence of postmodern thinking and postmodern themes in modern life. Subsequent chapters will specify these criticisms and research strategies that will provide clues to the design of empirical studies.

Social science desperately needs well-done field studies of organizational communication that address the relationships between information, ambiguity, uncertainty, and deception in the observed work of signs, or signwork. The surface features of organizational life, such as the growth of word processing, workstations, and high-technology record storage and use, must be understood as a function of the codes and power relationships governing their use. Institutional codes or rules for communication may themselves be manipulated, used, and played with to achieve pragmatic ends. Records are expressions of various forms of social compromise by those who create them (Manning 1977:Ch. 6, 1980, 1988a:Ch. 8). Absolute notions about organizational loyalty and integrity are subverted by situated rhetorics, which are themselves subject to reinterpretations and *deconstruction* (Norris 1982). Lies and deception are tied to self-serving so that ethics disappear under the bottom line (see Jackall 1988).

Social science also needs narrative studies, and studies of organizational culture that reveal life as it is experienced and "lived" (or at least talked about!) within the megaorganizations dominating modern society. Tales and narratives are to be considered not as so many representational truths, but as "as if pictures" of the social world, perspectival paradigms, and minirealities shaping experience. Talk of all kinds, as Erving Goffman (1974:Ch. 12) reminds us, is "loosely coupled" to the world. It serves to locate members of encounters in social relations rather more than in a physical or material reality. It is this very feature that makes social life possible: talk is a rendition of the world as experienced by the speaker, and in that sense talk functions to ground the speaker in a relationship to an audience, as well as to the events depicted. Hence, the centrality of gossip, work stories, jokes on oneself, and the like in conversations.

More studies are needed of the social production of knowledge and information. Information, especially acontextually presented official information or propaganda, is reified and takes on major importance in the media and in everyday life (see Ericson et al. 1987; Altheide and Johnson 1977; Johnson 1989). The social networks that generate this information and lend credibility to truth claims should be stripped bare of the pretense of objectivity and neutrality, and the hierarchy of credibility closely examined.

Research should explicate the links or contexts connecting signs and signifiers, and sets of signs and social life. For example, how is one to understand the nature of modern organizational communication and how it binds speaker-hearer or audience-performer?

A difficult topic, perhaps an oxymoron, is postmodern ethnography, more of which are needed. This is ethnography that reflects sensitivity both to the perspective and to the features of the age that gave rise to it (See Manning 1990a,b,c; Cullum-Swan and Manning 1990). What would such an ethnography look like? Here are some suggestions:

A postmodern ethnography focused on communicational process should show a concern not only for choice of the proper and suitable field techniques and methods, but sensitivity to the range of available modes of representation and literary *genres*. The novel, the journalistic report, the travel log, the anthropological monograph, and the photographic essay are equally valid modes of representation of a field of processes. These techniques and genres may be combined, and fragments and shards of events seen from various perspectives may dance in and out of a narrative. Events and lives seem less centered, and the self less remote as an explicable cause of events; thus, chance and indeterminacy, not causality or correlation, are central to experience.

Postmodern ethnographies should facilitate the development of new approaches rooted in a deep appreciation of the fundamental perversity and *unpredictability* of human conduct. New understandings of how people deal with uncertainties and the media-saturated nature of this experience are needed.

Postmodern ethnographers should write reflective and reflexive texts that take into account (interweave) the subtle demands of making sense of others' conduct as well as one's own. Also required is a sensitivity to the location of culture in discourse and in the *image* or model of reality that constitutes the *experience of the other*. Such writing requires an understanding that while studying societies as wholes in a comparative fashion, one should encourage systematic, often intertextual, integration of the native's and the observer's *perspectives*. It would appear that social context, that which the observer brings to the object, as well as the field in which the object is constituted, is critical in the analysis of the written representation of objects and in a sensitive work of deconstruction (Marcus and Fischer 1986:vii). This may mean playful adjustment of perspective, subject/observer roles, or modes of presenting materials. Such new modes of writing should not obviate an ability to set ethnographic questions and the ethnographic moment in broader political, economic, and historical perspective.

Relativism and historicism remain: social *spaces*, not space as a universal or transcultural concept, are to be appreciated, and *times*, not time, are to be valued (Harvey 1989). Much is also expected of intuition and insight, knowing and reporting what is unsaid and perhaps *unspeakable* (Tyler 1987). We return to these matters in the final chapter of the book in the section on postmodern ethnography.

Perhaps a general conclusion or recommendation can be stated at this point. A proper ethnographic study must analyze the role of context in meaning production and reproduction in full detail. This requires seeing how context transforms communication at each critical point within the organizational communications system.

Conclusions

This chapter contains important themes about the nature of communication and the social functions it plays in three types of societies. The knowledge society, and the societal type called by some postmodern, in which all facets of communication have become growth industries, are discussed in some length. Implications of these types of societies for field studies of organizational communication are discussed.

Communication functions in social context and in the structure of social and cultural relations, and cannot be studied outside them. In this book, the setting of focal concern for studying communication is formal organizations, social forms that are, to a greater or lesser degree, always embedded in larger patterns of economic and social organization. The material reviewed in this chapter should allow us now to consider the role of theoretic paradigms, or the assumptions about the social structures within which communication functions, in organizing studies of organizational communication.

Bear in mind the rather different theses about the role and consequences of information and communicational modalities in society pointed out in this chapter as you read further in this book. Close observation combined with a critical attitude to theories and models and observed behavior that sensitize observation are critical to bringing off excellent qualitative field research. Does the research discussed indicate such a radical shift in the paradigm within which researchers view their research and their research problems? Are the problems of management different if authoritative language is being undermined? In order to connect notions about societal-level influences on communication suggested by the above-described changes in social relations in modern society, to interpersonal and sociolinguistic bases for communication, more formal models of the functions of the sign and of the communicational act are needed, and these should be linked to societal context.

Paradigms in Communication Research

Introduction

Various loosely connected ideas or paradigms, sets of assumptions about communication and society, organize research on organizational communication. It is important to set these out at this point because the book will hereafter be written within the interpretive paradigm, which combines discourse analysis, semiotics, and the loose coupling metaphor.

The first section of the chapter takes up several paradigms within which organizational communication research based on qualitative or field methods is undertaken [adopted from Putnam (1982) and Krone, Jablin, and Putnam (1987); see also Fisher (1978) and Dance 1982)]. These paradigms reflect assumptions about the society in which organizational communication takes place. Several themes discussed in Chapter 2 are echoed here: the need to develop paradigms that reflect the fluid, changing, symbol-suffused character of modern society; the changing role of variously connected signs; the increasing prevalence of information and high-technology information processing. Even though these paradigms provide the basic assumptions on which research is based, they are rarely explicitly presented in a research publication. They are assumed, and can be considered the source of *images*, or root metaphors that guide and sensitize systematic thinking. As the philosopher Suzanne Langer (1951) has written, these images are the stock and trade of the mind.

Two broad views of communication, the interpretive and the functionalist, are contrasted here. The *functionalist paradigm* uses a few select root metaphors for communication, or ways of seeing one thing in terms of another, drawn from physics and information or systems science (e.g., "mechanistic," "cybernetic," or "organic"), to depict organizational structure and function. The *interpretive paradigm* includes work in the hermeneutic, symbolic interactionism, and ethnomethodological traditions. It is based on ideas drawn from dramaturgy and phenomenology. [For a more detailed discussion of these matters in the context of the theory of complex organizations, see Burrell and Morgan (1979).]

In later sections of the chapter, two of the most important ideas salient in the interpretive paradigm, *discourse* and *loose coupling*, are discussed. Some of the limits and problems associated with loose-coupling theory are noted in the last sections of the chapter. These sections outline the guiding perspective of this book, drawn from the work of Karl Weick (1979), which combines a sensitivity to the loosely coupled nature of communication with an interest in paradox, language, and discourse. This overview will enable us in subsequent chapters better to appreciate the intersection of theory and research that of necessity guides good scholarship.

Paradigms in Communication Research

The word *paradigm* is useful in discussing approaches to organizational communication. It should be remembered that the concept is "borrowed" and, like all borrowed concepts, is a bit shabby and shopworn, and can be slightly misleading. *Paradigm*, as used here, must be distinguished from its nature and uses in the natural and biological sciences. In communications research, as in sociology, there are no firm, clear, and exclusive schools that constrain and guide thought and research as there might be in physics, biology, or mathematics (Kuhn 1970). Many ways of thinking, or perspectives, are characteristic of the social sciences, but social sciences are not sharply delineated paradigm-based fields in the sense that physics is. This has several implications for research. The central ideas that organize communications research may be drawn from several paradigms, and ideas from one are not contradictory or mutually exclusive of ideas taken from other paradigms. Researchers draw on research from many disciplines, cite authors who are working within other paradigms, and are often more wedded to technique (e.g., statistical analyses) than to given theories. No critical experiments have the power dramatically to alter the nature of contemporary thought and procedures, and no key or fundamental texts contain *the* accepted conventional wisdom about a field's concepts. Finally, no broad, accepted theory detailing the nature of the basic phenomena of interest exists in the social sciences. On the other hand, critical experiments, key texts, and an abstract theory are found, for example, in physics, molecular biology, and DNA studies.

Bearing the limits of paradigms in social science in mind, we may offer a tentative definition of a paradigm as a set of assumptions about social relations (or actions) and social structure, and the elements of ordering and defining action (norms, values, ideologies). Quasi-paradigms also exist. A quasi-paradigm nears wide acceptance in social science; it will contain both explicit and implicit ideas about the nature of social reality. Quasi-paradigms guide research strategies or methods (such as field research, survey research, or experimental research), and even tactics or techniques for mobilizing research (statistical tests, economic models, documentary research). Quasi-paradigms contain dominant metaphors, or ways of seeing, and they are useful to group broad sets of ideas or theorists.

Functionalist Views of Organization and Organizational Communication

Putnam's excellent review argues that "the functionalist paradigm dominates the major research traditions in organizational communication" (1982.198). Drawing on her review, the following sets out variants on the functionalist view that will be contrasted with an interactional/interpretive perspective. Two subversions of the interpretive paradigm, discourse analysis and the loose-coupling metaphor, are discussed near the end of the chapter. The dramaturgical perspective of organizations, which guides this book, is an interactional and interpretive paradigm, and is the context within which the research approaches outlined in Chapter 4 will be discussed.

Functionalism

The functionalist tradition, inherited by communications research from scientific management and industrial sociology (which lives on now in business schools), embodies a concern with the effects or consequences of communication. This means that communication is seen as a means to achieving an official (managerial) end or goal. From management's point of view, the purpose of communication is achieving stated official (i.e., managerially defined) goals. Virtually all sociological theories of formal organization are suffused with the assumptions of functionalism (Perrow 1986). Functionalist theorists emphasize efficiency, rationality, goal attainment, and managerial control and guidance of communication.

Functionalism derives its heritage from F. Taylor (1911) and Chester Barnard (1938), and is enshrined in the tradition of scientific management. It addresses the manner in which communication (rational or not) serves to enhance the work performance of employees (therefore, by implication, tying it to reward systems and how they are communicated to employees), vertical and horizontal communication, command and control, and effective means of achieving outputs.

Counterthemes, sharing the same premises about human beings and their communicational patterns, emerged under the title of the (also functionalist) human relations school (Mayo 1933; Roethlisberger and Dickson 1939; and later, Likert 1961; McGregor 1960). Its adherents argued from a belief in the relevance of social relations as the basis for rewards, not merely formal monetary rewards, to good communication as a very significant vehicle for improving morale and increasing production. Thus, shared group ties, good interpersonal relations, personal security, widespread decision-making participation, and the like (early versions of Japanese management?) were advocated. Good communication rooted in interpersonal relations was seen as functional and as guided toward accepted ends.

After World War II, broader notions of conflict within the organization and between the organization and the environment were seen in the social sciences. A variety of functionalism, e.g., "natural" functionalism, associated with the work of sociologists Parson (1949, 1951), Selznick (1949), and the early Columbia-influenced Gouldner (1954, 1959) and Blau (1960) appeared. These writers emphasized adaptive and evolutionary aspects of social organization, balance or equilibrium maintained between organization and environment and internal forces. These forces included both the irrational and rational, and formal and informal organization. With the rise of conflict theories, systems/information theories arose and facilitated more diverse metaphoric thinking about organizational processes.

Systems/Information Theories

An important subtheory within the broad functionalist umbrella is the systems/information theory cluster (see Haas and Drabek 1973). The systems metaphor was adopted from biology and modified to include the naturalistic, evolutionary themes of post-Darwinian biology. Systems theories emerged from the influence of engineering and communications theory upon organizational analysis.

The works of Von Bertalanffy (1968) in systems theory, of Burns and Stalker (1960) in sociology, and of Lévi-Strauss (1963) in anthropology did much to demonstrate the utility of the metaphor of the "communicational system" as a basis for social analysis. Before moving on to the organizational implications of functionalism, it is important to review the "pipeline" theory of communication drawn in large part from systems theory.

Perhaps the most common construction of organizational communication is what might be called the "pipeline" model. This model sees senders intentionally sending messages (as preestablished units) along a channel or medium of communication to be received as understood by receivers. A caricature of the pipeline theory of communication, one that would see the sender standing at one end of some channel, with messages known to have been received when receiver acknowledges them, assumes that communication is a relatively closed and unproblematic process. It assumes the (shared) orientation of sender and receiver, a nonproblematic channel, and standard units of information as content. Meaning, or that which converts data into information, is seen as an allusive and secondary aspect of information transmission. This model was developed by engineers whose interest was the transmission of units, where "operator error" was of little interest when compared to the capacity of the equipment to carry the stated number of messages at a given level of noise, quickly and cheaply, between two points (Shannon and Weaver 1964 [1949]).

This sender-message-channel-receiver model of communication, modified by Jakobson (1960), is widely used in social psychology. Much communicational research uses an (often unexamined) pipeline model that sees "irrationality," "inefficiency," and "dysfunctional organization" as a result of the intrusion of unwanted noninformational aspects of message processing. It may be useful for attitudinal and reductionistic studies, but is of little value for dramaturgical analysis, which studies symbolically articulated performances in social context (including various and changing audiences) (see Rogers and Rogers 1976). As we see later, this pipeline model conveys a dubious and rather flat model of human communication and of sentient human beings, and it has therefore both moral and intellectual consequences. It ignores what is most human about us—sentiments, passions, excess, blindness and collective ignorance, and the embodied nature of social life. It relegates what is primary to secondary position: the symbolizing and language use by which human beings select, retain, or reject environmental stimuli and their images of these matters contained in their recipe knowledge (Schutz 1962), stereotypes, rules of thumb, and taken-for-granted-assumptions (Garfinkel 1967) and communicate these to others.

In systems theory, organizations can either be seen as "open" or "closed" systems, depending upon the degree of influence that outside messages and forces have upon internal communication patterns (Scott 1987). What is viewed as an organization is an "organizational system": a layered system of subsystems arranged hierarchically usually by authority, and linked by communications. The principal function of these systems is to process information, and this in turn shapes internal structure in some dynamic fashion. Complex feedback and regulatory functions maintain internal equilibrium and a niche in a market or a position within a set of competitors. Uncertainty maintains an important function, as does coping and use of strategy by organization members around characteristic patterns of uncertainty (Crozier 1964). The focus is upon patterned activity, rather than individual actors and their functions within the organization.

The capacity of the organization to maintain its boundaries is very critical to organizational survival. Variants on this theory, which combine information theory with functional-evolutionary theory, are called "evolutionary" or ecological theories of organization and focus on survival and growth as compared with decline and death (Rappaport 1967, 1968, 1971, 1984; Freeman and Hannan 1989; Young 1988). Whereas the early functionalists emphasized the role of normative ends, social values, or rules in defining organizations, the later form of functionalism makes communicational processes themselves the defining characteristic of formal organizations.

Interpretive Views of Organization and Organizational Communication

Theories Revealing Variations on Rationality

Several recent developments in organizational analysis have moved away from the narrow individualistic rational-decision model that is featured in the rational choice theories and classical decision theory. March and Simon (1960), John Meyer and associates, and Weick (1976, 1979, 1988), moved functionalism from its focus upon purposive action and narrow forms of rationality to explanations of socially patterned variations from rationality (Elster 1985). They altered and sharpened the focus of research on the informational-based, cognitive decision structure of organizations, and have modified the open-systems perspective.

March and Simon have shown that decision-making is based on a variety of factors other than information and that even stated organizational purposes are often vague, unknown to the actor, or multiple in character. Decisions are a function of prior actions of organizing and are shaped by social matters. Communication is often as much about symbolic matters, ideas, beliefs, and assumptions as it is about information (March and Olsen 1976; Feldman and March 1981). In this view, organizations possess an "invisible design" (Feldman 1989), which stands independent of known norms, rules, and values. This emergent order is nevertheless communicated tacitly, through routines, and has an ordering effect over time.

Meyer and Rowan (1977) have argued that organizations without a clear task base, especially those in the public sector, will decouple from—maintain a distance from or avoid clear evaluation from—the environment by means of myths and ideologies. These maintain organizational boundaries and autonomy. This freedom or autonomy is reproduced within organizational segments in which results and evaluation, rewards and tasks, goals and means are loose and seemingly uncoordinated with the stated official goals.

Weick introduced (1976, 1979) and elaborated the metaphor of loose coupling (see Orton and Weick 1990). Weick sees loose coupling as a central metaphor for organizational analysis and *organizing* as the process of patterning organizational communication. He has argued that loose links or loose couplings exist between information and action, deciding and information, organizational subsegments and the organization as a whole, and an organization and an environment. The loose-coupling metaphor has generated a wide range of innovative organizational analyses (Orton and Weick 1990).

Loose coupling is a formal cognitive model of how people respond to, define, and label organizational "things." Loose coupling, in that sense, captures the actor's subjective perspective on complex and often interlocked choices and systematic actions (Weick 1976:2). Enactment is the means by which "thoughts," "decisions," and meanings are displayed; it is a form of creating understanding because enacting an environment produces the "raw data" from which meaning becomes clear.[1]

The concept of loose coupling draws on Simon (1969), and is a conception of contrast based on relationships within and between systems and subsystems. If systems are composed of stable subsystems, then relationships *within the subsystems* may be tighter than relationships *between the subsystems composing a system*. (Weick 1979:3). The concept then requires comparative, systematic, processual research based on a design that uses such differences as data. Using the concept of loose coupling to describe a system flashes an *imagery*, or dances a metaphor for characterizing complexity. This imagery differs from the imagery of systems theory, of interdigitated hierarchically integrated closed systems, or of a competing, adaptive organism within an ecosystem.

In research influenced by the loose-coupling metaphor, organizations are seen as some combination of internal problem-response routines, patterns of variously uncertain external environments, and structures of authority (Meyer and Rowan 1977). Complex organizational structures are seen as developed rather than as constituted a priori. Emphasis is placed on the creation and maintenance of symbols and symbol systems that either (a) reflect "reality" (material, technological) or (b) create reality. Decision-making and the bases for deciding, such as the interpretation of interpretations (hermeneutics), are seen as shaped by various noninformational matters. Stories and tales may aptly and succinctly render a version of some problematic within the organization (the nature of authority vs. the role of individual choice). Myths that explain the existential problematic at the root of the organization (e.g., the notion that policing controls crime, even if crime is beyond control) are central to understanding stability and legitimation. Some emphasis is placed upon the importance of negotiation and the emergent negotiated order that emerges from inner and intraorganizational transactions (Maines 1977).

Semiotic and Dramaturgical Theories

Semiotic and interpretive theories focus on the symbolic or representational aspects of organizations, and on the differential use of symbols to account for and mark social relations. Semiotics can guide field research sensitive to the importance of semiotics as a means to elaborate the shape of the social mandate of the organization, its overall ideologies, codes, key symbols, and practices (see Manning 1987a). Some variations on structuralism are relevant for the study of organizational communication.

Semiotics is the science of signs, and studies how signs mean in everyday life (Eco 1986). The most general features of semiotics are found elsewhere in more detailed summaries (Eco 1976, 1979; Hawkes 1977; Saussure 1966; Culler 1975).] Semiotics, which is based on a model drawn from linguistics, studies representations or signs, and although language is but one among many sign systems (chemistry, fashion, manners, highway signs, music, Morse code) it is taken as paradigmatic.

The basic concept of semiotics is a sign. A sign is the result of a mental connection made between a sound and an image. It works in contrast to other sounds and on two levels: the series of "horizontal" items to which it is connected (as words are in a sentence) and in "vertical" associations such as metaphors or clusters of similar meanings. The largely "unconscious" model of the workings of signs learned by the communicant functions in tandem with structure to produce meaningful communications. This is the great advance of semiotics: objects, meanings, things, words, indeed any sign vehicle that carries a message, have no inherent meaning. They become meaningful only in context. Thus, a basic proposition of semiotics is that system precedes meaning.

The original ideas of semiotics are associated with the writing of the Swiss linguist Ferdinand de Saussure. His ideas are important in communications research for two reasons: because they provide the fundamental theoretical structure of most modern linguistics and because the model of linguistics (pioneered by Lévi-Strauss and others in the social sciences) is a source of metaphorical or analogical thinking about social relations.

Several features of the sign should be noted. The combination of a sound ("cow") and an image (picture of the cow), an expression (or *signifier*) and a content (or *signified*), when linked, mentally produce a sign. Yet, a sign cannot exist alone. The sound and the word in conventional terms are heard as one, but meaning comes from *arbitrary* (culturally determined) contrasts. Any meaning is a result of difference or contrast between two items, linked at another level, typically, for example, by simile or metaphor—"the police engage in a war on drugs" that is, association of one idea (policing) with another (war); synedoche—a part stands for the whole or vice versa—police are "the long arm of the law"; by opposition—hot vs. cold, up vs. down, red vs. green. Other *tropes*, or modes of linking signifier to signified, such as extended irony, are widely used in the social sciences (Brown 1977, Darley 1983a:396).

Since the connections between expressions and contents are arbitrary, the context of the linkage is important. In fact, various meanings can be attached to given signifiers. The same signifiers can be linked to different signifieds, given a context. This leads to puns, figurative by- and foreplay, and when extended, to metaphoric configurations of social relations. Think of the homophonic list (1) *you two*, (2) *you, too*, (3) *you two*, and (4) *U2*. In the first three examples, one links the words to someone other than the speaker, or the disembodied other, and in the last example to the twentieth letter of the alphabet and the second number in a system of counting, more than one and less than three. Within the context of rock music, the latter representation, *U2*, also signifies an Irish rock group and reflexive identification (as in "we, the singers, are you, also"). *U2* also indicates the American spy plane piloted by Francis Gary Powers, which was shot down over the Soviet Union in 1959. Although concrete referents can be easily identified in the sentence, "Go and get the ball," not all ideas have specific locations. Abstract concepts take meaning from the setting or context of their use, e.g., "profits," "the bottom line," "justice," "scholarship," or "love." The relationships between words and actions, in short, are culturally defined. In French, water is *eau*, in Spanish, *agua*; the same thing is, in that sense, indicated by different sounds.

Signs are also clustered into meaningful sets as a result of codes and coding. The process of coding, which is a mental and therefore cultural activity, entails grouping a set of expressions and a set of contents, messages, by some ordering principles. Think of Morse code, a way of interpreting dashes and dots as words. Codes may be variously tight (as in mathematical formulas) or loose (as in American etiquette), and the relationships between the signs in the code may be analogous (treating a man as if he were a "pig") or homologous (mathematical formulas). When the relationships are analogous, they work on connotation, and in lengthy versions lead to extended figurative exercises, allegories, tales, myths, legends, and political ideologies.

One narrow definition of culture is what we assume they know they know and what we assume they know they know we know. Since the *interpretant*, or that which links expression and content, changes given the context, changes in the interpretant lead to changes in meanings. (In one of the above examples, "rock groups" are the assumptive interpretants, while in another it is "national security"). Interpretation by individuals using shared codes produces stable meaning. Meaning does not inhere in the signifier (a word, a gesture, a symbol, or a collective action).

Links made between signs in context indicate types of social relations. The links may be direct or indirect. Two sorts of meanings are critical in communicational analysis. *Denotative* meanings are associated with or carried in part by the sign vehicle (that which carries the expression such as an automobile, or a dress), while connotative meanings are more general and broad such as "gender" or "class," which might group the signs displayed by or on a dress ("very feminine," or "very fashionable"), a car (a BMW indicates a "yuppie on board"), or a suit. [These meanings can be clustered either as a list, or within or by association with a paradigm.] In everyday life, however, both metonymy and metaphor work simultaneously to produce meaning. Consider, as an example of the combination of metonymic and metaphoric meaning, the word *yuppie*. *Yuppie* is constituted initially as a metonymic associatoin—young, urban professional—and was probably originally used by advertising or computer people to name a variable for entering data onto a computer for analyzing buying or consumption patterns. Since "hippies" were the synecdochical group (as a part, they stand for an age, period, or decade) representing the cultural (connotative and even mythological) sense of the sixties, the extra *ie* or *pies* was added as a rhyming pun, and by analogy suggested that yuppies are the hippies of the present day. *Yuppie* was reified, or used as if it referred to an actual interacting collective unit, or a status group, real people with shared life interests. As a result of this, a single indication of the "yuppie life-style," such as "running shoes" worn to work with suits or dresses, was seen as one part of an entire symbolic repertoire (see below on overcoding). *Yuppie* as a group was used as an ironic pun with hippies as synecdochical (part = whole) indicators of the era of the sixties (a connotative and metaphoric association). *Yuppie* now is used as a term of derision for any currently popular or fashionable life-style preference or status symbol. Perhaps it captures envy and resentment of those who are ambitious and successful, just as *hippie* spoke to envy and resentment of those of middle-class origins who apparently rejected the conventional ideas of ambition and success. The word became an ideological weapon for the media and others to use to confer meaning. Created by the media for their own meretricious entertainment purposes, the term now begins to shape selves, choices, and experiences. This sequence of changes in location, referent, and use of a symbol's meaning might be considered a semiotic spiral amplified by the media.

Metaphors are one type of trope, or style, as are irony, synecdoche, and metonymy (Burke 1962; Manning 1979a; White 1980; Richardson 1990). In taking on a trope, or writing style, one asserts a way of seeing the world. In this sense the paradigms discussed above are extended metaphors or allegories of communication. To say organizations are systems is really to say that they are like systems for the purposes of this analysis, or that they are like living organisms or machines for the purposes at hand. It is good to hold metaphors loosely, for they conceal as well as reveal. The dramaturgical view taken here, for example, may mislead one into reading too much into an action, just as a machine metaphor of communication based on the pipeline theory may lead one to read in too little!

When a metaphor, or a way of seeing one thing in terms of another, is extended, as suggested above, one finds *metacommunicative* strategies, or ways of sizing up situations that encompass time and space. Organizations operate fundamentally by providing members (and clients, customers, patients, etc.) with organizing metaphors. Myths, allegories, tales, and legends are extended metaphors that incorporate motives, histories, values, and purposes of whole groups, organizations, or societies. When these ideas are explicitly political, or explain power and authority relationships, they are termed ideologies.

Semiotic concepts, taken together, are a means for prising open the culture that lies within and behind even very simple messages such as greetings—Hi, Hello, How are you? Hey! Yo! Good morning, Cheers, and so on. Messages are *indexical*, or partial indications of the work of signs, in metonymic, metaphoric, and other associations. Strings of signs are clustered as messages or texts, and become tropes, or ways of seeing, in time.

Many communications are ambiguous, and often they "float" because the conventions are not clear. This is increasingly true in complex, media-satiated societies. Thus, forms of power and authority, operating through rituals and ceremonies, serve to "pin down" meanings and stabilize the links between signifier and signified. The ritualized posturing and federal government propaganda that accompanied the attempt to convince people that something was being done about illegal drugs in the United States in 1988–1990 employed the metaphor of a "war on drugs," connoting violence, an enemy, targets, and eradication and/or total surrender to isolate one drug, "crack cocaine," and its users. This concealed the primary drug-related health problems caused by mood-altering prescription drugs, tobacco, and alcohol, which are used by all classes and races. It was instead an attempt to sanctify alterations of civil liberties (e.g., locker checks and drug tests at work), and the use of violence, and to mystify and dehumanize the victims sacrificed to the conventional morality. The expression *drug* is equated with illegal "crack," and a new sign, with connotations of risk, addiction, death, and crime, comes into being and stands as the basis for a "war."

Recently, for example, Giddens (1984), drawing on the works of Goffman, Cicourel, and Burke, has explored how meanings (and time and space variations on them) become a part of the structure of organizational action. Organizational structure is on the surface the elements or patterns of rules, and social relations (encounters and face to face copresence) are articulated by discourse and ideology (Gidden 1984). Rather than being dependent upon information, organizations are embedded in *trust*, and must deal with equivocality and uncertainty in information and noise. Surface relations must be seen in terms of a deeper code or structure that makes sense of the often conflicting surface events. An environment from which communication flows must be interpreted and constructed, regardless of the networks from which the communication emerges or arises (dense, close, loose, tight, redundant, etc). Processing of information means that data are chunked, coded, organized mentally in narrative and tales, formatted within by organizationally sanctioned forms and means, and made symbolic. In short, raw data become encoded cultural materials within organizations (Weick 1979; Manning 1982a, 1988a). The material constraints are reflected in organizational discourse and not the other way around. These ideas are consistent with the perspective of this book.

Paradox and the Double-Bind Concept

A primary variant from the functionalist perspective highlighted in the dramaturgical perspective is the role of paradoxes, contradictions, and double binds (see Bateson 1972; Watzlawick et al. 1967). As discussed above, organizations, although they are socially constructed frameworks for the interpretation of communication, become in time *reified*, or *defined as real*. This means that they are socially constraining, objective, and defined as having an existence "external" to individual actors. They are social facts. The power and authority of organizations are in the final analysis symbolic, but they are seen as real, and therefore are real in their consequences (Thomas and Znaniecki 1918–20).

Organizations contain a slender thread of rationality that dominates rhetoric and accounts for decisions, but on close examination, many rationalities coexist with a dominant rationality. Multiple realities or perspectives differ as a result of the organizational roles and locations of individuals. They exist within organizations and pattern perception. These realities are sustained because short- and long-term aims, goals, and objectives, and personal and group agendas, although rational, may be inconsistent or in contradiction with each other.

Some messages may be given readings that are paradoxical or contain elements of mutually exclusive action demands. These may be informal messages, rather than directives, and are simply taken for granted rather than understood explicitly. In the police, for example, detectives are expected to produce clearances (an organizationally acceptable outcome such as an arrest, confession, or warrant for an arrest) of crimes by gathering interviews with witnesses, victims, and alleged offenders, undertaking investigation of the facts and evidence gathered, and making telephone calls primarily. Yet they are expected to keep up with their paperwork. The first produces more paperwork, and one cannot both gather more material and reduce the material at hand. This is a paradox resolved in an organizationally acceptable fashion as we shall see below.

However, a simple paradox may be embedded in a paradoxical cycle (Putnam 1986), or a series of mutually contradictory messages that evolve over time. In this case, the two alternatives posed are "nonexistent alternatives," sometimes expressed in commonsense terms as "you can't win for losing" or "the faster I work the behinder I get." In policing, a paradoxical cycle arises in patrol work in disorderly areas. If one uses the arrest sanction to control order problems such as loudness or hanging out on corners, it increases the citizens' animosity to the police and reduces their willingness to give the information and support necessary to police such an area. If, on the other hand, one uses violence, threats, harassment, and informal sanctions on youths, then police authority may become personalized, or seen as radically motivated. Citizens may nevertheless protest to the media that "nothing is being done" about the drug problem or "crack houses." This may lead to "self-help" (Black 1983) actions such as burning reputed "crack houses" and to a loss of police authority in such areas. The "no-win" nature of this paradox remains for officers because either approach leads to inefficaciou٠ outcomes and responses.

System contradictions or mutually exclusive alternatives may reside within a system. The police orientation to crime control is such a system contradiction (Manning 1977:Ch. 9) because there is an apparent contradiction between the objectives and consequences of concerted efforts to attain them. Organizational analysis, as discussed below (Chapter 6), must identify the sources of contradictions and paradoxes as points calling for careful research, and must identify the characteristic responses of the organization studied (see Putnam 1986:163–65). For example, an important strategy used by organization members for responding creatively to contradictions is *metacommunication*, or communication about the binds inherent in the messages. Research should establish the nature and content of these contradictions as well as the range of patterned responses possible. These questions are best answered within the framework of a version of the loose-coupling perspective combined with discourse analysis.

A Theoretical Framework for Organizational Analysis: Loose Coupling and Discourse Analysis

It is now time to draw together some of these theoretical strands. We must explore the relevance of the connection between the concept of loose coupling and discourse analysis for field studies of organizational communication. We have already suggested that the concept of loose coupling is a subtle and vexing one, and that the many definitions of loose coupling suggest closer analysis of the relationships between the concept itself and the guiding subparadigm, metaphor, or perspective of loose coupling. This analysis, in turn, will permit a more refined discussion of discourse and coupling.

Loose Coupling

Loose coupling is the central concept or metaphor within a perspective or *frame of reference*. It is not a theory in the sense of a set of formally stated logical relationships from which inferences, propositions, and hypotheses can be derived. As a perspective, loose coupling provides accounts of states of systems, internal and internal-external transactions as sustained by cognition, and technology and structure.

The loose-coupling concept and the loose-coupling metaphor both draw on the imagery of open-systems theory. Proper use of the loose-coupling concept, if this formulation is true, would appear to require the existence of at least two identifiable, organized (hierarchically ordered?), articulated (joined by at least two variables) systems, or a system and its subunits or subsystem, with known transactions occurring within and across them.[2] These two articulated systems of analytic interest are assumed to be joined such that variables can be named and operationalized to measure the relevant relationships. Of special interest to Weick are *changes* or responses measured over time, across concrete instances, events, processes, or organizations. Changes in the shape of organizational systems resulting from adaptation made possible by loose coupling are also of interest.

Connotations, or implicit meanings, play an important role in the paradigm. The 1976 Weick article contains at least 15 implicit meanings of the concept (p. 16). A useful example of the importance of connotations as a sensitizing device, perhaps, is the kinds of adjectives used to describe relationships said to hold between subsystems, systems, events, acts and intentions, formal goals, and actions in (Weick 1979). Words such as "eventual" "occasional" or "negligible" suggest patterned ambiguity in the relationships to be studied as well as the effects of social context (or contextual effects) on their meanings. Linking relationships are described using words that are commonly or likely to be indexical (context-bound) in character.

Loose coupling is useful in exploring dynamic processes.[3] It is a temporal metaphor for logically organizing sequences of interfaces, interlocks, cognitive maps, and networks (cf. Cohen and March 1974). Loose coupling is the key feature of the idea (see Chapter 4) of organizing. This focus suggests that neither producing meaning, or the subjective interpretation placed on events, nor organizing itself is a direct product of systemic relationships of the kind suggested by variable analysis.[4]

Any formal model of coupling is subject to shaping by social context. These shaping forces produce patterned ambiguity. The capacity to capture these subtleties makes the loose-coupling perspective a rather nuanced way of looking at particular organizations. At least two important sociological sources of patterned ambiguity exist. The first is the effect of *context* on meaning (Weick 1976:10). Analytically, context is defined here in part as what is brought to an interaction and in part as an emergent product of mutually interactive dependence relationships between more than two people in an organizational frame of reference. The second is the *location of cognitive processes of interest within organizations*. Where do these lie: in group divisions, loyalties, collective memories, rituals, and traditions, in short, in an organizational culture? [These two forces change the nature of the content referred to by altering the *form(s) of coupling* of interest.] Loose coupling thus has many meanings because it is a rich and variegated polysemic concept, and it is central to a metaphoric rendition of organizational dynamics and organization-environment transactions. Some facets or aspects of the perspective are now discussed.

Loose coupling provides a contrasting conception to certain overly rationalistic theories of organizational behavior, and is especially apt in settings in which people are inclined to account verbally for their behavior in terms that deny ignorance, error, or nonrationality. Loose coupling refers to various metaphoric renderings (descriptions) of observed anomalies and apparent paradoxes identified within functional theories of social systems. The perspective is antifunctionalist and ironic, best seen in contrast to its near versions in ecological or open systems theory. This critical stance shapes the examples and gives the arguments an almost poignant quality.[5]

Throughout his work, Weick refers to the limits or constraints on understanding, and the way in which "enactment" substitutes for full understanding. There is a sense in which Weick "meditates in writing," considering as he does the nature of the human condition, and the esthetics of existence, as did Weber when he noted the inevitable growth of rationality, "the iron cage," in modern society. The argument concerning the conditions under which loose coupling evolves and is sustained is an investigation of the dimensions of the human spirit. It implies the need for choice and autonomy over centralization and authoritative determinants of collective action. This brings us to the central role of discourse in loose-coupling research.

Discourse and Coupling

Discourse analysis is the study of talk, both formal and informal, and written texts of all kinds. Discourse is found in chunks and pieces and is studied in units larger than the sentence (Potter and Wetherell 1987:7). Discourse analysis takes many forms, from quite detailed formal strategies, to less precise and general analyses of historical developments in social relations guided by structural change (Foucault 1977). The overall goal of discourse analysis is to link coherent discourse with other patterns of social relations. Unlike sociolinguistic approaches that use artificial or fabricated instances, discourse analysis chooses to study the "natural" and to combine the situated study of practices with talk. It seeks to explicate how the creation and maintenance of social relationships is expressed in talk.

Both the concept of discourse and modes of coupling play a central role in the analysis of organizational communication. The central role of discourse is revealed if one sees it as the means by which the complexity of the environment, as defined by participants in the organization, is translated into organizational action. Causal indeterminacy characterizes environments conducive to loose coupling. Causal indeterminacy is perceptual, verbal, and attitudinal, and refers to actors' shorthand summaries of the environment. Loosely coupled processes, in short, speak not to the nature of the external environment, but to the nature of the reality of the perceived environment. Perceived complexity exists for many reasons: because actors lack sufficient insight, facts, or accumulated systematic knowledge to work out cause maps, because this is in the nature of the material and or social world observed, or because this is a generalization based on empirical data gathered on some types of environments (Burns and Stalker 1960).

In research influenced by loose coupling, one might ask what features of the material or social world correlate with loose coupling. What are the conditions under which loose coupling rises (cf. Meyer and Rowan 1977; Orton and Weick 1990)? Of particular interest in this regard is the role of history (the development of organizational structures) and technology in determining the evolution of organizational communication patterns.

Role of Discourse in Organizational Analysis

Discourse is widely understood to shape choice and define options (some of the following points are adopted from Manning 1987b:85–86). Discourse serves to formalize knowledge that is vague, tacit, and assumed. Central in the functions of discourse is "knowledgeability" (Giddens 1984:2–5ff.), information known but the precise effect and cause of which is not well understood by actors. As Giddens points out, the sources of motivation are diverse and include both conscious and unconscious factors; and the degree of understanding of discourse is both conscious, denotative, and connotative, as well as semiconscious and not well understood. Further, any set of actions will contain the possibilities of producing unanticipated or unintended consequences. Praxis, or explicit and pragmatic action, so overvalued in management texts, produces a consciousness that Giddens terms "practical consciousness" (p. 7). Practical consciousness, in turn, interacts with discursive consciousness or awareness of what one is doing as reflected about and discussed. Signification, or the representation of action, interacts with properties of social systems. System or structure is in some dialectic with practice, leading in time to enstructuration (Giddens 1984:25).

Discourse research can speak to the formulation of the conditions for the production and reproduction of social systems. In formulaic terms, structure : language :: speech and practice (relations). The interaction of the two "sides" of this formula leads to enduring social systems. Language and speech provide the "rules of the game," tacitly known, and upon which people draw.

Several additional features of organizational discourse are important in defining research targets when studying organizational communication in the field:

1.   Organizational discourse includes in its focal concerns a view of resource base, the location or mapping of problematics, and trust in the environment, as well as a set of techniques, modes of assessing that environment, and hypothecated (official) aims.

2.   Organizational discourse creates a set of codes (implicit and explicit), which include ways of interpreting and sharing these interpretations for organizing responses to alterations in both the physical and social world.

3.   Organizational discourse contains, signified by key terms, clusters of problematic paradigms, and ideological or connotative metaframes for stabilizing the world in counterfactual terms (Weick 1979; Luhmann 1985).

4.   Organizational discourse frames reality (provides rules for deciding "What is going on here"?) and sets out the units (culturally defined and carried by sign vehicles) possessing the force to enact a role (Greimas 1966).

5.   Discourse produces means by which "new data" are selectively perceived, retained, and believed (Weick 1979:135).

6.   Organizational discourse maps ideas, symbols, and chunks of meaning upon nature, creating emergent ideas about nature, or "cultural bias" (Douglas 1987).

7.   Analysis of the character of the cultural bias of organizational discourse is important in understanding how conceptions of the nature of the world are transposed into "facts" and practices in organizations. Cultural bias is the authority that defines the relevant facts or information and is the basis for assumptions underpinning those facts. It both constitutes and sets out the nature of organizational problems. Bias is distributed within organizations as well as across organizations.

8.   Organizational discourse contains explicitly stated biases that stratify preferences among types of risks internally and externally, enhancing some modes of uncertainty (information absence or overload), and depressing others.

9.   Plural rationalities or multiple social worlds will emerge and persist in organizations, especially within organizational segments, for coping with forms and kinds of uncertainty (see Fischhoff et al. 1981).

10.   A linguistic or semiotic model of organization is a framework or heuristic for discovering differences by which utterances are defined and selected (Lemert 1979a:86). Reasoning employs tokens of problems located in semantic or discourse fields (McPhee 1988; Toulmin 1958).

11.   Explanations based on semiotics would seek to discover the principles that organize previously encoded values and signs about signs, or social organization and differentiation (MacCannell and Mac-Canell 1982).

12.   Key concepts, once elicited from interviewed organizational members, can be linked to semantic fields, roles and tasks, and the organizational mandate and discourse (ideology) of the organization (Barley 1983; Manning 1987a). The relevant kinds of meanings will include denotative, connotative, and ideological-mythological meanings.

Organizational discourse provides insights into how the organization organizes itself, orders itself without design (Feldman 1989), and maintains its central mission and meaning to its members. The range of meanings that it permits and rewards, especially of its core terms, is a sensitive indicator of the fundamental paradoxes the organization faces.

The Role of Enactment and Loose Coupling

Organizations maintain loose links with the environment(s) by which they manage and cope with vicissitudes. Weick argues persuasively that organizations encode and decode information in an orderly way and so respond to or enact an environment. The processes of enacting ensure organizational stability and reduce ambiguity to a workable level. It is as critical to establish the nature of the enactment and coupling processes as it is to study the enstructuration process (as seen above). Organizational discourse contains the *linking* and enacting processes essential to sustaining the place of the environment in the material as well as the symbolic world. Consider these aspects of the central concept of enactment:

1.   Information processed by human service organizations, for example, is *reactive*, and response to such communication is loosely coupled, lagged, or sporadic and erstwhile to responses.

2.   Organizations, as Feldman and March (1981) usefully summarize, are typically *overloaded* with information. Yet organizations believe information is in scarce supply at decision points. More is gathered than is needed, yet it is always said that more time and more information are required. These propositions are believed to be in the nature of the case, regardless of the level of information current within the organization.

3.   Decisions are taken and priorities are established largely through the use of organizational routines (Feldman 1988a,b,c,d). Routines, in turn, are carried out backstage, are informal, and nonexplicit. Routines serve to control or ration organizational resources (Lipsky 1982).

4.   Organizational communication systems are used to maintain autonomy and discretion, to produce and solve uncertainty within organizational segments. Individuals use communication systems to cover themselves in official terms, in both defensive and offensive fashions (Manning 1979a:13–14).

5.   The reflexive knowledge of actors of decisions and the flow of information constantly alters and redefines the context and meaning of messages. Organizational segments, technology, specific task and role sets, and the encoding and classification of messages, embed information (Manning 1988a).

6.   The conditions of constraints on time, effort, memory, concentration, and resources and conflicts within organizations mean that decisions, some of which are found in texts or messages, are always taken using situational rationality, and are accounted for variously.

7.   The study of accounts, or rationalizations or excuses for action (Scott and Lyman 1968), and their changing form and content, is a primary tool of organizational analysis (Potter and Wetherell 1987).

Combining the concept of loose coupling with discourse analysis is a useful theoretic tool for examining the internal and external functions of organizational communication.

Conclusions

This review of paradigms within communication research suggests that the concept of communication is multifaceted and context dependent. This basic point is seen not only within organizations, but in the theories used to describe and account for the conditions under which various kinds of communication take place in organizations. The notion that discourse is constitutive of organizational relations, producing and reproducing them, and that these ideas, in turn, are loosely coupled to each other, provides a powerful imagery of organizational communication. Through talk (discourse about itself), the organization enacts (shapes, defines, marks the boundaries of) itself. Although individuals perceive their meanings and position to the "plurality" as unique, they are embedded in objectively known shared meanings and collective representations having intersubjective validity. In this sense, they are both interpersonal and collective, both intersubjective and contextual.

These and other ideas drawn from the loose-coupling perspective and the semiotic and dramaturgical perspective will continue to shape the examples and arguments presented here. The concepts of discourse and enactment are revisited in research reported in Chapters 5, 6, 7, and 8. In the next chapter, the last in Part I, several studies are presented as exemplars of excellent qualitative field research. We also return to discourse analysis in the final two chapters of the book.

II
FIELD STUDIES

Examples

Introduction

This chapter reviews selected illustrative studies of organizational communication in part to set the stage for Chapter 5. The chapter outlines some practical issues, provides a basis for studying organizational meanings, and identifies themes in qualitative organizational studies. In the rest of Part II, Chapters 5–8, field studies of organizational communication focusing on external communication and internal communication are presented. All the chapters use themes drawn from the interpretive theories described in Chapter 3.

The Basis for Selecting Studies of Organizational Meanings

Meaning—its patterning, location, and consequences within organizational context—is central to interpretive studies of organizational communication. An organization, among other things, is a means for encoding and interpreting messages, providing the forms into which signals sent with the intent of communicating are placed. If this statement is true, then organizations are, at very least, also forms within which communicating about communication takes place. Organizations provide the communicational units into which the flow or stream of messages (from either external or internal sources) is cognitively partitioned and messages are distinguished one from the other. Organizations contain (show, entail, display) the cultural units (and the sign vehicles) that carry messages through the organization. The boundaries across which the messages flow constitute the principal subsystems of the organization.

This meaning-based notion of organization as an open communicative system implies that organizations do much more than simply process messages having various informational content. Organizations shape and pattern messages in the first instance as a stream and later as a number of discrete units. Organizations are minimally an assemblage of codes and formats in which messages are placed, and the context within which they are rendered sensible. The formal processes of message movement are in some dialectical relationship with the informal modes of communication indicated by such concepts as the "organizational culture."

As Putnam, citing Weick (1979), writes, "Communication, then, is not simply an event that takes place within a container where people transmit oral and written messages. It is a continual process of creating and/or reaffirming interpretations through the interlocking behaviors of organizational members" (1986:152–53). Communication can be studied in many ways, but the purpose of this chapter is to identify a small number of studies that most creatively uncover the process of "reaffirming interpretations through the interlocking behaviors of organizational members." In this sense, these studies will provide useful models for field studies.

The studies reviewed are not simply studies of discourse in the form of accounts, or justifications or excuses for action, or merely performative utterances (see Potter and Wetherell 1987). The studies include analyses of organizational structure, technology, and roles and tasks that pattern the noninformational aspects of message-processing. As such, they are not merely studies of the verbal. Communicational research correctly includes more than individual thoughts or selves; it focuses on the organizing of meaning, or enactment, placing message-processing and messages within a framework of interpretation, of interlocking and enacted meanings. Analysis must be undertaken of the constraints furnished by patterns of organizational structure, the roles and tasks of the members, and the dominant technology.

Table 4.1 presents the studies and their foci, and will provide a format for the following discussion. The methods and authors of the studies are shown in column 1. Column 2 shows *what* meanings are of interest and also gives a list of *where* the meanings are studied. The *why* is implicit in the method chosen as well as what might be called the theme(s) of the studies, in column 3. *How* the meanings are to be studied and the analytic form used to present the findings are given in column 4 and complete the table. The dimensions that organize the table also provide the chapter's framework.

Table 4.1. Selected Studies of Organizational Communication

Method; author (1)	What meanings (data); where (2)	Why; themes (3)	How; form of analysis (4)
1. Semantic/ semiotic (Manning 1988a)	Calls to police in "segments"; operators, dispatcher officers in two departments	Syntagms, paradigms, ordering, priority, processing, rules	Flow charts, figures, trees-algorithms
2. Semiotic (Barley 1983a)	Funeral director interviews; funeral homes	Routines, disposals, display, removals	Semiotic charts
3. Discourse analysis (Cicourel)	Dr.-patient interactions; hospitals, clinics	Text-discourse relations	Algorithms, detailed examination of written records and observation of interviews
4. Folktales (Martin et al.)	News clippings, interviews	Paradoxes; social integration	Illustration of key themes in stories
5. Textual exegesis (Sudnow 1965; Waegel 1981)	Interviews, observation; records of crime	Case processing	analysis of words, codes and organizational outcomes through observation and interviews
6. Narrative analysis (Bennett and Feldman 1981)	Court discourse; recordings, observations	Link talk to organizational procedures and practices	Microanalysis of talk—pauses, turns, etc.; structure of narratives
7. Loose coupling (Manning 1980, 1988a)	Fieldwork	Describe the nature of the coupling; compare organizations	Analysis of communication flow in two organizations
8. Fieldwork (Jackall 1988)	Business ethics interviews	Describe and account for ethics in large U.S. corporations	Link vignettes to organizational goals, career aims

The topics and studies reviewed are chosen for several reasons. These are excellent studies that I have read with appreciation and profit over the years. They are also well written and designed, and have been well accepted in the field of organizational communication as indicated by frequent citations and discussion in the research literature. They are also explicit in their focus, data, and analytic procedures. Significant attention is given to the nature of organizational meaning, rather than general or broad societal meaning. Conversely, they entail, but are not exclusively, studies of individual perceptions, attitudes, or individual-message interactions. The chosen studies are *organizational*, and they view an organizational communication system (OCS) and codes as more than a sum of aggregated individual attitudes and beliefs. The studies range temporally from analyses of brief encounters or events such as calls to the police or attorney-client interactions, to longer communicational sequences, up to and including long-term relationships that may stretch over years. In this sense, they focus more on the extant codes and their use than on the creation or suppression of codes, or the interactions that alter or change the organizations' modes of organizing. They could be called, as are most social scientific studies, "conservative."

The following section discusses the columns in Table 4.1: (1) the general method and author(s) of the studies; (2) the meanings (data) gathered in the research; (3) why such data were gathered and to what theoretic questions the research was addressed; (4) how and where the data were gathered and the themes in the analysis.

Discussion of Research Modalities: Selected Studies

Semantic/Syntactical Analyses

P. K. Manning (1988a) studied two large urban police organizations in two countries (England and the United States) both of which used highly refined centralized, computer-based call-processing to handle calls made on a centralized 911 line, by using observations, records analysis, ethnographic fieldwork, interviews, and tapes of calls to the police [see Manning (1988a, Chapter 2) for details]. The police communications (PCS) system in both organizations was divided into three segments or subsystems: operators, dispatchers or zone controllers, and officers. However, in the British force (BPD), the operators were housed in a central office building, and officers and dispatchers shared an ecological area, while the midwestern police department (MPD) placed operators and zone controllers together in a central building and officers were only in contact with the organization routinely via the radio. In both organizations, operators answered calls, sorted them out as police relevant, referred or terminated them, classified the relevant ones using computers, and passed what was shown on their computer screens to dispatchers either by radio (BPD) or printout (MPD). If they required further attention, they were passed on to officers via radio in both systems.

The messages in each subsystem were divided mentally into syntagms, or units of meaning, such as time of the call, nature of the incident, classification, and address. Each of these elements can be read off independently as a denotative meaning or bit of culture, or they can be combined, using a mental code, into a set of paradigms or metaphorical associations that connote something about potential police action. When, for example, the crime of rape is noted, it denotes "serious crime" and is automatically granted first priority by the computer. To officers and dispatchers it also connotes "good police work" and "crime work" that is honorable and important. Each message is *undercoded* in respect of police ideology (Eco 1979:135ff., Manning 1986). Paradigms are used to cluster messages into sets or groups such as "action," "nonaction," "closed," "crime," and "noncrime," and items within messages are also sorted into paradigms that are indicative of the nature of the call. For example, officers are interested in the name of the event, the classification given, the time they received the call, and any remarks such as "weapons" or "man on the scene." These are gathered as the elements of the assignment signifying a potentially good call. On the other hand, a call with "domestic" elements (constituted of syntagms such as classification, name, and address perhaps if known) is seen as a nuisance, ambiguous, and potentially dangerous (Davis 1983).

Messages take meaning from both similarities and contrasts with other messages within a message stream (they have synecdochical links to each other). Their contents are sorted and oriented to with culturally shaped lenses within organizational subsystems. Messages are vertically stacked (given priority) and placed in other associative contexts within organizational segments, as well as horizontally partitioned into types of messages (by incident content and by classification code) and metaphorically grouped. Organizations contain a set of relatively fixed sign functions that are, or appear to be, fixed because organizational structure, technology, roles and tasks, and interpretations are in part stabilized as cognitive. But there is no tight link between the event in the world, the call made about this, the incident produced by the operator, the assignment and the job, and the resultant outcome. Texts are always in some *situationally patterned* relationship to unstated or *deictic* knowledge, noise, and a field of activities. A message focus is always in part misleading because any message is always at least to some degree a function of background features unaccounted for by the sign functions assembled in the message. Organizations are rooms for echoes of texts, and echoes are a part of the rich and varied sound collections characteristic of organizations.

Semiotic (Code) Analysis

Stephen Barley (1983a,b) applied semiotic analysis to key domains in an occupational culture, in this case "the funeral director's understanding of his various tasks" (1983a:393). The articles set out in very clear fashion the semiotic method, drawing on ethnosemiotic (meaning in a group or cultural context) assumptions, using eliciting, observation and inference, and abduction. It is a model of interweaving data and theory. Barley, in short, observed and conducted interviews in a community-oriented funeral home in a metropolitan neighborhood in an eastern seaboard city, which he termed "a local funeral home," that served a community of Catholics of Irish, Italian, Polish, and Lithuanian ethnic descent. He aimed to "uncover basic units of semiotic analysis—signs that have relevance for funeral directors" (p. 399), and tried to discover just what these were as well as the codes by which the signs were made meaningful. He sought a broad understanding through interviews. Then he formalized the work by specifying the *domains* (areas in which categories placed shared at least one feature) and eliciting, a technique of questioning that involves asking, about an item of interest (let us call it X for this discussion), What sorts of X are there. . .? The categories and subcategories in each of the 56 domains were initially identified. In theory, these domains and subdomains have a linear quality such that they can be arrayed as ordered trees or algorithms. [See Needham (1983) on polythetic classifications and Kay and Berlin (1969).]

Some of the domains clustered or were seen as connected by commonalities, which were further pursued by Barley and mapped. These were ideas like "naturalness" of the appearance of the displayed body, and "putting people (family and friends) at ease." These are connotative meanings that build on the denotative meanings arrayed within the domains. The unity within domains was checked by questions about each item as well as differences between items in separate domains. The semiotics of funeral work were analyzed in three codes: posed features, furnishings, and removals. Each of these was related to the overall wish of the director to maintain control of the performance, to manage and smooth the flow of events, and to make the funeral "natural" and "normal." In pursuing this theme, Barley draws on and extends the classic work on the dramaturgy of the funeral by Robert Habenstein (1962).

For purposes of illustrating his method, let us consider the code of posed features (see Figure 4.1). After the body is cleansed and embalmed, it is posed, and eyes and mouth are arranged to give rise to the interpretation of the set of metonymic signs that metaphorically indicate "peaceful sleep." The idea of a living, sleeping person is opposed to the dead person (two distinct domains of metonymic signs result—the signs are arrayed as shown in Figure 4.1). On the other hand, the posed corpse (left side of the figure) is associated metaphorically with the sleeping person, both of which are opposed to the unposed corpse (right side of the figure). The body is meant to resemble a living person by converting metaphorically the metonymic signs that are shared with the posed corpse and a sleeping person, and by the same token to suppress the similarities of both with a dead, unposed corpse. The funeral director intends, according to Barley, to have participants read the series of metaphoric associations between peaceful sleep and the posed corpse as "natural" and that this reading of the signs will ensure a smooth, unproblematic funeral. The contrasts between a smooth and a disrupted funeral are found above the line in Figure 4.1 and are connotations of the denotative meanings contrasted below. This oppositional structure from bottom to top is the source of meaning, because as Barley writes, following Saussure, "Signs have no meaning unless they are contrasted with other signs in a system" (Barley 1983a:404). Barley concludes that his three examples of codes—posed features, furnishings, and removals—only one of which, the code of posed features, was explicated here, are based on identical denotative contrasts, metonymical arrays of metaphoric signs arrayed as metonymic signs that suggest that "oppo-

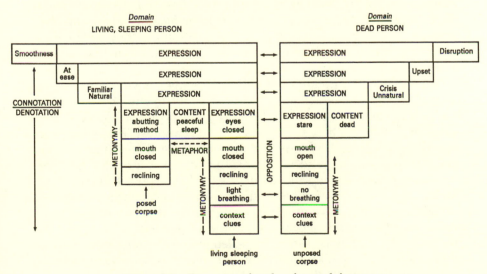

Figure 4.1   Diagram of code of posed features.

sites" are similar. "The redundancy of the coding rules at the denotative level is reinforced by synonymous, and hence redundant, connotative codes. Taken together, the three codes converge to form an interrelated semiotic system" (p. 410).

In these two papers, Barley illustrates the power of a semiotic analysis of organizational communication. The communication analyzed is reflexive in that it characterizes the setting, and that the setting is in part defined by the present of these denotative meanings and connotative redundancies.

Text/Discourse Analysis

Aaron Cicourel, a sociologist who began with a general phenomenological critique of social research methods (1966), and then published a detailed ethnomethodological analysis of juvenile justice (1970), has in the last ten years written a series of brilliant analyses of the relationships between texts (written sets of signs in organizational contexts, in this case, medicine and hospitals) and discourse (in this case, observed and recorded interactions between doctors and patients in a clinical setting). In the course of this research, he has mounted a devastating critique of conversational analysis (Cicourel 1975, 1976, 1981, 1985, 1986). Simultaneously, he has addressed a central question in structuralism: How do people communicate in organizations using several different sense modalities, in quite different settings, using the symbols and assumptions of diverse microcultures or social worlds? How do they draw together information, coding, storing, retrieving, recoding, and reconstituting it when necessary, using long- and short-term memory? How do they combine data to make sense, e.g., placing within the flow of discourse nonverbal materials such as gestures and postures, intonation, accent, speed, and register?

An untested assumption of structuralist semiotics is that these processes and integrative activities are carried out in the shadow of the model of language. Is language *the model* that embeds or is central to all forms of communication as Barthes (1970:11) argues? This view is reflected in the conceit of conversational analysis: that syntactical and structural features of the social organization of talk, especially the "middle management conversational devices" (Levinson 1983) like turn-taking, next-speaker selection, and topic selection, effectively account for talk's ordering. Cicourel argues effectively that a verbally based notion about ordering ignores the multilevel character of talk, and the integration of somewhat formal knowledge and the formal knowledge of professions like medicine and law with everyday conversational metaphors, slang, and elliptical remarks (see Goffman 1983a).

It is quite clear from this research that *formal knowledge*, such as the knowledge of disease entities, their etiology, pathology, and prognosis, displayed by physicians in interviews is in tension with and contrast to *local knowledge* expressed by and characteristic of patients. Commonsense knowledge understood within a hospital, such as the meanings of tests, their costs, time frames, and diagnostic relevance, and bureaucratic rules concerning diagnoses, admission, release, and the conditions under which insurance covers various afflictions are used to organize the care of the patient and are used by physicians without recognition of the patient's ignorance.

Cicourel notes that language is limited (for obvious reasons) in its capacity to convey fully all that is communicated in an encounter. Much of import is communicated within a medical transaction by nonverbal matter: postures, gestures, the degree of shared emotional tone in the interview. The ongoing nature of the patient-doctor relationship is not entered on the medical record, but is often relevant to treatment decisions as well. The precise care given the patient within the hospital may not be known by subsequent physicians reading a medical record. A few key points may gloss a long discourse by the patient, or a few boxes may be ticked to summarize a medical history taking several minutes to recall, piece together (since the information may not necessarily be given by the patient in the format-provided order), organize, and write down on the record (Cicourel 1975). Writing and listening may be mutually exclusive activities, so that periods of writing, when the physician is looking down, may be those in which other important communication is ignored, not seen or noted. Capacity to recall different kinds of information, especially abstract knowledge rather than local knowledge, may differ for doctors and patients.

Cicourel seeks to identify and link what people use to connect what others *say*, usually as heard in *chunks* (phrases, sentences, and whole sequences connecting as themes in what is said), with their *understanding* on the one hand ("what someone really means" or meant to say) and what is *written* by those with the official authority to do so. Of course, the question can be reversed: one can ask how what one reads is "translated" into what one says about a text. The institutional locus (the "where" in Table 4.1) is large teaching hospitals in California. Cicourel has observed doctors and patients communicating in order to understand the how and the why—how and why doctors "translate" patients' talk into subjective and objective cues, medical diagnoses, medical records, and even a set of treatment regimens (see also Paget 1988).

One of Cicourel's studies (1986), for example, analyzes detailed data from observation of medical interviews, doctor-patient interactions, and the interview protocol itself to draw subtle connections between types of knowledge (formal and commonsense knowledge) and the endlessly indexical (something that stands for something else in context is indexical) and context-dependent nature of human communication. With his analysis he orchestrates important critiques of conversational analysis, the methodology of interviewing, aspects of artificial intelligence, and the modeling of speech acts. Central questions are raised about speech pragmatics and semantics. He argues for textual analysis in which the analytic unit is larger than the utterance, speech act, or the sentence and in which meaning is seen as being structured by underlying patterns and practices and emerges through and by the attributed meanings given to context-bound statements. The central question of survey research, how answers to questions are seen as indices of social organization and structure derived through the translation and back-translation of statements, is elegantly stated.

This is naturalistic observation. Cicourel focuses on the conversational *stream* rather than elements, sentences, or phrases, or microscopically examined sequences, to see how participants construct the sense of an ongoing interaction combining their local knowledge, feelings here and now, past experiences, and routine understandings of how others gloss, summarize, and chunk large bits of their encounters with others with the questions asked by the doctor. How do they wait and see to explore confusions? Do they draw on the resources of their knowledge of the use of various tropes, irony, sarcasm, jokes, and poetic or autoreferential features of talk, to integrate and make sensible the interview? He has employed both "top-down" or narrative models of talk (Rumelhart 1975) as well as "bottom-up" approaches based on listing the sequence of questions between physicians and patients (1975). Cicourel, a Spanish speaker, has also examined carefully the consequences of both written and verbal translation from Spanish to English (many patients in the clinic studied were Spanish-speaking), the relationship between medical records and interview transactions, between interviews by specialized medical personnel and interviews by general practitioners, and how deaf and hearing speakers differ in their understandings of a textual analysis or of instructions and assistance in the classroom (Cicourel 1973).

Given the constant use of formal interview schedules and protocols in all kinds of client-serving bureaucracies, understanding the relationships between these eliciting devices and local or personal styles or knowledge is critical. Cicourel (1986) addresses the question of the relationship between formal and local knowledge, between text and discourse, between modes of understanding and their integration over the course of a conversation, and between some imputed code and an ongoing sense of understanding. His analysis is refreshingly embedded in pragmatics (Levinson 1983), or the social notions that embed language but that cannot be derived from it directly, and in very careful exploration of both taped and observed doctor-patient interactions.

In these researches, Cicourel has explored the basic question of the fits of various kinds and forms of communication. He shows clearly that the authority of the physician screens information and gives him or her the cultural authority to "hear," "see," and record some facts and not others, and to define the nature of the problem about which the patient seeks advice.

Text/Records/Interpretation

Two excellent examples of studies of the relationships between organizational assumptions reflected in records and organizational outputs (decision-making)[1] are David Sudnow's (1965) studies of public defenders in a large California county and William Waegel's (1981) studies of general investigative detectives in a large urban police department.[2] Given a focus on textual analysis, they both gathered interviews, made observations in court and in offices, and examined case records. The theme of the two studies, the ways in which records can be read as features of or revealing aspects of interlocking behaviors and meanings, was predicated on assumptions about the nature of the communicational process and the text-discourse link. They viewed records as reflexive, revealing the audiences who read and used them, the writers who created them, and the behavior reported in the official texts. The aim of the analysis was to describe why and how these interpretations fit into organizational roles and how communicational processes reinforced this "fit."

These criminal justice functionaries acted in the capacity of information workers. They had to screen facts, assemble them into cases for organizational purposes, negotiate the meaning of the cases jointly in interaction with their organizational colleagues, and produce reasonably complete cases within some time frame. Both assume that time and other resources are scarce, and both assume that the persons alleged to have committed the crimes, if named or known, are truly guilty.

Studies suggest that the level of work load affects the pattern of typification (Emerson 1983; Manning 1988a). Since in both organizations studied the work load was high, the differentiation among cases was quite refined and served to maximize effort on cases "with potential." Waegel suggests that where work load is high, typifications may become essentially final judgments (Waegel 1981:275). In both settings, individuals with legal authority to decide feel under pressure to produce and to keep paperwork up to date. The tactics by which this is managed differ. Let us look at the "what"—the work accomplished.

The public defenders read case reports collected the previous after-noon along with their interviews with defendants the morning before the trial. The large number of cases that must be processed in court every day, and the tight, heavily scheduled court dockets limit time available. To reduce complexity to manageable variety in a routine fashion as well as to observe schedules and demands originating outside the setting, e.g., court schedules, *typifications* emerge as tools to charac-terize quickly and efficiently or typify the essential features of the case seen as relevant to the operations of the public defender's office. The urban detectives work with time and production deadlines, and pattern their decisions in response to these organizational pressures.

Sudnow uses the term *normal crime* to denote the typifications used by public defenders in a public defenders' office in California. Normal crimes are "occurrences whose typical features, e.g., the ways they usually occur and the characteristics of persons who commit them (as well as typical features and typical scenes), are used and attended to by the P.D." (1965:262). These typifications, in turn, are critical to the normal routines of the court and are assumed to be relevant along with the assumptions that all the players in the drama are moral and are engaged in "doing the business of the court as it should be done." The participants are role players, who are routinely playing the same role. The prosecutors and defendants are part of a team locked together in a mutually useful set of bargains.

As noted above, the typification and the behavior or facts it encom-passes are not independent, but linked in a dynamic fashion, each affecting the other. There is further a tension between the *instant case* (the case being considered at any time) and the types currently in use to decide in the setting. The question asked is, Is this in fact a typical "rape"? The focus in both the Sudnow and Waegel works is what might be called the *code,* or the rules that order the meaning of the communica-tion, although that word is not used. How is social coding done? In a sense, the research question is how the facts noted in a particular case fit the contours of an identifiable general type. Careful research including both observation and interviews suggests that much is brought to the case that in no sense is there to be read. No case could be "taken as read": it is always interpreted within the perspective(s) brought to the case by those framing it, processing it, and deciding its disposition.

In organizations a sequence of considerations seems to operate. The features of a specific case are compared with the routine case or a typical case of "burglary," "rape," or "robbery." The first organizationally based problem is, What is the potential for the case to achieve my ends? In Waegel's work, detectives were able to allocate resources (their own time largely) differentially to achieve a higher number of closures (some of which were arrests), to suspend a large number of cases (around 80 percent) with little or no work, and to keep up their production figures. In the organization described by Sudnow, lawyers made a series of assumptions about the case that guaranteed little refined differentiation between cases: they assumed that the person was guilty, sought typicality, and were cautious about exceptions that were atypical crimes for this community. There were also two troubling subtypes: normal crimes committed by those who maintained their innocence ("recalcitrant offenders") and typical crimes committed atypically.

Let us now further examine the dynamics of case-processing. Detectives focus on the offense, the victim's life-style, race/ethnicity, class, and the possible "clout" or connections of the victim. These constitute the set of items forming the *code*. They also organize the written investigative reports. Once the code is known, however, a question remains concerning how the code is to be used by encoders (police detectives in this case) and how it is mapped upon the preestablished case report format.

Case interpretation involves (1) deciding how identifiable the perpetrators seem to be, (2) normal social characteristics of victims, and (3) the settings in which the crime took place (at home, in public, in known areas of the city). These, taken together, confer meaning on the crime and outline a strategy for handling it (Waegel 1981:270). The central question is *credibility* or trust: much hinges on the degree of credibility of the *source* of the information (this varies between cases of victims of "face-to-face crime" and of property crime). The second consideration is based on commonsense understanding of white and black victims and their life-styles and habits. The setting determines the degree of importance of the effort, e.g., a lower-class area inhabited by drunks is an important cue. After this information is known, the typicality of the incident is determined and the core features (victims, life-style, and place) are combined into an interpretive scheme. This encodation suggests the level of effort required to solve the case and produce an arrest. The degree of typicality results from a tacit phenomenological comparison of features of the instant case and the shorthand typifications used in the police for sorting and categorizing such cases. Some fitting and squeezing may be necessary at times to fit a case to a paradigm. Written reports, in this event, may be distorted or "fudged" to confirm the desired outcomes. This description of case-processing obtains when the cases being considered are routine (information is present and there is little unusual public or media attention) and the work load is normal or routine.

Sudnow's analysis also documents the generality of typification in case-deciding. Sudnow observed that public defenders who are assigned to defend indigent defendants use a sense of typicality that is offense specific. This becomes a tool that modulates between a charge and the necessary category of crime viewed as reasonable for a plea bargain once the person agrees to plead guilty. It is a tool for reducing uncertainty, given a set of known facts and exigencies of organizational functioning. Sudnow argues that the link between the charge on which the person was arrested and that for which he or she goes forward for prosecution finally (after the plea bargain) is what he terms "normal crime." This is an offense-specific typification, which is not determined by the logical or actual facts of the case or the necessary link of the charge and the bargained charge, but by "situational inclusion," i.e., how they are seen to be connected by the defenders and the prosecutors. The idea of situational inclusion entails the manner in which the offense was committed, the social characteristics of the offender, types of victims, and named sorts of criminals or social types of offenders, such as "narcos," "burglars," or "rapists." The general features of normal crimes in Sudnow's analysis focus attention on the offense types, not on the particulars of a given crime or criminal. The particulars are often not of statutory relevance (do not define the evidential features of the crime) and are community and setting specific. The offenses are understood in terms of the ecological features of the settings in which they occurred.

Normal crimes and typifications of criminal records are both part of the taken-for-granted grounds for working and getting along within the organizations studied.[3] They are understood as relevant to the business of the court, and are attended to and understood by participants in the court system. The police, likewise, learn to accommodate themselves to these practices. Necessarily, these features of cases are learned by public defenders and detectives so that they can work within the system, be successful, and meet the minimal expectations of colleagues.[4] Typifications are both social and psychological in the sense that they are useful for organization members to accomplish work tasks, but are also intimately connected to and a part of the social organization, routines, and assumptions of the bureaucratic organizations in which they are found. They form an important part of the commonsense knowledge that all normal participants are soon expected to possess, use, and understand, often tacitly and without specific verbal cues. These "unstated recipes" work for the reduction of original charges to lesser offenses viewed as "reasonable" by all participants (save the defendant, whose views do not count), once the bargain is agreed. The question asked by legal actors is, Does this case fit the normal case?

Telling Tales out of School

A central question in organizational analysis is the role of communication in creating and maintaining organizational structure. This question has been answered in the past almost entirely within the rhetoric of rational and formal organizational communication. The role of informal communication has been eschewed, or seen as an obstruction to achieving the ends of the organization. This is clearly false, since informal aspects of organizations can facilitate or not the ends of the organization, and formal communication can either serve these ends or obscure and confound them. It is most clear that the question of integration and noncoercive and non-sacred-based organizations (Etzioni 1975) is clearly revealed in the collective identification and sense of organizational identity that develops within a segment of the firm. Thus, there is a current vogue within organizational studies of communication to study "organizational folktales." These are often linked to studies of organizational and occupational cultures (see Frost et al. 1985; Van Maanen and Barley 1985; Strine and Pacanowsky 1985). In this section, I summarize themes in the narrative analysis of organizational culture.

One component of organizational culture is the stories, stylized renditions of events, and the personal narratives that people tell about themselves. One view of organizational culture and of the stories found therein is functionalist. Stories are *functional* in that they help to resolve individuals' sense of ambiguity, they resolve fundamental dilemmas about the location and consequences of responsibility and accountability, they serve to increase morale and integration, and they maintain the ambiguity of organizational action (Martin, Feldman, Hatch, and Sitkin 1983; Brown 1990; *Journal of Communication* 1985; Martin 1990). Stories have an implicit and explicit structure, which makes them enduring, useful in chunking and coding information, and appealing. Much of the research draws on cognitive psychology and on anthropological studies of myth.

A related, and not mutually exclusive idea is that stories provide the *ritual and expressive materials* by which identities are sorted out and attached, roles are established, postures and attitudes are danced, and meanings and interpretations are spun out within an assumed world of cultural symbols and signs (see O'Donnell and Pacanowsky 1983; Pacanowsky and O'Donnell-Trujillo 1984; Strine and Pacanowsky 1985). Actors produce images of each other, cues read as miniscripts and enact social conventions (Trujillo and Dionisopoulos 1987). Tales, or retellings of shared meanings, express a culture, apart from any functionalist reading of what they do for or to the organization as a "rational entity."

In a succinct and powerful outline of "organizational communication as cultural performance," Pacanowsky and O'Donnell-Trujillo set out an antifunctionalist rationale for the centrality of symbolizing performance qua performance as axial in the interlocking meanings that are organizations. Processes of performing "cultural performances" that mark ritual relations, passion, and feeling, and that provide sociality (articulate verbal interactions), politics, and enculturation or socialization are key domains for studying organizational communication. In their view, "a culture is not something an organization has; a culture is something an organization is" (1984:146). Their summary is well stated:

> As organizational members engage in the communicative performances of organizational life, they reveal through their implicit or explicit commentaries on those performances the ways of making sense of their particular cultures. In the same way, as members perform rituals of the culture, they reveal the particular temporality of the place. As they perform the passions of the culture, they reveal the particular drama of the place. As they perform the socialities of the culture, they reveal the particular smoothness of the place. And, as they perform the politics of the culture, they reveal the particular strategies of the place. As these revelations continue to be interpreted and reinterpreted, the newcomer and the veteran (and the observer) can come to appreciate the subtleties of organizational culture. (p. 146)

Note that the first sentence above links "communicative performance" and "organizational life." The authors adopt a reflexive view of culture that locates "culture" directly in the readings individuals make of symbolizing behavior, and communication of the meanings of specific performances. Culture, in their view, is "making commentaries" on the performances of others. It is not the behavior seen as a conventionally clear set of signs, the expressions, or the signifiers that are of exclusive interest in this view. They turn attention to *how* these signifiers are tied in context to contents, to signifieds, how the signs mean, and how such meanings are the basis for responses to the performances in the first instance. Culture is produced as an interlocking series of sensible meanings: performances taken to communicate to self and others meanings that are in turn shared with the audience affirming and confirming those responses (Weick 1979:110–117).

As my analysis of the themes in a police funeral [and its functions as myth, drama, ritual, and form of enactment (Manning 1977 Ch.1)] suggests, police tales function to set out the boundaries of the occupation. They label activities and stabilize the uncertain characters police meet ("scumbags," "assholes," "maggots") and assert that both teller and audience are valued and tough. Tales of failure set the moral limits of responsibility of the police and the public. As Van Maanen (1988) notes, tellers of stories omit some detail and editorially tailor a compelling narrative that heightens the exciting and omits the boring, the inconclusive, and the illegal and immoral. Stories function within an occupational culture, but they are quite multifaceted, and their themes can be read in different ways. In other words, to point out that police stories have functions does not reveal the different functions they have in different contexts of telling.

Stories can be turned, or read "upside down," as well as "back to front." As many narrative analysts note, the overt and rational content of the stories, especially those gathered in organizational context and linked to the occupational culture, are *two-faced*. They present frightening contingencies—firing, loss of promotion, proximity to death—as well as provide solutions to inevitable dilemmas and paradoxes. They also tap unconscious human fears: death, separation, loss of work. Any theme of survival and coping is made possible by the existence of a problematic, the vicissitude. Although one can see stories as serving to integrate and facilitate, they also alienate, maintain social distance, and maintain *ambiguity* (Boje, 1991). Every success story implies the reality of failure, each rendition of the conquest of a difficulty signals the potential loss, each story that glorifies the top of the organization reflects on the banality of life at the bottom, and so forth. Some overt themes suppress others, and so stories reveal power (Martin 1990). The function of stories and tales in marking ambiguity and paradox can be explored usefully.[5]

Narrative Analyses

W. Lance Bennett and Martha Feldman, in *Reconstructing Reality in the Courtroom* (1981), base their analysis on the structure of legal stories. They seek to uncover how law and stories intersect. They present a formalized system of analysis of narratives in the courtroom. Their techniques are well suited to institutional analysis; they have generic features for the analysis of legal and other texts. Many alternatives to this style of narrative analysis also exist (see Goodall 1989; Rosaldo 1989; *Journal of Communication* 1985; Martin 1990; M. H. Brown 1990).

In themes well illustrated by this research, Kim Scheppele observes that courts are institutions in which the unspeakable is and must be spoken (1988:3). She continues to argue that "law is an interpretive activity" *(ibid.)*, and that in courts, two kinds of *texts* are interpreted and interpolated: the social text and the legal text. The legal text may be a regulation, a case, a law, or a previous decision, while the social text may be an event, a longer story, or a practice. Legal decisions are thus the reading, deconstructions, or interpretations of social texts in terms of legal texts (1988:86ff).

This succinct summary might well apply to any setting in which stories are told, in the offices of various professionals—doctors, lawyers, accountants, professors, therapists, clergy—and in governmental bureaus where services are rationed. The aim of discourse analysis using tales told in such settings is to provide a coherent account of how order, sequence, grammar and syntax, and form are mutually signalled and understanding is maintained over the course of reading a text or hearing a tale. The mandate of discourse analysis, as is true in these examples, is to understand and explore speech using as a basic data fragment chunks of discourse larger than the sentence. Levinson (1983:286) states that the aim of discourse analysis is to identify the units and then formulate rules or principles that explain or appear to account for the credibility, coherence, or consistent interpretation of longer tales using the basic units. One focus is to ask how and why certain tales or narratives are more persuasive or "succeed" as tales.

Bennett and Feldman (1981) provide an elegant example of the analysis of courtroom stories (observed in court, and then used experimentally). They set stories told by witnesses within the formal constraints of the procedural rules of courts, arguing that courts permit and provide the conditions for "ritual presentations," constrain what is told to certain types of admissible information, and limit the range of interpretation of the meaning of the tales. The structural features of the courts— the rule of evidence, order of speaking, and presentations, in short, the formality of the court—permit jurors and others present in the court to convert items placed within the framework of everyday judgment into the framework of legal evidence. Stories are an everyday form used for this purpose: an "everyday communicative device . . . a communication in the context of a defined collection of actors, means, motives and scenes" (p. 7).

Stories are plausible or not, given a coherent structure. Narrowly construed facts are not key in this, nor are elements taken alone. Whether viewed as credible or not, the tools used are the functional tools of legal work and a central feature of courtroom drama. They work as dramatic encodings of everyday life, create emotional responses and factual inferences, convey information, and signal and display outcomes; they can be compared and assessed with respect to courtroom functions (pp. 8–10).

Bennett and Feldman employ Kenneth Burke's (1962) basic dramaturgical concepts—*scene, act, agent,* and *purpose(s)*—to analyze stories gathered in classroom and court. The authors first identify the logical units of legal stories, and set out their understanding of the empirical and logical, esthetic and normative connections between the elements within the stories. Some stories, they argue, are more coherent than others, and therefore more adequate to accomplishing the work of the court.

The authors provide a set of criteria to assess the central action of a story and how it is to be interpreted. They derive a series of formal rules such as, "empirical connections are drawn between the elements of the story and clear logical connection is made" (Bennett and Feldman 1981:49–60). They rely on the structure of the narrative as they analyzed it, not on the perceptions, feelings, or judgments of the actors involved in the courtroom drama. They thus, as do many structuralists, set aside or overlook the role of confusions, misrepresentations, failed stories, differing standards of truth, evidence, and modes of persuasion. They recognize the pragmatic aspects of a story, that some stories may be told "better" than others in court, but they do not pursue the implications of this. The court, for them, is a social institution for sorting out the acceptable reading of the legal-social text (to adapt Scheppele's terms here). Clear understanding among participants would ideally produce fair and just outcomes. They conclude that to the extent that people can grasp the central point of a legal story and test the adequacy and completeness of a story, they are able to make sense of courtroom proceedings. [For an opposing view, see McBarnett (1981).]

Loose Coupling

Karl Weick's concept of loose coupling (1976, 1979) has a wide range of application and has served as the basis of several studies of organizational communication, including *The Narcs' Game* (Manning 1980). Recall that the concept of loose coupling takes its power from an implicit dialectical difference: it is always relative to (or compared with) some other type of connection within the domain of interest to the investigator (Orton and Weick 1990). Thus, in Weick's work on educational systems, he notes that the relationships between various "teachers," considered as a gloss for the teacher subsystem of a school, are tighter than those between teachers and principals, and the latter subsystem is thus (more) loosely coupled by contrast with the closeness of the teacher-teacher subsystem. On the other hand, police in the patrol division or "officers" as a subsystem are loosely coupled to each other, but relatively tightly coupled to their radio as a source of work (Manning 1988a). The idea is complex: both groups or subsystems, teachers and patrol officers, as elements within organizations *are simultaneously loosely and tightly coupled.* This suggests that items or concepts are always multifaceted and wound together like strands of a rope, in Wittgensteins' terms. They are related to each other by the context within which they are viewed, and their meaning is thus, to a considerable degree, context dependent, not context free.

Loose coupling as a metaphor, or way of seeing, is also a way of not seeing something. The fact that a few relevant and specified relationships are noted by an investigator to be loosely coupled states, at least by implication, that other relationships of interest in the same domain are not. They are tightly coupled in the sense that one can predict outcomes, or behaviors, relatively accurately. So, if one can predict that officers on patrol will reply routinely to radio calls, and carry out an assigned job, e.g., go and have a look, one cannot so readily, given the facts contained in the message sent out on the air, predict whether a written report will be made, the content of that written record, or the name given to the outcome produced by officers' appearance on the scene. The latter actions or "outputs" are affected by variables or considerations other than those provided by the radio message. Records are thus loosely coupled to the call (one could consider in this case the call as synecdoche for command or "the organization"). One could also predict that records are loosely coupled to both the organization and the call.

One implication of this formulation of loose coupling as a perspective is that such metaphoric images of organizational action are likely to bring anomalies to the surface. Police organizations are hierarchically ordered and formally structured to produce immediate and unquestioned compliance; some would label them "paramilitary" bureaucracies (McNamara 1967). Yet aspects of police work are highly discretionary, decentralized, under little supervision, and subject to little evaluation (Jermeir and Berkes 1979). Police are found sleeping on duty, taking bribes, and running personal businesses on the side, all while nominally "in service" and "on duty." Police are under tight control and supervision when involved in demonstrations, labor disputes, and parades. This variation in coupling within one organization cannot be accounted for by a single set of other variables such as "potential for violence" or "perceived risk," since "routine patrol" can be both violent and risky. The explanation for this apparent anomaly is that officers are loosely coupled in respect to routine calls and tightly coupled when involved in policing masses of people. The organizational form, one would assume, has evolved to maintain both tight and loose coupling as a central feature of the relationships between officers and their supervisors.

Both subjective and objective factors are at work in producing and maintaining organizations with loose coupling. Loose coupling is a common structural and procedural feature of many social systems, but it is also found when one examines the meshing of ideas and the social construction of interlocking meanings (Gronn 1983). Subjective and objective features produce and sustain looseness of coupling in the specified areas. Let us consider the example of the drug police (Manning 1980).

Transactions between system members in drug enforcement units and the police organization as a whole are characterized as loosely coupled in respect of the degree, frequency, strength, and kind of responses exchanged between narcotic agents and the police organization's central command and control system. For example, they are not expected to use the general force channel(s) on the radio, instead using their own channels, and they do not monitor closely or respond to routine non-drug-related radio calls. They are also loosely coupled to the social world of drug-using and -dealing. As a result, it is not possible to predict the degree, frequency, and strength of the responses, e.g., number of raids, search warrants executed, arrests made, seizures by the drug police of "drug markets" on the basis of the unit's size, amount of buy money for drugs, information in the files, or the size or viability of the "drug problem" in the city. This is true because the drug police are loosely coupled to the larger police organization and the public in terms of calls for service and because they are loosely coupled to supervisors and evaluation based on performance. They maintain structural autonomy by behaviors such as radio use, independent action on investigations, failure to report details of their activities to their sergeants, and manipulating the official record of money they carry (Manning 1979a). The structure of policing in these ways is both tightly and loosely coupled, and the actions of the agents serve to sustain the autonomy and discretion identified. Thus, both subjective and objective factors contribute to the conclusion that police organizations are loosely coupled.

The *reflexive* aspects and consequences of loose coupling have been quite considerably underplayed in research. *Reflexive* refers to the extent to which action has its own referent. The degree to which that self-referentiality is a central or even defining feature of that action is a variable. Take another example from the social world of policing. In one police organization called "Suburban," cases were assigned to drug officers to investigate. These were usually a result of telephone calls from the public (such calls were rare, but in Suburban County, the head of the police wished to maintain an image of the police as a service agency). The more one was assigned these calls, the lower one's status. The converse was also true since the low-status young officers were given these cases to investigate. Senior investigators, thought to be the most clever, were rarely given these assignments (or did not carry them out if they were given them). In this situation, officers were loosely coupled to these case assignments because number and kind of cases coming in was not the basis for assignment or work load among the investigators. Moreover, since those officers thought to be more skilled did have to work them from time to time, the basis for assignment was not "status" alone, but a combination of status, what cases the skilled officers were working at that time, and the level of shared information sergeants had about the activities of their investigators. These matters were defined in part by context, or definitions of shared meanings of status and skill in drug investigation, but also were produced by the actions of skilled officers who avoided their sergeants, lied to them, constructed stories about the kinds and level of investigations on which they were involved, and generally maintained the public front that they were always working on at least one "big case." The capacity to avoid assignments was partially structural, since supervision was not close generally and assignments were made informally, but it was also a function of the beliefs shared among members of the unit about the kinds of cases worked by skilled officers. Officers knew very little about the others' workloads and this ignorance was also a socially constructed feature of peer and investigator-sergeant relations in this unit (Manning 1980).

The concept of causal determinacy used by Weick to describe the nature of the environment(s) in which loose coupling is likely to develop suggests a degree of perceived complexity in an environment that is enacted, or acted on, such that distrusted data are checked and the results are fed back into subsequent selection of data. The Weickian conception is based on individual cognitions, but it may refer also to operating stereotypes or images of the environment. Metaphorically, the idea of enactment of a causally indeterminant environment fits well with my observations of the choices and actions of drug police. They lack information on the level of use, kinds of drugs used, and the structure of dealing (at both the wholesale and retail level) in the communities, and rely instead on discrete, individual actions and choices of cases worked and types of closures brought to them. They acted so that they might see the nature of the drug problem, and selectively retained the information so obtained. In this sense, the environment was not determinantal of cognitions and choices. It was socially constructed, rationalized, and accounted for, and these enactments, selections, and retentions produced constraints on future actions. Perhaps this is a good example of causal indeterminacy because officers believed they could not predict the nature and quality of their next bit of information which might become a case, and thus discretionary action, loosely coupled to the inspection function, permitted the organization to enact its mandate.

Loose coupling is also a contextual matter because it is produced as a result of interorganizational comparisons rather than as a result of measurements of a level of coupling. In policing and in the British Nuclear Installations Inspectorate (NII; discussed in Chapter 5), subunits within the organization are more or less coupled than others, thus providing a basis for specification of the nature and kind of loose coupling found. However, the degree of coupling can also be examined comparatively across organizations. Metro and Suburban police drug units were both loosely coupled to the larger organization. But when the links between the officers and a set of critical bases for centralized (sergeant and/or lieutenant) control (handling of money and evidence, search warrant procedures, and informant files) were compared, important differences were found. These features of control were loosely coupled with the inspection/evaluation function. Suburban was much more tightly coupled than Metro. Suburban supervisors had many more written or official indicators of activity to use to assess officers' performance than did their counterparts in Metro. The consequences of this can be revealed in several outcomes, e.g., search warrants enforced, level and kinds of investigations, seizures (size and value of seizure and kinds of drugs seized), which favored Suburban in the expected direction.

In summary, the loose-coupling perspective is not based on a formal system of propositions or logical deductions. It seeks to capture and illuminate (a) the multiplicity of perspectives in organizations based on various shared intersubjective realities, (b) the changing nature of consensus that pins down ambiguous meanings in organizational context (e.g., movement between two points while the two points themselves are moving), (c) the content affecting the forms of ordering data into the categories of ecological change, enactment, selection, and retention, and (d) the limits of metaphoric and analogic thinking about organizing and organizations.

Charting Moral Mazes

The sociologist Robert Jackall recently published *Moral Mazes: The World of Corporate Managers* (1988), a monograph based on a set of three interconnected field studies of American corporations (see also Goodall 1989).[6] This work illustrates organizational communication in the broadest sense, since he is studying the ordering of careers and work within an organizational structure, and providing us clues to understanding the meanings of the most general working rules he discovered among the white-collar tribes. The point here is that organizational communication is illuminated by informal observations since much of what people say that gives a context for their behaviors is ironic, backstage, and metaphoric.

Three core studies constitute the book: a corporate conglomerate (where he focused on the chemicals division), a public relations firm, and a large southern textile company. Focused interviews (done in 1980–1985) followed a period of background interviewing (p. 143; 40–50 in each corporation). His work identifies and probes the ethical and moral standards ostensibly guiding corporate decisions. He sought to discover through interviews and field observations what is viewed as correct, or "right" behavior by managers. He seeks to generalize, perhaps mistakenly, to all of American corporate life.

Jackall's thesis is found in a long quote from an executive: *"what is right in corporate America is what the guy above you wants from you"* (p. 6, italics in original). This quote, if generally accurate as a description of managers' ethical concerns, is a chilling statement of ethical "principles." Since this view of organizational life is not that encountered in the public relations materials and general depictions of organizational conduct found in the social science literature, the research methods and perspective on which it is based should be clearly understood.

Data.   The work relies exclusively upon excerpts from recorded and typed interviews, reproduced in edited, grammatically correct, and rather sterile snippets. Verbal accounts, reported events, and rhetoric are featured rather than behaviors. Jackall seeks to present the "typical," presenting a version or kind of corporate ideology, or conventional wisdom, "what works," rather than detailed descriptions of differences between the organizations, their divisions or segments, or various types of managers.

Settings: Where.   Jackall focuses on the world of ideas: ideas about success, about patronage and exchange, "looking good," and patterned uncertainties. He sets these ideas in a broad organizational framework that demonstrates their context-dependent nature. Although Jackall describes in rich detail the imagined moral world and career concerns of these executives, he does not describe the physical setting, the places, the times, or the geographic, economic, or political climate in which these corporations were embedded (Calhoun 1989). The content of managerial work, the nature of the decisions made, and their consequences are glossed in favor of setting out the managerial attitude toward the vicissitudes of work. Although the details of the work of these managers are omitted, along with the particulars of their leisure or social life, their views about "what it takes" and their imagery of the interpersonal demands of their work preoccupies these (mostly) men.

Focus and Theoretic Questions.   Jackall juxtaposes implicitly the moral framework of Weberian Protestantism and the themes of the "Protestant ethic," which elevates above all efficient, diligent, honest, hard work as a means to salvation, with the Machiavellian concerns of these managers

(1988:191–192). Work and salvation are loosely coupled in their world of work. Managers seek to please their superiors, to avoid being seen as making a mistake, and to know instantly the right "spin" to put on an event or what sort of image is to be projected. Jackall shows how, once reified and sedimented in bureaucratic form, the work ethic no longer fully guides decisions or shapes career concerns (Mills 1951). The objective rules and procedures that etch "success" are always ambiguous, either too broad ("watch the bottom line") or too specific ("do not hire after the 15th of the month") to permit rule-following alone to produce success. Managers read the rules, values, and ideologies in order to make *situated decisions* that reflect the realities and constraints of the here and now (Mannheim 1949; Manning 1980). Authority is not an abstract entity, but is *personalized*, much like the feudal authority described by Weber. Rational-legal authority seems a sheer veneer. Legitimation is acutely sensitive to personal relations to the expectations and power of those above oneself [much as organizational life is described in the first few pages of Joseph Heller's *Something Happened* (1975:9–13)]. Since the vicissitudes of work, of the economy, and even of the aims and purposes of success itself cannot be read off or predicted from the contours of today, much work, time, and effort are devoted to managing the appearance of success.

Much of what is considered managerial work in formal terms is accomplished in meetings, and most of the rest in gossip and apparent conviviality and good humor. There is a constant tension, as Goffman (1959) suggests, between the front and backstage of corporate life and careers. Attachments and commitments are strikingly superficial and mercurial; managers are ready to redefine and rearrange their thoughts upon the occasion of a promotion or demotion of an immediate or one-step-removed superior. The air of the corporation stinks with approbation, dread, and fear of failure. Because in the absence of serious standards, success is defined interpersonally, one pattern of authoritative relations can vanish as quickly as the smile of a used-car salesman only to be replaced by another.

In contrast to the idle notion governing rationalist theories of organization, that organizations (and one assumes careers) are structured by information and the more accurate prediction of the future among the successful, *chance (appears) to rule here* (Jackall 1988, p. 79 ff.). Changes in governmental regulations, in governmental tax practices, or in the health of distant and unknown foreign economies echo in these organizations. Causes of events and their consequences, and praise and blame, are not even matters of "moral luck" (Williams 1981), but results of a mere concatenation of events. The centrality of luck and chance truncates the assumed connection between hard work, merit, and success, and leaves managers clinging to a patron. They endlessly interpret and reinterpret events to *enhance dramaturgically their own appearance of success, or to minimize damage through apparent failure.* They seize the moment, read the drift, and scrupulously watch out for number one. Jackall's quotes demonstrate how the open-ended, broad notions of "success" and "career" are understood.

Roles and Players. These managers see themselves as players, in the Goffmanian sense, people who seek only working consensus, avoid responsibility for their actions, manipulate symbols, people, and things to their own personal advantage as they see it in the moment, and who owe no acknowledged responsibility to product, corporation, stockholders, consumers, or others (cf. p. 145ff.). Furthermore, the basic rules described by Jackall seem to be antithetical to a consistently responsible life, for they are such things as (my inferences): avoid criticism of the "higher-ups," avoid any value commitment that might interfere with pragmatic action, avoid being saddled with responsibility for any failure, don't go over the boss's head, and, in short, to get along go along. Furthermore, the primary rules of loyalty to the boss and personal expediency are always context-dependent ideas that require socially correct readings of others' readings to ensure "survival." In this way, the "other-directed" man of the late fifties, the white-collar or organization man, and the empty actor-as-politician manqué of the eighties are made flesh and now live among us.

Meanings. Jackall shows that managers live simultaneously in two social worlds: the one of abstract notions (or signifiers) of "profit," "authority," and "success," and the one of concrete meanings loosely attached to given decisions. Jackall shows that the "top management" sets broad goals and pressures subordinates to do the necessary to accomplish the mission. Thus, Who says? is a mental question posed by managers to any command, mission, stated purpose, or value state. Ironically, the degree and kind of abstraction needed to make tough business decisions, as is true in all organizations, is based on *acontextual* readings of concrete processes of production, the skills of real people, actual events, and the smells, sounds, and sights of labor. This commitment to abstraction, that Veblen called "trained incapacity," frees managers from transcendental values or constraints. The book concludes that corporate managers treat ethics as no more than a quest for personal survival and advantage (p. 204). But does this mean that the efforts of managers to manage meaning produce or ensure success? No. Jackall describes a horrific world constituted by and for only superficial advantage, unconnected to notions of trust, friendship, honor, or even production, a world peopled by Goffmanian actors.

Even being well polished and superficially adequate to the situated demands of modern corporate life does not mean that one surely succeeds. Far more than the self is at issue. Events other than interpersonal discourse, symbol manipulation, front and backstage management are at work: Shit Happens, as they say, and it engulfs even the most carefully constructed managerial corporate personae. Crises are side-stepped, like an NFL tackle, but they are often reconstituted at another level, or for an incoming manager.

A methodological paradox arises at this point. If this is an accurate description of corporate life, then corporate executives will deny its versimilitude (Van Maanen 1989:313)! The validity of a narrative cannot be established solely by the teller. Jackall has spent many years studying corporations, and appears to be a part of that world socially; he has written this as an ethnographic story, rather than relying on theoretical premises or organizational theories. He tells about things as he sees and hears them, and in their ragged and somewhat shabby form. He makes foreground what is background in the positivistic correlational studies of organizations published in the *Administrative Science Quarterly*.

In this grounded study of organizational discourse, quotes demonstrate the loose coupling between statement of purpose and actions, between work and reward, and between hard work and success. The question arises, What is the nature of interpersonal or subjective realities that obtain in such organizations? How did Jackall, for example, develop the trust necessary to elicit the cynical and self-serving vocabularies of motive presented here? In these sympathetically rendered stories, the "dark side" of organizational life—failures, firings, and demotions—is not presented. Although examples of mistakes and errors of judgment are provided, they lurk in the background, and are the unspoken difference that provides information on this corporate life. The radical individualism of American ideology leaves no little room for nonindividual explanations for failure. Yet the book demonstrates that from their own perspective, these managers are mere objects of others' decisions, swept away by unpredictable malevolent forces, and shaped by unforeseen and perhaps unforeseeable events. Furthermore, since a basic assumption of the interviewees is that everyone lies to cover themselves, make themselves look good, or put the right "spin" on a story, *there is little belief in the idea that truth will rectify a situation or clarify events* (pp. 182–83). It may not be possible to separate the "honey from the horseshit" (p. 161). In these corporations, stories and tales create a socially constructed and intersubjectively sustained reality through what Jackall calls "symbolic dexterity." Like public relations firms generally, managers learn a style of self-presentation that rationalizes and justifies whatever happens, and sees it as predetermined and somehow inevitable. Yet events are subject to individual choice and can be controlled to one's advantage. That seems a fundamental paradox.

Conclusions

This chapter presents selected studies of organizational research based on important distinctive features of the studies as well as their similarities. Having summarized and evaluated these studies, it is now possible to draw out some points that might sharpen future qualitative research. This conclusion is a kind of review of the relevance of these studies for the future ethnographic study of organizational communication.

Foci

Some of the examples explicate the "folk logics" of informal communication within organizational structures (folktales and narratives) and communication with clients (Barley and Cicourel). Others analyze patterns of communication with the public at large or external communication (Manning on communication to and from the police). Formal communication central to managing the mission of the institution and bearing on societal or collective well-being are well described in several studies (Manning; Bennett and Feldman; Sudnow; and Waegel). Organizational communication as rhetoric (see Manning 1977, 1987b; Beare 1987) aimed at self-modification or *autopoesis* (Luhmann 1986), the public or organizations communicating with themselves, has been illustrated (Jackall 1988; see also Broms and Gahmberg 1983). (*Autopoesis* is discussed in more detail in Chapter 8.)

These studies possess important similarities. The concept of social context is well and fully addressed in most of the studies. Indeed, it is perhaps the central concern of most of them. They are often comparative and use the case study method (McPhee 1990; Ragin and Becker 199X). All reflect an interest in identifying units of discourse, and the narrative forms of expression, or typifications. Some adopt relatively more formalized analytic techniques (Barley and Manning). All illustrate, implicitly or explicitly, the role of contrast and similarity in context. This is an essential feature of the creation of meaning. Some provide details of the social construction of the technology of communication (the channel in Jakobson's model), while others examine aspects of the emotive and expressive features of talk (especially the folktale materials). Others examine the relevance of codes and coding (Barley and Manning). Few mention the autoreferential nature of communication in formal organizational settings, the fact that communication both defines a setting and is a feature of it. (Aspects of autoreferentiality are discussed further in Chapters 5 and 8.)

Ambiguities

Some matters are not well discussed in these studies. The studies reviewed rarely examine the *referent* of signs. They discuss signs in organizational contexts in which the referents are assumed to exist as an integral component of the participants' social worlds. Careful observation and interviews, systematic ethnographic work, is required to explicate this matter of referentiality further. The target or audience for communication is sometimes less than clear, although Barley and Cicourel are specific about the targets or the client or patient. Manning's analysis does not include examples taken from individual messages and callers, but makes a case for the relevance of both the workload and message stream as well as internal meanings of the messages driving the encounter with the caller. One might assume that content shapes the encounter with the citizen when and if the officer arrives at the reported scene. The matters of information, equivocation, ambiguity, and the field are not well articulated in these studies, although credibility is a central matter in several (Bennett and Feldman). Temporal and spatial alterations (and alternations) in meanings are limited at in several works. Ethnographic studies are well suited to provide detailed analyses of the rich background against which messages are seen and understood.

The research reviewed provides information on the where and what of the meanings studied. It discusses the why of meaning. The techniques vary in their precision and, indeed, in their reliability and validity (see Kirk and Miller 1985). Researchers doing ethnography seek validity and to reflect, insofar as possible, the "native's point of view" (Geertz 1973).

Future Issues

The studies reviewed raise several fundamental theoretical questions to which future research should be addressed. Does this research reveal underlying codes that enable people to integrate various modalities (e.g., to talk about paintings, write programs for symphony performances, illustrate books)? If so, how do people integrate them over the course of conversational exchanges? These studies also raise the question of relationships between structure (pattern, constraint, language, and code) and process (change, choice, speech, and coder). Giddens (1984) sees this as a matter of relations between structure and action, and this interface is the surface along which micro-macro connections between structure and process will be drawn (Orlkowski and Robey 1991). This may be a central question in organizational communicational research.

An ongoing debate exists between those who favor a top-down approach to narrative meaning and those who support a bottom-up model The limitations of the Bennett/Feldman approach (more or less top-down) to tales can be seen in Cicourel's analysis. He points out the constraints of using a purely top-down view of the structure of tales and their communicative capacity. Recall also the subtle arguments used by Sudnow and Waegel to link typifications to organizational practices. Suffice it to say that the way tales are interdigitated with institutional structure is only partially grammatical and syntactical, and their coherence and credibility are only one dimension of their role within institutional structures (see also Jackson 1990).

An interpretive view of social action maintains a reflective and enmeshed view of communication. Several of the studies reviewed used stories as data. Stories, as Van Maanen (1988), Hunt (1989), and this volume argue, also communicate about setting, role, messages, and the nuanced connections between the teller of the tale, the listener, and the audience. Van Maanen (1988) retells tales from various studies as well as his own tales in three different voices. This question of perspective or voice is addressed in Chapter 7. Do people tell the truth? Jackall found that people told him, "Do not believe what people tell you, even what I tell you." If lying is a common feature of organizational communication, and making oneself "look good" is an essential feature of a business career, how does a researcher discern intersubjective meanings?

Subsequent chapters address the question of *how* best to carry out ethnographic research. We begin in Chapters 5–7 with examples from my fieldwork. This is the basis for a "model" of doing fieldwork.[7] Chapter 9 sets out an approach building on these exemplars and other work. The focus will be on roles, targets, settings, codes, interpretations, coders (actors' roles and tasks), the functions of the sign using Jakobson's model, and analytic techniques. Chapter 10 discusses aspects of narrative voice and postmodern ethnography.

Internal Communication I: Two Ethnographic Studies of Communication

Introduction

Internal communication is central to organizational functions. It is a multifaceted matter, as the examples in Chapter 4 suggest. Yet, recent writing in organizational communication focuses narrowly on the problem of how actors produce a degree of routine certitude in processing and organizing communication (see Kreps 1990:Ch. 1). What is clear can only be known if one identifies the context in which communications occur, including noise, equivocality, and ambiguity. This suggests that in order to proceed further on our quest for organizational meanings, definitions in hand, we *require extended, detailed, qualitative, ethnographically rich examples of organizational communication derived from explicit theoretical premises.* Communication takes place in groups, organizations, and encounters and is to some extent always "setting specific" and context dependent.

Communications studies should specifically and explicitly spell out the context-dependent aspects of communication as well as the generalizable and transsituational aspects. This means combining in a thoughtful fashion a theoretically grounded approach with appropriate methods and techniques. One of the most useful ways to place studies of communication in context is to play with metaphor and use allusion; to strive, using theory and concepts, to incorporate open and defocused thinking when investigating and writing about specific concrete examples (Manning 1979a).

The next chapters take up internal and external communications, in part to contrast them and in part to explore comparative qualitative methods. They frame ethnographic work and theoretically driven analyses in communicational processes. This chapter provides examples of internal communication, while Chapters 7 and 8 focus on external communication.

A Research Agenda

One can readily discover rich examples of organizational communication embedded in the metaphoric language of Karl Weick. Using metaphors to cast about for the language that best captures the process of organizing, Weick explores the open text of communication. No one as yet has more lucidly captured the inadequacies of functionalist and closed-systems models of communication. His ideas continue to sensitize field research. A thematic quote setting forth the essence of his approach, taken from his evocative and important book, *The Social Psychology of Organizing* (1979), underscores a few of the significant problems implicit in the study of organizational communication. The quote places the study of communication aptly in organizational context and raises several key questions central to any ethnographic, qualitative study of communication. It also guides the two field studies presented in this chapter.

> The basic raw materials on which organizations operate are informational inputs that are ambiguous, uncertain, equivocal. Whether the information is embedded in tangible raw materials, recalcitrant customers, assigned tasks, or union demands, there are many possibilities or sets of outcomes that *might* occur. Organizing serves to narrow the range of possibilities, to reduce the number of "might occurs" the activities of organizing are directed toward the establishment of a workable level of certainty. An organization attempts to transform equivocal information into a degree of unequivocality with which it can work and to which it is accustomed. This means that absolute certainty is seldom required. It also means that there can be enormous differences among organizations and industries with respect to the level of clarity that they regard as sufficient for action. Members of organizations spend considerable time negotiating among themselves an acceptable version of what is going on. The activity itself is preserved by the phrase *consensual validation* and the content of the activity is preserved by the phrase *reducing equivocality*. . . . [A display is always] equivocal and people turn to their similar associates for help in sorting through the meanings and for help in stabilizing one of them. (Weick 1979:6, italics in original)

Several points bearing on field studies of communication should be taken from this rich and provocative outline of the broad mission of studies of organizational communication. This quote provides a mandate for studies of organizing or "communicational ordering." Weick points out, or gestures towards, the elusive, allusive, and sometimes invisible materials from which such studies are created—communications of all sorts, and he asserts their centrality to the organizational mandate. In so doing, he notes the importance not only of locating and establishing the "workable level of certainty" characteristic of an organization, but the possible variability in this notional level of clarity and certainty within an organization or across organizations. Importantly, he indicates that uncovering the processes of negotiating meaning is key to describing and subsequently understanding how and why organization members act as they do.

It is important to note that Weick does not assume that the aim of communication is always direct, serving the instrumental achievement of organizational goals, nor even that such communication always achieves its intended purpose. For example, creating and maintaining ambiguity is a central feature of all organizations. Organization members, in part to maintain their autonomy and discretion (Crozier 1964), also require a level of apparently shared consensus in order to work out their vague lines of collective action. Multiple and overlapping social worlds exist within organizations, as well as shared themes of unity, metaphors of ordering, and mission (Dingwall and Strong 1982).

Members do seek consensual validation (i.e., agreement between the participants that may or may not possess external validity) in order to reduce equivocality (average doubt about the sender of a message). Implicit in this formulation is the idea that noise and ambiguity attend all messages and that the routinization of communication is one of the primary functions of an organization. It is also the case that actors *hedge meanings* and avoid telling direct truths or falsehoods, or dissemble to avoid being confronted with their own lies. They use information and if possible manipulate people with information. Furthermore, the tacit grounds for order and ordering are not verbal, but are based on trust (Garfinkel 1963; Shapiro 1987; Rawls 1990). These are two contrasting sources of order, the verbal—the explicit and the formally rational, and the tacit, unexplicated, routine grounds of everyday activities (Garfinkel 1964, 1967).

Classic conceptions of bureaucracy, derived from Max Weber (1947), can be quite misleading. They see organizations as rule governed and hierarchical, held together by goal-oriented communications, whereas from a communicational perspective they are multicentered and multilayered networks of many sorts of messages, grounded on trust, practical working rules, and "make-dos."

Weick turns our attention to the study of what is communicated and how, and how it is made sensible for practical purposes, rather than assuming an ideal type of organization, such as a rational-legal bureaucracy, and the communication that such a model entails. Communications are constrained by social organization, and organizing is always organizing by someone in some social location. We now explore some of the processes of organizing discovered in two field studies.

The Cases: The Nuclear Installations Inspectorate and the Police

The two studies presented here focus on police communication and decision-making as well as on the processes of policy formation and implementation within a British regulatory agency. Both used field methods, interviews, and a modified form of semiotic analysis. Both are further discussed in Chapters 6–8.

Methods

The Regulation of Nuclear Safety. HM Nuclear Installations Inspectorate (NII) has overall responsibility in the United Kingdom for ensuring that the nuclear industry maintains the safety of its plant and operations. It does this by a variety of means, e.g., inspections to monitor compliance with licensing conditions as well as with international radiation standards, emergency procedures, formal and informal meetings, correspondence, licensing negotiations, and persuasion. Unlike the Nuclear Regulatory Commission (NRC) or related agencies in the United States, it is not a legal rule-making body, but has adequate ministerial authority to set and enforce the conditions of acceptable operation using "principles of nuclear safety" (NII 1982a), including fining or temporarily closing a plant and/or reactor, or revising the conditions of licensing. Its work is guided by the "reasonable practicable means test," which sets questions of possible modifications and designs, and plans within an economic context with respect to the equipment (especially its age and operating efficacy and productivity), management, and staff of a particular plant being considered (formal cost-benefits calculations are neither attempted nor desired) (O'Riordian Kemp and Purdue 1988).

The NII, at the time of study (March 1984–March 1986), was headed by a chief inspector and his deputy, and is composed of some 103 persons allocated into five branches. The first branch is devoted to operating plants, the second monitors the planning and building of plants approved and in process, the third regulates fuel reprocessing, and the fourth has responsibilities for future plants. The fifth or policy branch (created March 1986) is charged with policy development and implementation for the inspectorate. Each branch is headed by a branch head, and contains three or four sections headed by senior civil servants. There are around 25 people in each branch, save the policy branch, which has about 6 members. In March 1986, all but one of the branches of the NII were located in a large office building in central London. The fuel-reprocessing branch is located at Bootle, near Liverpool in the north of England, some 100 miles from London. In May 1986, the majority of the NII staff and management moved to Bootle. The chief inspector and his staff and the policy branch remain in London. The entire inspectorate has since undergone a further reorganization.

The four operating branches are divided functionally between "field inspectors" and "specialists," although this is not a rigid distinction, since many of the specialist experts have served as field inspectors and most of the field inspectors are also specialists. The specialties represented range from mathematics and physics to various kinds of engineering, and the specialists' training has taken place both in and out of university programs. They are white scientists and engineers, all but one of whom is male.

The material reported is based on interviews and fieldwork done in the NII between March 1984 and March 1986.[1] The overall aim of this work was to integrate notions of policy with the structure and function of the inspectorate and, having done that, to explicate the relevance of a metaphor that policy-making was a process.

Policing. This work drew on previous studies of policing. It consisted of a general overview (Manning 1977), an analysis of specialized facets of policing, including narcotics work (Williams, Redlinger, and Manning 1979a; Manning 1980), and PCSs (Manning 1982a, 1986, 1988a). Details of these studies are found in the references, but suffice it to say that all the studies were comparative, involving more than one organization, and all but the narcotics studies were cross-cultural and involved fieldwork in England (London, Manchester, and the West Midlands) and the United States (in several large cities including metropolitan Washington and Detroit). The studies were based on taped and handwritten interviews, participant observation, and records, as well as tapes of calls to the police. The study reported here focuses on the PCS, details of which are provided elsewhere (Manning 1988a) as well as above.[2]

Analysis of the Field

Organizational communications are embedded in several fields or sets of social forces that affect and pattern decisions. Since one of the most central concerns of organizational communication is the relevance of information and context to decisions, communicational analysts must see decisions and the decision field as central to their studies of organizations. The *field* in which decisions are made involves all those matters, objective and subjective, which shape a decision or account for an outcome. The notion of a field entails, as well, the horizon of matters that are known possibly to affect a decision under certain conditions, but do not do so on a predictable basis. This will be called the *surround* (cf. Bourdieu 1977). Fields subsume the more detailed interactional encounter or the specific organizational context. The communicational setting (one might call it, following Kenneth Burke, the stage or the scene) is a place characterized by a pattern of authoritatively ordered relations in which a conventionalized set of exchanged signs is interpreted by shared codes.

Semiotics, as we have seen, sensitizes analysis to a search for the interpretants that make possible the connection between the sets of signs (e.g., words in a verbal exchange) lodged in a given text (a record of a call to the police) taken as messages and the organizational context within which they are processed. Organizational rules, traditions, and authoritative relations constrain these connections. Semiotic analysis of communication thus should not simply be preoccupied with signs in context, or signs about signs, social organization, but the constraints upon communication in addition to those given in speech or the structure of semiotic systems.

Just as communications are constrained, fieldwork on communications is similarly constrained. It is possible that fieldwork-based analysis of communication and decisions is shaped substantially by (1) *constraints, material, and other objective structures*, (2) *settings* in which it is carried out, (3) *interpretive issues* central to the organization, (4) the *level of abstraction* at which discourse occurs, and (5) *crises and turning points*. These are the stuff of organizational dramas. Organizations differ in their potential for drama, indicated in part by notable crises and turning points. These dramatic materials, in turn, shape the range of available and useful tropes or *metaphors* relevant to the field study itself (Manning 1979a). These five points are used to report on selected aspects of communicational patterns in policing and the NII.[3]

1. Constraints. Clearly, material technology as well as "objective facts" act as constraints upon fieldwork in any setting. These "facts" have to do with the structural characteristics of the setting and the content of the topic of study; the nature of the material objects relevant to the study; and physical conditions, weather, climate, and the degree of physical and psychological isolation. In the police studies, with the exception of my work on the technology of organizing a response to public calls for assistance (Manning 1988a), these limits were not apparently difficult to overcome. This was due in large part to the consequences of negotiating successful access to an organization. Once access is negotiated at a given level of the organization (this may be renegotiated or require continuous negotiation), scenes can be observed, and key themes of the work can be analyzed. Talk, or discourse, can be checked against action; tales can be compared with observed scenarios; contradictions between ideology and practice can be explicated, and the salient critical points in communication and resultant paradoxes noted. These data may derive from both formal and informal sources.

The operative constraints with respect to objective facts were different in the NII and in the police organizations studied. It was not possible to "overcome" or "work around" these constraints, because the salient action was paperwork, the decisions were taken privately, and the settings of interest were largely individual offices. The material technology of nuclear power generation was daunting, complex, and only partially visible. The focus of the agency was upon careful paperwork, meetings, telephone calls, and consultations; and the several relevant sites for inspection (some 18 reactors in England, Scotland, and Wales) were widely dispersed. The questions asked NII members about the nature of nuclear safety were in part based on knowledge of technology, although my understandings were not deep (I had not studied college-level physics, for example). Furthermore, the reactors, although they are ideational and conceptual in the sense that they are seen as having character, or "personality," themselves are differentially accessible to the senses. For the most part they are sealed and covered in concrete and steel, and are permanently closed to view, although some portions of reactors and turbines are accessible by cameras, X rays, or video cameras. Even the turbines and electrical generating equipment are massive and unavailable to scrutiny except during routine outage and maintenance cycles. Processes of fuel storage and removal, as well as loading procedures, are dangerous, secretive, and well hidden from view.

In part because of this, regardless of the scientific database NII members use, many decisions must be based on judgment and made inferentially because one cannot see or examine the part, or because the subsystem is too complex or is in complex interaction with other systems. Some relevant parameters at issue remain guesses or hunches, good estimates (e.g., the probability of a wind at a certain height blowing in a given direction and speed across a given site carrying just released radioactive material over London, and how many persons would die as a result). Some guesses are intended to stimulate creative thought about likely responses and planning for emergencies and other rare events. For example, the meltdown of a core, any safety agency's second worst nightmare, took place only once, at Chernobyl. This is the single example, on the basis of current information revealed by governments, in the nearly 50 years of nuclear technology and experimentation. On the other hand, the Three Mile Island catastrophe wrought major changes in American nuclear safety regulation, and produced echoes in Britain, although since no pressurized water reactors were then in use in Britain, there was some smugness about the event. Some organizational problems result from utilizing the (somewhat higher) British versions of international standards for radioactivity. NII works with reasoned approximations of many matters central to its mandate, and accepts that this is a realistic, if not comfortable, public and private position.

2. *Settings.*   Two features are of interest here: the themes, or symbolic repertoire, represented in occupational displays, and the social structure of the two organizations.

Police.   Key *themes* in policing have evolved partly as a result of police departments' traditional organizational form (McNamara 1967; Manning 1977) and partly as a result of the police's occupational subculture (Holdaway 1988), and some are shaped by the law and the common-law tradition. Police are action oriented, and action and violence are both everyday occurrences and a part of police stories, their occupational culture. Violence also forms one basis for the division of labor within a police department. The primary locus of symbolic and self-affirmatory action for officers is "the streets"; they control people in situations where violence may be required (Bittner 1970). The police engage in fairly visible social control functions, and at least part of their activity is verbal, public, visible, and accessible to the senses. Police, for the most part, are educated at the high school level, come from lower-middle-class origins, and bring a working-class style to the organization and the occupational culture of officers below the rank of sergeant (Manning 1979a). Police devalue abstraction, intellectuals, and intellectualization, and overvalue (from the intellectual's or administrator's point of view!) direct pragmatic action to manage, dismiss, or solve an immediate problem. They view themselves as "people of action." They possess no general theory of policing or of human conduct, and their technology, although sophisticated, is embedded in traditional organizational tasks and structure. They rely on commonsense judgment in face-to-face encounters with people (Wilson 1978).

The *structure* and social organization of policing is based on the traditional assumption that as a monitoring and inspectorial organization, the police should maintain the maximal number of people "on the ground," observing and gathering information. The police are highly dependent on citizens for this, but in the years since World War II, they have become increasingly dependent upon the telephone and 911 systems as the primary channel for sending and receiving messages, and computers and related software for data-processing and storage. Their work is uncertain, demand is sporadic, and most of their assignments emanate from the communications center, rather than from their own choices to intervene. Most events they encounter are outside their direct control. Police work within a bureaucratic and decentralized command structure, and the work force, usually two officers riding in a car, is dispersed widely in an ecological area. The police possess high discretion, are rarely closely supervised, and value autonomy and personal authority. Their work, although visible to some segments of the public, is invisible, except in crisis, to their immediate supervisors (Jermeir and Berkes 1979).

Nuclear installations inspectorate. The symbolic aspects of marking the meaning of work, or *themes*, in the NII, among the inspectors, branch heads, and the chief, clearly differ from those found among the police. If these rather complex matters can be summarized, it could be said that NII inspectors are thought oriented, and most of what passes for "action" consists of reading, condensing, summarizing, commenting upon, or "minuting" files, reports, and documents, and passing on to others internal memos, reports, and scientific documents. Inspectors occasionally make a field site visit, but for the vast majority of the time, they work at their desks, using their telephones, attending meetings and conferences with colleagues within the NII and with the three licensees who produce electrical power and plutonium. (The most important of these three licensees is the CEGB.) Much of the valued work is "invisible" to the naked eye—one sees paper move and hears words spoken, decisions discussed, and gossip shared, but the movement of paper, the constant shuffling of files and records, is something of a blur. It is not easy to "see" a decision made. As civil servants with considerable higher education and training, NII people value abstraction, reasoned judgment, good sense, careful analyses, and systematic evaluation. They seek clarity and precision in their own writing and speech and value it in others. In the English manner, they value understatement, subtlety, and irony, and rarely like overt confrontations, disagreements, or direct sanctioning of others. Their preference in relationships with the representatives of industry is a constant dialogue that relies on good conscience, honesty, and humor. Although they view themselves as scientists and engineers, they see themselves as translating scientific principles and ideas into working judgments about matters social, political, moral, economic, and technical. One might call their central problems "sociotechnical" insofar as they monitor the products of the interactions between human beings and technical systems such as the nuclear reactor and related various components, subsystems, and systems. In this way, they stand between the "scientific" and the "political" or policy world of public safety. They see their work as "scientific." Yet, of necessity, science is a discourse or form designed to resolve disputes and for organizing discussion, while the ultimate purpose and justification for the work of the NII is not science, but ethics, morality, and politics. In this way, the NII inspectors stand in relation to science as the police do to law: both science and the law stand as resources for use in conflict situations.

The inspectorate monitors events, and is *structured* to ensure routine high discretion. The essence of the mandate is to ensure licensee compliance, while still maintaining the production of power and plutonium, and to do so by case-by-case analyses of individual sites and reactor circumstances. The mode of social control is conciliatory, and the style of relationship amicable. Other matters are central to the structure of NII: its dependence upon the industry for information, its indirect role in maintaining national defense capacity, and its final (unappealable) authority to close down, fine, or decommission a reactor. It is subject to the ebb and flow of work determined by the quasi-governmental organizations licensed to produce electrical power using nuclear reactors: the request for licenses, and the wish to modify a plant or change the conditions of the license. NII inspectors are dependent, furthermore, for information, evaluations, and scientific assessments produced by the scientists employed by the power producers or their subcontractors. As Heimer (1985a) has noted in the context of oil drilling in the North Sea, information dependency increases organizational dependency and the assuming of risks on behalf of the more powerful organizations. This "dependency" is a constant irony to the inspectors since they are asked to judge, often on short notice, the quality of scientific assessments made by other hired scientists about, for example, the relative contribution to "safety" of a new fire control scheme or radioactive emissions tracking system. The decentralized nature of the NII—branches acting in large part as semifeudal baronies, and relatively little communication other than between branches one and two—means that great discretion lies within the branches and at the individual level. The greatest discretion lies at the bottom of the hierarchy—with the inspectors. Very high value is placed on individual and branch autonomy and decisiveness, and little close supervision is carried on. (Some section heads monitor the work flow of their workers rather closely.) The cumulative pattern of decisions is usually only known to branch heads when a crisis occurs, when a decision is needed, or when a complaint is lodged by the generating board about some decision.

3. Interpretive issues. Matters problematic also differ in the two settings. The level of verbally explicit detail provided in my interviews was higher in the NII than the police, and the phrases, terms, concepts, and reasoning were scientific in character. It was assumed that I knew more than I actually did know about nuclear reactors, although I was not patronized or treated as ignorant. (I was, in fact, relatively ignorant.) Many of the key questions about the safety of the reactor were cast into scientific terms, if not jargon. Nontechnical issues, and social questions associated with reactor safety broadly defined, were rarely discussed.

4. The level of abstraction. The correlative levels of abstraction at which the questions of nuclear safety were debated, discussed, and outlined in the interviews were consistent with a very high level understanding of the implications of loss of public trust, yet there was an abiding unwillingness to engage in public debate or to educate the public about the risks of generating electricity by nuclear power. Lay opinion was not considered relevant to the technical questions the NII weighed. Regardless of these overt and verbal differences in conceptual powers, the similarities in respect to policymaking between NII and the police studied were striking. The varied, concrete, illusory, and changing meanings of "policy" in policing were reproduced in the NII. That complexity was expressed in technical terms rather than in the somewhat more earthy, direct, and concrete terms used by the police.

5. Turning points and crises: dramatic moments. There are few dramatic turning points for members of the NII. The licensing process, although central and problematic, is a lengthy one, often requiring a number of years to complete. The records of events that punctuate the career of a reactor site are housed in a huge cabinet, and decisions are minuted in files. There is little finality about any of the work done, because it is essentially negotiation. One reactor I visited had been under development for over 18 years, and had yet to be licensed. Even the elevators were under constant repair. In short, it is not easy to study bureaucrats when the "paper trail" itself is so vast and complex as to be inaccessible, and any simple depictions of the process are caricatures. Key matters are unavailable to the senses. Of course, major crises, altering the surround, arise unexpectedly as a result of disasters at home and abroad, and publicly known major accidents.

6. Metaphors. Police think in dramatic terms, and they highlight drama, conflict, distrust, action, control, struggle against evil (crime), and serving the interests of the high morality of the state. They are engaged in a constant struggle for sustaining the idea of moral and social hierarchy. The metaphors in the NII, on the other hand, are reasoned cognition, science (both concepts and analogies), sensible and careful planning, trust, and mutual cooperation in the interests of achieving shared aims and objectives.

Comparative Observations

The implications of the above overview, organized by six themes, again underscore the importance of difference in context, and the necessity for systematic comparative analysis. A single case study could not provide the explicit contrast that systematic ethnographic analysis requires. The questions arising, set out in the earlier quote from Weick, now can be discussed comparatively.

1. What communicational *meanings are to be studied*, given that equivocation, noise, and information are a part of any message or message series?

In the case of the police, the source of communication was the PCS (see Manning 1988a:Figure 2.2). Although this has been mentioned earlier and will be discussed in detail in the next chapter, a brief review is perhaps useful. The PCS is the central system of call receipt, processing, and output to officers on the ground. A study of the PCS is reflexive. It is a study of communications, the focus of which is the actual concrete communications system. In that sense, it is a study in forms of metacommunication, or framing communication about communication. The system that carries communication through the organization is also used by officers to communicate both officially and unofficially with each other. Calls were converted into incidents by operators, the processing of jobs was done by dispatchers, and the assignments were given to officers for disposal. Beginning with an event in the external environment, some of which become calls to the police, the initial call, or communicational unit, changes label and location, and moves from the external environment through the organization, modified, and returns transformed to the external environment. Calls moved through the police departments studied, labeled as messages, jobs, and assignments. Some became the basis for records.

In the NII, since the primary role of the agency was to ensure that the industry observed a sensible or reasonable level of safety, in part by the licensing process, the resultant paper trail was a focus of the fieldwork. The meanings of key thematic terms, "license," "conditions of the license," "safe," and "safety policy," and the nature of the paper trail itself (not a term used in the NII) were the target of my investigation. I attempted without success to trace the flow of correspondence within the NII: the complexity of the paper trail was beyond my capacity to understand, let alone produce even a remotely adequate rendition. The volume of paper generated, circulated, and filed was overwhelming: for example, a full 4 by 6 by 2 foot steel upright cabinet held the correspondence between the NII and the industry, called "the safety case," for a reactor nearly on line. The resultant gloss on the process that I wrote was a stage-based outline of licensing, its turning points, crises, and outcomes as described to me in interviews by senior officials in NII.

2. *When* are these meanings to be studied? Are there routine points at which communications can be studied, or are there crises best suited for extracting data?

Routinized organizational *times* at which meaning is transformed were clearly evident in the studies of the PCS because the police organizations studied were organized around three segments or subsystems (operators, dispatchers, and officers), and these in turn contained symbolic indicators of the movements of the messages through the PCS. The relevant communicational units (a social form that carries a message) changed as the message moved. The meaning of the message changed as it arose and was defined within the citizen's or caller's world, was processed within the organization, and became one of the bases for officers' actions. Powerful and various noninformational matters shaped message-processing. My fieldwork focused upon four variables that affected, shaped, or patterned the message or communicational unit as it moved: technology, codes and classification, roles and tasks, and interpretive work (see Chapter 6). As the message moved, its meaning was transformed, and the consequence of this motion was to fix or solidify certain meanings and to make others more unstable or problematic.

On the other hand, in NII, there was no neat central theme or flow of communication through the organization, unless one glossed it with the phrase, "the safety case." The safety case could be tied to a specific site and a named reactor, but any safety case involved collaboration between the parties, alternatively audience and performers, inspectors, specialists, and their counterparts among the licensees in the nuclear industry. Thus, communication was affected importantly by the power and authority of the social worlds and segments with which the organization communicated (Kling and Gerson 1978).

3. *Where* within the organization are meanings to be identified? Specifically, in what segments, vertical or horizontal in character, or defined locales or subsystems, are they to be best studied? Time (that is, organizationally defined time) of meaning and place of meaning are analogous in this study.

In the police organizations, everyday/anyday time, or citizens' time, was converted within the organization into several types of time. The citizens' calls were converted into clock or mechanical time by the computer-monitored operators, into the "police time" of the dispatchers and officers (some of whom worked on a concept of "my time"), and into the standard time of the administrators. These are forms of "organizational time." "Officers' time," based on their priorities and sensibilities, dominated decisions and actions at the lower levels of the organization and set the priorities for actions. Administrators, or those above the level of sergeant within the police, focused on written records and crises, so were virtually reliant on the time sedimented in records, clock time, and officially noted duties. These times had correlates in the channels used, in the form of verbal communication on the telephone, and in a computer file created by the operators and sent on as a printed copy to the dispatchers who use the radio to assign the job to an officer. If the radio message is acted upon by the officer, verbal interaction and observations on the scene may become a written record. Times, locations, and channels are partial indices, or signifiers (expressions), referring complexly to each other. Thus, time was not a universally shared idea, but one that resided in layers of the organization. The "where" of a message implies the time governing its movement and eventual disposition.

In the NII, the paper trail was an indicator of the progress in the activities surrounding licensing of a reactor. These activities can be called stages. This was roughly indicated also by the location of the case in one of the several branches within NII. It would center first in branch four, "future reactors," then move to branch one, "in progress," and then to branch two, "operating reactors." At each stage (and in each branch) in this natural history, considerations of safety could be raised, either by the specialists or by the inspectors, and these questions, doubts, and reservations were addressed further in intrabranch discussions and conferences. Furthermore, each new submission, report, or meeting could produce a recycling of questions, disagreements, and redefinitions. On the other hand, levels of communication were not set, so that inspectors could be communicating with plant managers, regional managers, or scientific experts at the headquarters of the CEGB. Communication took place in a maze, a rhizome, a tangled network of messages flowing within and between branches, between NII and the parent bureau, the Health and Safety Executive, and between the Health and Safety Commission in the Ministry of Trade and Industry where NII was located, and other ministries (especially Energy, Defense, and Environment), and finally between the NII and the actual licensees. It was less a trail than a multilevel moving glacier, very complexly connected beneath the surface.

4. *How* are meanings "pinned down" or shaped into "a workable level of certainty" within the two organizations studied?

For the police, what is done on the street is seen as the very essence of the work, and definitions of "good police work" are located there. Notions like "you had to be there" and "don't second-guess a street decision" and the constructed, shifting, and fluid nature of street reality are axioms that serve as fundamental sources for reducing ambiguities in meaning. That is, if a written report or an investigation produced an account that differed from the account of the officer on the ground, his or hers will be assumed to be closer to the truth, preferred as more accurate [this accuracy is itself seen as problematic and negotiable (see Hunt and Manning 1991)] than the management level report because "you had to be there." This mode of negotiating the truth of an event, in turn, is contradicted by notions of administrative responsibility, the rules and regulations of the department, standing policies, and volatile public opinion as reflected in the mass media. The ambiguity of meaning is pinned down in the most powerful way by trust in the source, Who was there in the event?, secondarily by departmental authority, and finally by the law and courts. In the NII, meaning is pinned down in the first instance by narrowing the focus of concern to the technology within and around the reactor. The means of establishing sensible outcomes is structural. Control by the top management of the organization works by default. Wide discretion exists at the bottom, and problems are allowed to "float up" only when not directly resolved (or when they languish and die) at the bottom of the organization. The third mechanism is the series of taken-for-granted assumptions about the social reality of the reactor. NII members believe that reactors are safe, that the industry is trustworthy, that the public entrusts the NII to use good sense, and that the mandate is secure, and the public believes that technical and scientific questions are best left to the experts (the NII) rather than widely debated. What is decided about everyday operating standards by the NII, in the end, is reified as guaranteeing safety and this presumptive test, NII approval of a license, is taken as adequate evidence of the existence of safety by the public.

Comparative Analysis

These examples can be used in the interest of making somewhat broader points as well as providing categories for a comparative organizational analysis of communication. It has been argued that communication pins down all that is taken to be fact, and reaffirms that utterly arbitrary but essential distinction between facts and values for organizational members (Scheppele 1987). Weick (1979) points out that what, when, where, and how this "pinning down" happens makes a significant difference in the process of meaning production, or what might be called the conversion of social events, things "natural," into organizational categories and jobs, things "cultural."

In the two settings, NII and the police, the themes of the work and organization differ, a distinction that can be crudely glossed by saying that the approach to work is governed by an "action paradigm" and the approach to the organization by a "thought paradigm." This is a matter of emphasis, of course, as police frequently think and NII inspectors do act. The constraints vary as well, with the NII representing a high-technology, paper-oriented, regulatory agency and the police representing a low-technology, action-oriented, control agency. Both are certainly open systems, but NII is formally charged with anticipating the future and reducing the risk of nuclear accident or the release of radioactivity. The NII, perhaps of necessity, relies on the industry for information, resources, personnel to carry out research, and its goodwill and trustworthiness (Heimer 1985a,b). The police rely on the public for information and support. The structure of both organizations is "bottom-heavy." Discretion and operative control over decisions lie at the bottom of the organization, in the hands of the police officers and the inspectors, while public accountability rests, ironically, at the top. Both contain horizontal and vertical divisions that modify the noninformational context. The communicational units in the case of the police are discrete, time-bound, organizational responses to events, while in the NII these units are seen in processes, abstract definitions, and thoughts about thoughts and about technology, which stretch imaginatively far into the (unknowable) distant future.

In the police, high and positive evaluation of autonomy and freedom of decision can be traced to the ways in which events on the street are managed, even when eventually resolved by internal processes or when shaped prior to the officers' receipt of the message. Police eschew paper, concretely define their personal focus, style, and locus of control, and use the public metaphor of decisiveness and implicit violence. The policy deny, perhaps correctly, their dependence (directly for information, cooperation, and support, indirectly for employment and benefits) on the public. Since they act essentially as a screening agency for the criminal justice system, they maintain independence by focusing on their discretion in permitting the passage of the case into the system or not, e.g., by arrest or not, rather than on the nature of the outcome of the case (Reiss 1974). In the NII, the values of "muddling through" and considering and legitimating the licensee's "safety case" meant that NII members were creating the mirror into which they looked to see themselves. The paper trail, or the safety case, is the organizing metaphor central to their mandate. However, since it was negotiated and they were dependent upon the licensees for information, the sought-for "workable level of certainty" was transactional and intraorganizational in character. It had a somewhat ironic character; and it has been suggested elsewhere that NII complies with the licensees' standards rather than governing and regulating the licensees (Manning 1987c).

Communication, even explicit commands and directions, is not everything. Tacit and consensual validation of central ideas like "safety" or "crime" remains organizationally problematic, in part because, like the police on the streets, the NII inspectors *presume* that their actions control, shape, alter, and manage an uncertain, vague, elusive feature endemic to complex technology and social organization. The object of study here, communication, is both a feature of the settings studied and constitutes or renders them visible to participants. However, mere metaphors of drama cannot avert nor capture the horrendous potential actuality of a nuclear disaster.[4]

Conclusions

An agenda seized from an evocative quote from Karl Weick, in the form of a set of categories by which fieldwork might be organized and focused, was advanced and illustrated by a comparative analysis of two field studies of organizational communication. Some conclusions and lessons for the field were drawn. We are now positioned to consider another aspect of internal communication in the police.

6

Internal Communication II: Paradox, Routines, and Resolutions

Introduction

The theme of this chapter is paradox and its resolution in organizations. The overall aim of the chapter is to set out some relationships between message analysis, paradox, and various solutions to or resolutions of ambiguity in organizational communication. The previous chapter addressed comparatively processes of internal organizational communication and their study. This chapter steps back; it is reflective. It contains a series of inferences, signposts, and directions for the study of internal organizational communication. These inferences grow in part from the analyses and data presented here and in part from the theoretical perspective that informs this book. Some of the theoretical sources drawn upon here include Karl Weick's notions of organizing, Luhmann's (1986) concept of *autopoesis*, or the self-reproduction of communicative patterns in social systems, and Bateson's concept of the double bind. Cooper's rather difficult Derridian perspective on organizational communication as a solution to differences within a context is also used (see also Quinn and Cameron 1988). The chapter analyzes modes of message analysis in two police departments.

Message Analysis

Recall the three segments or subsystems within a police communications system—operators, dispatchers, and officers—and also that organizational actors in all three segments both screen calls and shape the nature of the response to any call. A short version of the process is that police operators screen initially all calls, passing most on to dispatchers, who selectively forward them to officers.

Operators in the police organizations studied maintained a detailed set of understandings about how to make sense of a call prior to transforming it into an incident. The average call takes some 15–30 seconds to complete, and tends to be somewhat "formatted" by callers (i.e., callers anticipate some of the questions, or wait to be asked for the relevant information without "rambling" on). It appears that many callers know what is expected of them. In order to pass into the system, a complete call (not terminated by either party) had to meet these preconditions: it was deemed to be about police business (not a wrong number or operator error in transferring the call to the police); it was complete (not terminated by either party); the caller was trusted. If the call met these conditions, operators opened a computer file and in effect translated the call from the language of everyday life into police talk. Let us consider as examples two summarized vignettes, one from the British Police Department (BPD) and one from the American Midwestern Police Department (MPD).

BPD "Stolen Car" Call

A telephone call comes into central police communications center on a 911 line around 9:15 A.M. from a young-sounding person with an foreign accent. He stumbles, mumbles, and then says (with some difficulty in speaking English) that he wants to report a stolen car. The operator listens with a careful mind to deception. She asks the caller to give his name, his address, and where he is calling from [a telephone booth or "call box" outside his place of work, as it happens]. "Your car was stolen, you say?" she asks. She asks for and gets the particulars of the car—make, year, color, and registration number [equivalent to the license plate number in the United States]. The operator asks the caller if he has made his last car payment, a question he finds confusing and befuddling. [One assumes he did not know why this was being asked of him when he was worried about the loss of his car to thieves.] He finally mumbles "Yes . . . I think so." She then asks if she can call him back shortly and he says "Yes." "At what number?" He gives the number of a call box and then says he is at work. Then he decides against asking calls to be made to him at work. He is confused and agitated. The operator puts the caller on hold, checks a list of repossessed autos she has at hand, and discovers that his car has been repossessed [towed away and stored somewhere] by the finance company. She comes back on the line to ask if he owns a Cortina, etc. [the details of the car he provided earlier], to which he responds "Yes." The operator tells the caller just before she terminates the call, "Your car has not been stolen; it has been repossessed because you did not make your last car payment." "Oh . . . ahh . . . thank you. . . ." "Good-bye," replies the operator.

MPD "Stolen Car" Call

The operator at the emergency center answers, "Police. Where is the problem?" [The computers are programmed with a fixed algorithm of choices beginning with the location—address, street corner, named place. In the absence of the location, the computer will not allow the operator to proceed without an "override" of the program.] A person with "educated speech" says, "I'm calling from a phone booth, but my car was stolen around the corner of Posh Street." "What is the address of the phone booth?" the operator inquires. He answers, with some irritation, with the street corner and says, "My car is a Datsun SX400Z and was stolen from where it was parked around the corner." She takes the particulars of the car, the approximate estimated time when it was stolen, and tells him to wait for an officer to come and take a report.

Comment on the Calls

Considerable organizational work is displayed in the processing of these two calls. Making some general points about this processing will permit specification of some general rules and principles that serve to enact, or socially encode, ambiguous calls in both departments. First, the nature of social *ambiguity* is well illustrated here: ambiguity lies not in the nature of the facts presented to the operator, but results, is created, and is socially constructed as a result of the dialogue between the operator and the caller. Ambiguity emerges, in part by the interaction between the caller and the operator, and their conjoint dialogues serve to produce an actionable choice and authoritative meanings. In the BPD call, detailed questioning such as is shown here is rather unusual. The BPD operators, unlike the American operators, have no set format or set order of questioning by which they must extract the needed information buried in the caller's discourse. No organizationally mandated order is required. The exceptions to the use of the routine format, and the ritual use of question and answer, illustrated here are revealing. The exceptions seen in this BPD call suggest one basis for a nonroutine treatment or a "normal form" modification of the usual pattern of hearing the call, opening a computer file, and sending the message on to the dispatchers for assignment to officers. Police operators are oriented primarily, but not exclusively, to the cognitive function of the words or signs (message; Jakobson's model). They exclude various interpretive possibilities about the call—that it was about a past event, that it was about a dream or fantasy, that it was a poetic exercise, that it was a prank or joke. They check the channel, as do the callers, saying, "Do you hear me?" "You're talking too fast . . . I can't understand you," and suppress response to the emotional tone of the caller unless the caller threatens suicide. If suicide is threatened, operators are under strict orders to respond to callers personally and even treat them like human beings: keep them on the line, listen carefully to them, alert others to the problem, seek medical assistance for the caller, and so on.

In the BPD call, the operator was oriented to the caller and to the poetic aspects of the message (the register and intonation of the caller's voice and the speed at which he spoke). If operators orient to accent and content in some interaction, as was the case in this call, it is revealing of "normal practice" (which is to ignore this as irrelevant to the "facts of the call"). Note that the operator did not encode this as a stolen-car call. It was termed an "information-only" call. In the BPD call, the operator suspected that the caller might be an "Asian," and might not realize his car might have been repossessed and not stolen. She also knew the area from which he called, an area of low-income "Asian" (meaning people from the Indian subcontinent) and West Indian residents. She believed something about the caller and the call, and pursued a line of action to establish or rule out what she already believed to be true. Such reasoning can be exaggerated in horrendous cases where operators believe a scene is not a shooting, proceed to deny a car, or merely reassure the caller while violence is in progress. The example does not have to be horrendous to make the point: belief embeds facts in ambiguous calls.

In the MPD call, the caller telephoned from a street in a well-known area of good restaurants and shops after lunch, and his information and position were taken and processed without further question. He was told to wait for an officer (officers are not always "requested" by operators, nor do they always go) to take the report. Let us consider some further nuances of processing potentially problematic calls.

Subsystem Effects: Operators, Dispatchers, Officers

Decisions about the disposition of calls are subsystem specific, i.e., the working rules that govern these decisions are not uniform across subsystems, iterative, or transsituational. The questions concerning the meaning of the call, and the silent mental dialogue that they cause, are not identical in the subsystems, although the questions are functionally equivalent. The process of organizing messages is not truly iterative and recursive. It is, rather, analogically sequenced and ordered. Calls are seen not as homologous and formally comparable, but as analogically alike, and the analogs are to be sought. The available tacit knowledge used by operators to orient to the calls, such as information about time, place, the location of the problem, the types of calls, and callers, is also used to organize the meaning of the brief, elliptical, and sometimes puzzling content of the call. Context, or assumptions brought to the call by the hearer, tacit information inferred from these calls, are important data for analyzing calls. This type of decision-making *interacts* in a complex fashion with the information content of the calls. Here are some "rules" discovered in each of the three subsystems.

1. *Operators* send on all calls that they do not refer or refuse, and all accepted calls must be encoded or given a classification (a number). Calls are classified not by mutually exclusive binary logic assigning something to *either* an *x* or a *y* category (but not both, "maybe," or "could be"), but by means of an apparent *analogical system* of metonymy, metaphor, and paradigmatic association, which says in effect, This call is more like the other calls I labeled in this fashion (gave this classification to), and less like those I labeled in that fashion or otherwise. The classification given the call makes it a type or an index, one of several that resemble an imagined prototype of the concepts "burglary," "auto theft in progress," or "rape" (Rosch et al. 1976). Calls, appearances to the contrary, are not discrete units, but are seen as a stream affected by the context of other calls being processed at the same time, by previous calls like this one (synecdochically related), and by future calls yet to be made. Their resemblances, one to the other, are situational and sporadic. In the BPD call described, a file was not opened because the operator, a police officer, distrusted the caller. Operators maintain beliefs about the nature of elements in the world as reported to them, and these beliefs embed the "facts" given by the caller. For example, the closer the source to the police, (or near police), the more trusted the message, regardless of the detail provided. Operators, once they have made this determination, close off the conversation, telling the caller a unit has been requested or that the police will "call 'round," and generally ignore or refuse to attend the phatic and connotative aspects of the message. As a result, dispatchers verify and reify operators' decisions and take on faith the notion that the call they receive refers to events in the real world, "out there." Once that is decided, they proceed on that basis, discounting inconsistent facts and anomalies.

Calls are typified, put into formats using accepted or normal form inclusions and exclusions (Bottomley and Coleman 1980), much like the typifications used by prosecutors (Sudnow 1965). In other words, operators and dispatchers routinize messages in accepted ways. Dispatchers and operators "send everything down" in part to ensure that they are not vulnerable to the claim that they did nothing. Protecting oneself from criticism is generally accepted as the norm and widely termed "covering your ass." The messages are translated and back-translated such that when the officer arrives on the scene he or she can shape it to the actual scene encounter. Calls must not therefore be classified in such a way or read out on the air in such a fashion that they could not be otherwise described or classified, once the officer reaches the scene. This concludes the self-covering and self-protecting exercise.

All messages are located in a web of tentative relations in the "outside world" (the social world of citizens, the location of most of the callers, a world partially shared by the officers), the worlds of banks and stores with alarms, and the social world of the organization within which the operators and the dispatchers work. These three distinctive social worlds have varying degrees of redundancy, coherence and information potential.

The web of tentativeness frames any message so that it is read as: "although the message reads this way, it always could have been, and may well be otherwise." "You have to be there." It is assumed that truly to understand the emergent, unfolding nature of the reported event, one has to know the context. The most trusted and authoritative report-ers are police officers who are or have been on the scene.

2. *Dispatchers* work with at least once-processed materials (or twice or more since the caller has processed the object and turned it into an event prior to calling the police). When the point of an incident is not imme-diately clear, "rules of thumb" are used by the dispatchers to classify and act upon the incident, once they receive it. Like the operators, they must differentiate the message from noise, judge doubt and equivoca-tion, and separate the message from the field of other activities flowing on around them.

They first employ what might be called *the rule of social reality* to pin down the meaning of a call. The objects reported in the incident they receive have a referential reality and they exist in the here and now. They conform formally the operators' definitions, even if they doubt them unofficially.

Dispatchers use a second rule: *draw upon tacit knowledge of such calls.* They bring this background knowledge to the foreground. They might ask themselves: What have I done previously about calls "like this one"? Dispatchers frequently receive calls such as the two illustrated above. If they decided to assign an officer to the incident, they may consider: Do I know the area where the car was stolen? Where is it in the city, and what is its social composition? How frequent are car thefts there? What sort of car is it? Is it the sort favored by car thieves? (In Detroit, for example, the favorite target of car thieves is the Chevrolet Camaro, while in England, the Ford Cortina is a commonly stolen car. It is used for parts, and is easy to fence and sell.) They might further ask themselves: How long ago was it stolen (when did the caller report the event took place)? Was it said to have been taken from in front of the house or from the garage?

Was it possibly taken clandestinely by a teenage son or daughter, or an estranged, angry spouse?

The third rule used by dispatchers is: *assume the referential reality of calls*. Assume that this reported event happened as reported for official purposes. (This rule does not exclude holding and applying unofficial and informal understandings of the calls!) The operator's classification defines the event and the object of the call in the world, and converts it into a matter for police business.

Fourth, dispatchers, like operators, used the *rule of analogy* combined with a sense of versimilitude or "knowledgeability" (Giddens 1984) to interpret the content of calls. They ask: Do these facts seem likely? Are they similar to events (of this kind) I know personally?

A fifth rule advises dispatchers to *associate meaning with the timing of a call*. Calls on Friday or Saturday night describing a family fight are seen as "routine," as are morning calls about burglaries discovered right after storekeepers open their store.

These five rules or assumptions facilitate the encoding and processing of messages. They also mean that intended content, callers' needs, and the social world of real events are always secondary in importance to these rules and other organizational procedures for encoding calls to the police.

3. *Officers* orient themselves much less to technological, classification, and role constraints than do operators and dispatchers. Even message content is less important (with a few exceptions, e.g., mention of a personal injury, a suspect on premises, or a colleague in trouble) than are surrounding understandings, the field, and noise. A few key aspects of the message may be salient, and synecdochical or representative of the entire text. The interactive process between officer and radio message yielding a social construction of reality can be distilled. For officers, a few key points of information are determinate. Three simple paradigms, or associative contexts, exist within which a message (a radio call) can be placed by officers: (1) take action straight away, (2) take action in due course, and (3) wait and see/do nothing immediately. Work load affects the use of the latter paradigm. The higher the work load, the greater the number of calls within the "wait and see" paradigm. Of primary concern to the officers, aside from work load and message flow considerations, when they turn their attention to the content of the message, is the bearing of "surrounding understandings," or the field of meaning that surrounds the social context within which the message is seen.

The degree to which surrounding understandings pin down meanings to routine parameters and how changes in the surround produce changes in message meaning cannot be overemphasized. A lively example of the impact of surrounding understandings on the salience of items and the paradigms within which the messages will be placed is illustrated by 16 reported rapes of young school-bound students in Detroit in late December 1988 and early January 1989. It was seen as a series, and there was speculation that they had been done by the same person. The rape concern became amplified into a moral panic (Cohen 1979). School was adjourned for the Christmas holidays and media attention turned to the celebration instead. Police subsequently announced to the press that 1988's total number of reported school-related sexual attacks or assaults was 40 percent below that of 1987, and that overall the city's sexual assault figures were slightly down. [There were 1,187 rapes in January–October 1988 and 1,194 in 1987, a decrease in the official number of seven (*Detroit News*, 16 December 1988).]

Two discernible things happen as a result of a change in the surround. First, any rape call becomes high priority for all units. This may lead to clustering of units, swarming, and "call-jumping" to take calls directed to other cars. During this period, a reported rape or the possibility of a rape becomes a salient and *defining feature* of the call, making the surrounding understandings within which the message is heard now "another rape," rather than a "school fight." Second, change in the surround also changes the ordering of information bits or the salience of the units within the message. For example, a sexual assault or possible sexual assault report featuring an *address* in an area around a school, or reported near the *time* of school opening or closing, during this panic, will be given high priority, and the items underlined will be keyed on as relevant to the larger issue of "girls being raped on the way to school." Then, as a result, the call will be seen as one in a series of calls ("rape calls") integrated metaphorically. These features will increase the informal concern and priority given to a call containing these elements (syntagms). They are read off a radio call that might define it as an instantiation of "sexual assault," "rape," "rape in progress," or "rape just happened." Put another way, if an "assault," "noisy fight," or "person with a weapon," is heard by officers, they will translate it into a "rape" call. In the absence of the moral panic about rapes on the way to school, officers will see these calls as instances of "assault," "noisy fight," etc., and only by association as possible rapes.

As noted above, uncertainty and ambiguity are built into the structure of police communications. This is in fact amplified by the modern high-technology computer-processing of messages now used by most very large American departments (Larson 1990). The American urban police are increasingly dependent upon radio and technologically mediated messages rather than face-to-face encounters to mobilize them. They must take calls encoded in two other contexts and decode them for their own practical purposes. Officers must in effect "deconstruct" the call to think through the following: How does the call come to me as it does? What do I need to take from the call in order to act? What is its priority in my personal agenda? In many respects, what happens is that the apparent ambiguity and uncertainty in the call-processing system is resolved pragmatically by the actions of officers.

The elaboration of this theme or reduction of equivocality and ambiguity in policing and call-processing is a microcosm of the problem of resolving paradoxes in communication, but it has special relevance in public-serving organizations, and organizations that devolve authority and discretion to the bottom of the organization.

Paradox and Resolution

We can turn now to police message analysis for examples of paradoxical messages and their resolution. This exercise will, in turn, enable us to state some inferences concerning the study of paradox and ambiguity in internal organization communication.

The Double Bind

The anthropologist Gregory Bateson and his colleagues advanced an important theory of mental health and illness that has relevance to the study of communication paradoxes in organizations. The central metaphor was adapted from information theory and the key idea is that of the *double bind* (1972:201–27). The double bind arises when two messages with contradictory action implications are communicated at once (they may be contained in the same text or message). In Bateson's view, such messages are very destructive when communicated by an authoritative person to another, and serve in the long run to suppress the hearer's ability to discriminate such communications from others.

Bateson sees communication and communicational skills as essential to proper ego functioning and socialization. At the root of competent communication is the capacity to discriminate between items within a context, or to reframe a confusing message under a broader or more inclusive category. To communicate involves sensing *context* because knowledge of context makes it possible to discern the meaning of the elements in the message. The elements in a message are defined by what they are not—by their relation to other elements in the field or context (Bourdieu 1983). Communicants must recognize and draw upon the "differences that make a difference," which according to Bateson is called "information." Discerning difference is, as has been argued, based on the ability to differentiate messages within a given context, to shift associative contexts or paradigms, and to communicate about communication (to tell others how one is framing what has been said).

General logical types represented by names such as "stolen car" must be fitted to given *tokens*, or instances of generic types, such as phone calls that allege that a car has been stolen.

Discrimination among communicational modes, for example, between play, fantasy, humor, falsification, learning about such processes, and layered messages (a joke embedded in a story or lecture), either within the self, or between self and others, is essential to mental health or positive "ego function" (Bateson, Jackson, Haley and Weakland, in Bateson 1972). This discriminatory function is done in part by reading multiple types of signals in context, so that the expression said in frustration that "he should be shot" does not literally mean a person wishes another to be murdered, but that his or her behavior is so vexing that he or she, metaphorically at least, should be silenced.

Some family systems, according to Bateson and associates, contain problems that make it difficult for communicants to discern paradoxical messages, to mark differences between tokens or instances, and to assign them correctly to the logical types to which they belong. Think of how one detects jokes, falsification or fabrication, and learning by rehearsal (rather than the "real thing"), or learns to learn. Some kinds of systems, closed and intimate, where people have little chance to leave, may be characterized by authority figures, especially the mother, who send signals that confuse types and tokens. The ability to discriminate among instances and to frame them in different contexts may be severely compromised. The child in this situation feels he or she can't win. The schizophrenic personality uses unlabeled metaphors because he or she lacks the skill to assign signals to various types. This is also described as "concrete thinking," in the sense of being unable to redefine a signal as a metaphor, an allegory, or an ironic remark (p. 205).

Bateson states some five rules or conditions under which the double bind will predominate in interaction (p. 203). Families are (1) systems involving (2) two or more persons (one of whom is the "victim") with repeated experience, with (3) a negative injunction ("do not do x or I shall punish you") and (4) a secondary injunction enforced by threats of punishment (usually implied withdrawal of love) that contradicts the first negative injunction. This latter may be nonverbal, or a denial of a threat, or punishment. Threats of loss of love if the target person does not respond produce strong pressures to accept the first two conditions of interaction among children. The final condition, (5) prohibition of escape, is perhaps ensured by the threats explicit in the previous injunctions that bind members to the family.

Ironically, once these rules for communication are grounded and legitimated within a family, they "disappear," and in fact become invisible to family members. These rules become the implicit rules that seem to account, when legitimated and accepted within a family, for the miscommunication that maintains the double bind as a characteristic of communication in families with a schizophrenic member.

Bateson shows in his analysis, derived from intensive interviews with schizophrenic patients and their families at the Palo Alto V.A. Hospital, that children raised in family systems where double-bind messages were common, and who accepted them as being in the nature of the world, were subsequently unable to distinguish metaphoric from literal comments (or in the terms used here, metaphorical from metonymical associations). In Bateson's view, the disjunction of verbal and nonverbal messages is critical in producing the double bind. For example, a mother who says "I love you" while pushing a child away, or while speaking to it in a harsh and ominous manner, creates double-bind messages that are massively erosive of the child's trust. Which features of the message, literal or metaphoric, verbal or nonverbal, are telling? How should the child orient to the message?

As dependent children, the children studied were subject to repeated paradoxical or double-bind messages and they responded eventually by creating a kind of dual reality, or radically dissociating their feelings and thoughts. They could fly into a rage when any aspect of the double bind was perceived. In situations where discrimination is required in an intense relationship, where two orders of message are being presented in such a relationship, and the individual is unable to comment or make a "metacommunicative statement," the individual's ability to discriminate among modes of communication may break down (p. 208). In extreme, this is the root of schizophrenia, but it is common in all authoritative and/or binding situations.

This has become a model for the analysis of the genesis of mental illness, and for the analysis of paradoxical messages. Because this systems meaning approach to mental illness and to organizational analysis is so central to current thinking about communication, especially the relationships between verbal and nonverbal communication (Birdwhistell, 1970; Ruesch and Bateson 1951; Watzlawick, Beavin, and Jackson 1967), it is important to review the centrality and pertinence of the idea as well its limits.

The double-bind idea has important relevance to the analysis of organizational communication. There are some nonobvious differences between families and formal organizations, and these can be used to distinguish Bateson's formulation from the perspective presented here for the analysis of organizational communication.

Organizations and the Double Bind

Organizations and families share some similarities when seen as "communications systems," but they differ in several very important ways. These differences or limitations help to set the limits of generalizations made about the effects of double-bind communications on social organization. There are at least six important limitations upon generalizing from Bateson's model of the workings of the double bind to the analysis of double binds in organizational communication.

First, the nature of the ties that bind people together differs in organizations and in families. Organizational members are tied together in both informal and formal fashion. The principal mechanisms are commitment (which may have an expressive dimension called "loyalty") and contracts. They are not bound together as family members are what are thought of as "blood," "kinship," and/or affine ties. As people sometimes say, You cannot choose your family members. Second, organization members have explicit choices denied dependent family members. Organization members can "exit" (leave), they can object or "voice" (raise their voices in protest, political organization, or activism), or they can remain "loyal" (accept the situation as it is) (Hirschman 1970). Third, the time frame for communication in families and in organizations differs. While organizational communication may be endured for brief periods, up to 40 years or so, families of one kind or another nurture for virtually a lifetime. They are particularly critical in socialization. Families have an identity-creating and -maintaining function, and an existential dimension that is explicit in familial communication and only implicit in organizational communication. Fourth, the depth and character of commitments to families and organizations vary. The question of loyalty is only in part based on contracts. The formal nature of the obligation and alternative sources of messages that define and sustain the ties of the person to the organization vary in location and number. Fifth, the number, as well as the intensity, frequency, and quality, of the communications experienced differs. Employees are subject to authoritative formal communication through written and informal channels. Sixth, the ratio of formal to informal communication varies, as does the weight and quantity of informal nonverbal messages. Formal organizational communication, because it does not come from a source as loved and trusted as one's mother, and is relatively "open" to other authoritative sources for confirmation and establishing the validity of the message (organizational truth), is less likely to be "binding" in both senses of the word.

In other words, organization members have more options for coping with paradoxical messages than to family members. An organization member can see these paradoxical predicaments as merely pragmatic, and seek a number of immediate solutions. These include just "doing something," leaving the system, agitating for structural realignments and changes (in leadership for example), redefining the meaning of the messages in a different context, and metacommunicating about the meaning of these messages so that they lose their power and authority. In families, it would seem, only the latter options are available, and some children metacommunicate by reframing themselves as *both in and out of this crazy system*. Let us now reexamine the process of message analysis.

Organizational Paradoxes

Three forms of pragmatic paradox (Putnam 1986) are illustrated in Chapter 5's message analysis of calls to the police in both Britain and the United States. This should help us to visualize the importance of mechanisms for coping with such paradoxes in organizing settings. Some of the features of the double bind occur in everyday communication.

The first form is the paradox represented by the contradiction of an *official* version of an event, what is captured on tape or in written records, and an *unofficial* version rendered by observers of the event. Both of the calls described above were made to report a stolen car. One was not recorded as a stolen-car report, and the official record showed it as an information-given call (BPD), while the other (MPD) was written up as a stolen-car report. The context within which the facts were reported and coded differed, and only one was defined officially as a "stolen car."

The second sort of paradox is between the idea that a message has a *single (actionable) meaning* (with variable clarity) and that messages have *changing meaning* as a result of being interpreted at various stages or organizational subsystems. Think of only one variation in the meaning of messages: the temporal. Messages at the "front end" are encoded, collapsed, and enacted by operators as incidents on the basis of the processing rules for ambiguous calls and their tacit knowledge and imagery of the reported events as described in real time. Dispatchers, on the other hand, are oriented both "backward" to the event reported in the incident and the call, and "forward" to the job(s) they may have to assign the officers to perform. Finally, officers receive the call as a report of an event made into an incident and sent out to them as an assignment (a multiple transformation in time and space within the organization as well as real-time passage of a couple of minutes to hours or even weeks since the reported event), and are oriented bifocally as well: to the original call and processed form it now takes, and to the actual encounter, the social reality of the "external world" within which they must now act. Since the organizational form and different kinds of organizational time are intertextually woven into the radio call, there are times when a message may have quite distinctively different implications for action, depending on which of the forms are salient in the decision process (not even relevant to the content at this point).

A third sort of pragmatic paradox arises because the direct *rules* for information-processing invoked at each of the three stages in the system *generate and sustain ambiguity*. The "unreflective rules" (such as analogical reasoning, nonexclusivity in classification, tacit knowledge, and belief) may fail to order an incident, if, for example, ambiguity in the event remains in the mind of the operator and the dispatcher questions a part of the incident sent forward (this is rare) by telephone or radio.

How are these paradoxes resolved within the PCS? How do messages mean "the same thing" (as well as different things) for all practical, organizational purposes? What can fieldwork tell us about such processes? Let us consider the issues as suggestions to the field-worker.

First, the field-worker should seek to discover whether other, more general rules come into play to resolve ambiguities. Weick (1979:Ch. 4) calls rules of the sort outlined above *assembly rules*. As Weick points out, *diversity of ends is a given in organizations*, but routinization and a means focus enables work to go forward. In the police, these rules typify such matters as "you had to be there," "the officer is best positioned to have a look and to establish the credibility of the call," "things change," or "callers are not generally to be trusted." As the philosopher Wittgenstein (1969) has so elegantly (and elliptically!) argued, being able to do something repeatedly, as the police do, i.e., routinely to process messages and attend calls, does not mean that they understand in a singular fashion what is held in common by the object "domestic" or "man over the wheel."

Second, the field-worker should seek out the *routines* (Feldman 1988a), the repeated ways in which people process the objects that are at the center of the organization's mandate, e.g., decisions about students, about nuclear power, about widgets or screws, about cases processed by professional organizations of doctors or lawyers. Routines reduce ambiguity to manageable levels, produce accountability, and set expectations (Feldman 1988c). In the police, the PCS increasingly routinizes and centralizes control over police work, although it has little effect on crime or social order. Routines pin down meanings, that is, they obviate them such that they disappear into the doing.

Third, the field-worker should elicit and carefully examine the explanations and accounts provided by organization members at various levels for their errors, mistakes, and crises. What dramatic events do people refer to and about which they tell tales? Where do they happen? How are they resolved? What is the view of the causes and best solutions available for these problems? Why do they continue to occur?

Fourth, field-workers should begin to abstract from their notes and observations patterns of paradox resolution and general explanations. These may be accounts for actions that are part of routine crises. They should collect and synthesize the higher level explanations for errors and problems that might be called "policy," or "rules for deciding how to decide."

Fifth, when in the field, field-workers should carefully observe the *metaframes* (communications about communications) used to resolve the paradoxes that exist in the organization(s) studied. These metaframes, if well organized as a set of beliefs, are usually called ideologies, or existential groundings. For example, business people believe profit and loss statements constitute the "bottom line" by which allocation decisions are made and that money is the primary motivation for all market choices. Accounts for decisions are often given in terms of "bottom lines" and "profits and losses." Police live in a world governed more by moral contours than by profits and losses. Police believe that ultimately the world is a shifting change structure of lies and deceptions, untrustworthy people, and thinly constrained and self-interested perceptions and actions. Their judgments are personalistic, moralistic, and interlarded with concern for right and wrong. Neither police nor business people trust people very much, but their actions and their missions are different, as are their root metaphors for capturing this external reality. These *root metaphors* justify the elevation of their own judgments as well as their need to respond to the values and beliefs of those with whom they identify.

Sixth, field-workers should be aware that all such field observational problems are nested and "thick" in the sense Geertz (1973:6, 448) uses the term: an explanation, account, or set of connotative themes clustered as an ideology is a reading of someone's reading of behavior. Culture unfolds in the stories people tell to themselves about themselves (p. 448).

Resolutions and Organizational Culture

We now return to the significance of uncertainty in organizational communication. Rather than seeing uncertainty (unknown probability of a given outcome) or information dependence as a function of "gaps" in otherwise closed and rational systems, the perspective adopted here suggests these are endemic in communication. Uncertainty, an inevitable feature of all communication, is central to the analysis of hermeneutic processes revealed in close study of organizational cultures. These self-reflexive processes are reflected and sustained or structured into organizational communication. The aim of formal organization is to deny such gaps. The police provide an interesting example of the enstructuration of uncertainty.

The police must cope with uncertainty organizationally and as individuals. Some of the means of doing this have been described above under the categories of strategies and tactics. Other modes of coping with uncertainty in organizational terms can be noted (see also Manning 1977:317–19). Some principles govern police coping with uncertainty. We have already suggested something about informational strategies, but there are other strategies based on the celebration of the values of policing, or which have the form of *ritual*.

Policing is teamwork, and it relies on mutually oriented action to form the appearance of consensus to an audience. One of the most important principles of police teamwork is information-based: policing is the constant attempt to control the level and kind of public information. A second principle is based on a wish to conceal awkward acts or events and to reduce front and backstage conflicts by segregation of audiences. On the grounds that this assists their effectiveness in controlling crime, police use a third principle: they routinely lie and deceive the public and conceal many important decisions backstage. All of these ritualized activities serve to maintain the idealized front of policing and can be called ritual or "front work."

Nevertheless, there remain a series of latent or potential conflicts that ritual cannot obscure, or lies conceal. Teamwork often falls apart. Police cannot fully control the public access to their failures. They are forced to reveal evidence in court, or to provide budget rationales to city councils. There is often an internal conflict between the information that officers encounter on the ground or over the radio and the direction and guidance that administrators seek to provide and want to be seen to be providing. In short, informational and ritualistic strategies may come into conflict.

There is furthermore an internal aspect to the information/ritual axis that patterns the nature of how higher administrators cope with problems. Organizationally, some divisions within police create cases (vice and narcotics) or respond to facts and cases that have been once processed (detectives), while others are making cases and assembling facts for further processing (patrol).[1] This makes officers in these divisions differentially at risk and dependent upon the public. Police managers in some divisions are better positioned to control and guide actions of officers than others. Let us consider further how information and structure interact in police divisions.[2]

1. In the traffic, juvenile, and detective divisions or bureaus, guidance or policies are kept private and unrevealed. But such divisions typically require more guidance (even in an officer-oriented department). Greater administrative control means that lower ritualization is possible on the ground in everyday decisions.
2. Patrol, the most visible activity, is most information variable in character and is least subject to administrative control. The least controlled activity is most subject to ritualization by officers in response to their own feelings or uncertainty in enforcement.
3. Work in drugs or vice, in which the police initiate many of the cases rather than respond to public calls, varies in ritualization potential; it appears to be *neither* high nor low on the dramatic potential index.

External Communication and Internal Structure

This outline of sources of uncertainty and response in policing should assist us in developing some general propositions about the nature of the relationship between external communication and internal structure. The formal organization or division of labor within Anglo-American policing is revealing. It can be shown with reference to the American police that:

1. The greatest resources are invested in patrol and in maintaining personnel at the bottom of the structure.
2. The focus of supervision, review, and accountability is at the front end of the information-screening apparatus: the operators who receive and encode the calls from the public.
3. Uncertainty is seen as high in urban patrol work. This may be due to several factors—vacillations between high- and low-information states for the officer, the encoding or decoding of very elliptical and brief messages sent via the radio, etc. Questions about trust in the sender and source of the message as well as noise are abiding.
4. Uncertainty and ambiguity are built into the structure of police communications insofar as police are increasingly dependent upon radio and technologically mediated messages rather than face-to-face encounters.

These four points suggest that the sources of uncertainty and paradox in policing are related to the organizational-resource base of given segments of policing. It is assumed that information is a nonconstant factor in communication, and that meaning is created through the social definitions directed to the messages received. Thus, these actions and modes of coping are based on ritual unity and consensus as well as pragmatism.

A situational view of organizational practices and rules is implied as well, since these are modes of coping with uncertainty. The *situational view of organizational practices and rules* (including the practices of the police and their occupational and organizational culture) argues for the relevance of situated rationality (Mannheim 1949), or what Weber (1947) called "substantive rationality." This is a form of reasoning that says that decisions reflect the ways in which actors define and constitute facts and identify their audience(s), and the actors' subjective intent to understand the knowable consequences of any outcome such as an arrest, a disciplinary note, or an assignment. A situational view of information, especially written records, is taken by officers. The meaning of a piece of paperwork is defined in part by the audience to which it is directed (Who will be reading this? the writer must ask as he or she writes), in which the importance of the audience to whom the paper is directed is noted, and in part by the notion that rules are resources to be used to define situations. Rules are means through and by which the meaning of the occupational culture is animated. Rules and norms are resources that can be used to accomplish a variety of ends. It is unlikely, given this depiction of the nature of the work, that a police subculture is a tightly integrated set of norms or evaluative standards (which may be called rules, principles, or even practices).

It is possible to speculate about the relationships between this structure of information and information use and the nature of external police communications. Information patterns and management, and violence and its use both have discernible and empirically established relations. As a consequence of the distribution of information, police managers in some divisions are better positioned than others to control and guide actions of officers. This degree of control is related roughly to sources of work and information.

Information is related to violence. Given that Anglo-American societies are increasingly rational, instrumental, and practical in orientation, and that such behaviors are subject to a wide range of interpretation, police face increasingly complex environments. The more complex the crime and the social structure's range of permissible behaviors, the more police are faced with interpretive problems with respect to the social order they are meant to monitor and sustain. The more redundancy in social structure, the higher the social integration of the parts in an interdependent whole, the more possible is a ritualized and confirmatory police response to events. They must bring order to complexity and richly contextualized encounters; and they can do this either by adapting to the instrumental dimensions of behaviors (cf. Sykes and Brent 1983) or by further attempting to ritualize their responses and trying merely to conform with general expectations of police. The increasingly common response would appear to be a combination of media rhetoric and coercive violence under the mandate of authority (Reiss 1971; Rappaport 1971; Manning 1977:312).[3]

Uncertainty varies in its relevance to officers, depending on their position in the organizational structure. It also identifies problematic areas for police management as well as for the management of appearances. These distinctions between the degree of uncertainty in the work and the structure of the organization are also reflected in the police occupational culture. Occupational culture buffers uncertainty and assists in the dissolution of paradoxes.

Occupational Culture

Some aspects of the idea of occupational culture are edifying and can perhaps serve to describe and identify relevant pieces or sequences of police behavior bearing on the question of internal communication. Let us begin with the notion of tasks, and include the nature of the perceived or enacted environment (Weick 1979), police technology, and some aspects of the rank structure of the police.

The core *tasks* of policing, uncertain as they are, are traditionally defined and largely face-to-face, order-maintaining or ordering jobs. They are carried out with an unrefined "people-processing" *technology* located within a traditional *hierarchical structure*. The interaction of these factors (tasks, technology, structure) produces a set of attitudes and an explanatory set of beliefs rationalizing or justifying the work and its contingencies, or an ideology. The police officer on uniformed patrol is dependent on his or her colleagues and on the public to a considerable degree, yet the occupation emphasizes autonomy and discretion. The most important *theme* (or cluster of attitudes and actions) of the occupation is displaying, maintaining, and enacting *authority*. At its best, police work on the ground requires authority to be creatively displayed in quite variegated circumstances. Thus, dependency, autonomy, authority, and uncertainty are key occupational themes.

Several observers (Manning 1977, 1979a; Ianni and Ianni 1983; Punch 1986) have argued that at last two distinctive *social worlds* [Goffman

(1974:46) calls them a realm, or a limited and bounded area of shared meaning] coexist within Anglo-American policing. The first world is occupied by those holding the rank of sergeant and below. These might be called lower participants in the rank hierarchy. The second world is occupied by the administrative cadre, those of the rank of sergeant and above. Note that sergeants, like foremen in factories, are part of both social worlds, and are occasionally caught between them. These social worlds both unify and divide the occupation. Phenomenologically, the lower participants (called "officers," even though all sworn personnel are called officers, regardless of rank) and the administrative cadre are divided by different tasks, views, and access to organizational authority, life-styles, modes of ambition, and horizons of concern (the time dimensions of the work). They share an experiential base (all have served as constables or officers at some point, although not all have been members of the administrative cadre) and some assumptions about the nature of the work, and are bound together by task dependency. The *styles*, or modes of expression of one's social values, characterizing these two social worlds partially overlap and partially differ, and the meanings attached to the work differ.

Important corollaries of membership in one of these two social worlds exist. Some of the differences are matters of class or origins, but working-class culture, from which most police are recruited, supplies many of the most frequently noted *emblems* of policing: the emphases upon individual control of situations, toughness, machismo, hedonism, deprecation of paperwork and abstraction, and concrete language and description. Officers trade the lack of autonomy on the job for maintaining the working-class style (Katz 1965). One of the most important of these emblems, or symbols that collapse a set of attitudes and practices into a single word or set of signs, is control. The control theme is manifested internally in the detailed rules and regulations governing behavior, and the harsh punishment found in police organizations, the high standards of commitment required, the 24-hour conception of duty and its connection to sacred occupations that are "callings," and the actual risks of police work. In other words, the emphasis upon individual control is a dialectical reaction to historical attempts to restrict, control, guide, supervise, and otherwise make accountable the individual officer (Miller 1977; Bittner 1970).

In the social world of the administrative cadre, the emblems of the officers on the street persist; they remain surprisingly salient, as a ground against which to view the figure of intrinsic commitments to the values and satisfactions of the work. They think of themselves as "good police officers," and emphasize their "street smarts," "toughness," or past crime-fighting successes, rather than their administrative skills, wisdom as a manager, or educational achievements. Intrinsic commitments and satisfaction with the tasks seem analogous among the administrative cadre to the claimed autonomy of the lower participants.

The two social worlds of police are further internally differentiated by the nature of the bases of attachment (emotional involvement or morale) and types of commitment (unwillingness to leave the work) to a police career. These attachments can be seen in the "orientations" of officers, because the emotional tone or attitude of an officer is based on whether his or her attachments are to other colleagues at the same rank and in the same social world, or upward or downward (if in the administrative cadre). Within the two police worlds, officers may be laterally or vertically oriented. One may be upwardly oriented toward a rank one wishes to achieve, or laterally to one's peers or present rank. The most common orientation is horizontal and takes the form of what Van Maanen (1975) calls the "don't rock the boat," or "keep your head down and out of trouble" posture. Among those with lateral orientations, one's career anchorage can be accommodative or indifferent (Tausky and Dubin 1965). Informal networks that cross social worlds and are organized around political issues within the department, cliques, cabals, and other internal configurations, are very characteristic of police departments (Van Maanen 1974).

In the world of the lower participants, three themes—authority, uncertainty, and the resulting dependency—are primary. They are integrated by the two *metathemes*, or clusters of themes, called emphasis on "the job," and the idea that "good" or even "real" police work is restricted to that which they do on the streets. They lack much knowledge or understanding of the nature of the work of senior officers, and often deny its relevance. The administrative cadre, on the other hand, emphasize two other metathemes, the centrality of their authority and responsibility, or the metatheme of management, and the preservation of police autonomy within the political and legal system. This metatheme of higher authority focuses on coping with the broader political implications of police actions on the street. Administrators take the metatheme of "management" rather than that of the work or the job, and they view the aim of police management in the first instance as coping with the lower participants' subculture. Uncertainty reappears, although the uncertainty of administrators surrounds less the direct consequences of their work and more their dependence upon the good judgment, discretion (in both senses of the word), and competence of the lower participants. As James Q. Wilson observes (1968:69ff.), the police administrator is more worried about the mistakes and errors of the single officer that might cause organizational repercussions than in failing to carry out long-term policymaking and planning.[4]

Having suggested some aspects of the differentiation of the police world, it is not clear *how* exactly it serves to shape relevant "police outputs." Although I have presented it as a set of social worlds, themes, and metathemes, it may be more fluid and situational than these rather static ideas. The occupational culture may be something like a "strategic resource," available for the ordering and controlling of events, and providing the narrative form for occupational tales and renditions of the work. Storytelling occurs after the fact; it provides the *frames* (Goffman 1974), or set of rules organizing experience, rather than a set of specific norms or values. It resembles a set of tools to be employed on the jobs at hand more than a set of well-recognized constraints known in advance (see Swidler 1986; Horowitz forthcoming, Ericson et al. 1987). It may be that the differentiation of the police world is yet another form of loose coupling that protects and ensures the autonomy essential to the complex, shifting nature of the tasks, the traditional mission and mandate of the police, and the absence of formal theories explaining citizens' behavior.

Occupational Culture and Tight Coupling

The resolution of paradoxes can be seen in terms of our key metaphor, *loose (and tight) coupling*. The nature of the coupling between segments of an organization, between talk and the social world, and between the organization and the environment is a function of difference. We can explore this idea in the context of policing and its relationships to the sociopolitical environment.

The above summary of the police occupational culture suggests that policing is essentially loosely coupled with an environment. The recent work of Dick Hobbs, *Doing the Business: Entrepreneurship, the Working Class, and Detectives in the East End of London* (1988), suggests some of the important limits on the loose-coupling metaphor.[5] It clearly demonstrates that a form of tight coupling between environment and police organization can obtain. Hobbs provides several versions of the thesis of this subtle and persuasive book: "CID [Criminal Investigation Division—detectives] policing is congruent with the social order of the East End [of London]" (p. 215). He also writes: "[The police and the people of the East End] share certain key characteristics" (p. 1). He summarizes:

> The relationship between the [East Enders] and the CID is symbiotic; appropriately based on the trading of moral identities. The sharp entrepreneurship of the East Ender provides when appropriated and reworked by the detective a potent occupational front that distances him from the restraints of the administratively bound uniform branch. (p. 216)

Hobbs bases these generalizations on his considerable fieldwork (and life experience), a sharply drawn revisionist history of policing, and a rich and systematic dramaturgical analysis of the connections between the life-style of those living in the East End of London and the style of detective work practiced.

The above quotes capturing the thesis of the book also set out a functional triad constituted from three dramaturgically articulated social worlds: the *market* (constituted from pricing mechanisms, weak ties, and the rhetoric of capitalism and entrepreneurship) leading to the "commodification" of law and material objects; two participatory market groups (CID and the people of the East End); and the *cultural order* (shared language, accounts, and vocabularies of motive, symbols, and sanctioned strategies for coping with uncertainty) and the *social/ interactional order* (deals, exchanges, and reciprocities). In semiotic terms, the concept or signifier, *market*, is undercoded (seen in the connotative meanings associated with signs located in the two other social worlds) in the social and moral order, and in interactions between East Enders and CID detectives. One might say, in another semiotically derived phrase, that the cultural, social, and market orders stand as interpretants (the link between signifiers and signifieds; the unexplicated connections that, once made, complete a sign).

As a result of shared vocabularies of motive and participation in the same language games (my term via Wittgenstein), Hobbs observes that "East Enders are able to justify legal behaviour and neutralize illegal action by utilizing the rhetoric of capitalism" (p. 117). One stands for the other, and relationships in any one are shaded connotatively by relationships in the other. These minirhetorics, featuring such concepts as deals, turn-taking, and a belief in the aleatory nature of social life (based further on a belief in the importance of uncontrolled external events in shaping life choices), produce an isomorphic triad, three in one, or "doing the business." "Business" is a metaphor for the various forms— social, cultural, and legal—of ordering. (Of course, one might say that "the business does you"; it is a reversible equation.)

The dualistic themes (CID = East Ender) found in two interwoven narrative or story lines are integrated in the last two chapters and a postscript. The first triad of chapters (Chapters 2–4) focuses on the development of the police and the emergence of the detective function in the late 19th century, and the second (Chapters 5–7) charts the development of the East End as a morally, culturally, and economically independent place, marginal to the old-Roman-origins City of London (the financial center of the nation, called "the City" to distinguish it from Greater London). The final triad (Chapters 8, 9 and the postscript) argues for the mutually reciprocal structure and content of the two developed groups. This triadic organization replicates the triadic form of economic, cultural, and social exchanges that constitute the invisible infrastructure of "doing the business."

The analysis is carried out historically, comparatively, and economically. First, Hobbs shows how the East End developed as a place where new immigrants, often forced to survive by entrepreneurial skills because they were excluded from other markets, could survive by clever negotiation. It was traditionally seen as a "deviant place." It still is, and the relevance of this historically derived social and moral marginality to current practices is very convincingly demonstrated. Second, the book works on two sets of binary analogs. The first form of comparative analysis compares the economy and culture of the East End on the one hand with the rationalized market system represented by the City. The second form of analysis sets out the entrepreneurial culture of the CID in comparison to the uniform branch of the Metropolitan Police ("The Met"). A simple structural equation might take the following form: CID : Met = East End : The City.

Links are drawn between the contrapuntal themes found in detective work and in business. Parallels are drawn, on the one hand, between CID/detective work as innovative, entrepreneurial, risk taking, and risk making, and the rationalized, bureaucratic work style of the uniform branch of policing and, analogously on the other hand, between the East End, a haven of the striving, sharp, morally and marginally dubious, and the City, as the center of large-scale financial doings. These parallels are drawn carefully and systematically.

The book is a rendition of expressive and instrumental *ordering*, dramatic, economic, political, moral, vertically and horizontally, within and without the East End, but in so doing, it also demonstrates how, through deals, the market, and shared vocabularies and backgrounds, the CID and the entrepreneurial segments of the East End are tightly coupled. They are linked by several variables in a strong fashion, and the links work routinely in all transactions between detectives and East Enders.

The importance of this type of coupling can be seen in Hobbs's rich ethnographic depictions of what Weick would call "causal indeterminancy," or risk. Risk and uncertainty, chance, and statistical probability become enstructured by cultural rules for dealing, coping, serving, and reciprocating, among detectives (who turn a blind eye, exchange information, make deals, and use the concept of turn-taking to facilitate their careers) and East Enders (who turn a blind eye, exchange information). The emphasis is on oscillation (p. 13), process, and dynamics (p. 223), both within and between the two "cultures" (my terms). Cultural elements are important in stabilizing the coupling. Hobbs repeatedly emphasizes that elements of the East End masculine culture are reflected in the work style of the CID.

The consequences of these mutual dependencies are, of course, to facilitate the survival of both groups within the cultural milieux they partially share, and to provide the music for the dance of control being played out nightly, night after night, in various pubs and clubs in this part of London. This mutually nuanced control is shown to the reader bifocally, as metaphors make possible. The belief in self-determination and control of one's fate ideologically serves to mediate the market forces that fatefully and powerfully shape one's life. It also serves to maintain their marginality. And so, daily, is social structure reproduced.

Organizations and Information

In spite of the power of this evocative example of coupling and mutually shared coding, the example may be a rare one in modern organizational analysis. There may be no deep code in modern societies that sustains and animates its ordering processes, only a series of surfaces in vague contrast to each other. Imagery and media depictions represent a diverse set of nonvoiced views, formats, and taste cultures, lacking a binding and coherent center. The esthetic and the pragmatic are endlessly mixed in media presentations of events: things feel and words do, technologies are invested with love and desire, and people are used. The center of discourse drifts, and fact and value become elided.

In organizations, sensible meanings are crushed out of enacted or bracketed materials, some are selected and retained, and rules of thumb or of assembly maintain the conservative nature of organizational communication. Many recipes and realities exist, but some are more equal than others, as the pigs said in Orwell's *Animal Farm*. Expressive and instrumental communication are labels reflecting authority, not the content or intent of the act. Management has the unilateral authority to define the nature of the difference between the expressive, the symbolic, and the esthetic, unlike the peasants in Bali (Geertz 1973), and maintains the distinction reified in the writings of organizational theorists (Pfeffer 1981). Some few cause maps (perceptions of social causation within an organization—Weick and Bougon 1986) of matters considered to be "substantive" outcomes are authoritatively set by those at the top, and these are defined publicly as determined by external resources and power dependence relations. In practice, it is impossible to make this determination since all decision-making is circular. That is, some decisions come looking for answers, decision-makers come to make decisions, or are "looking for work," and solutions are worked out looking for issues to solve. Information is both signal and symbol (Feldman and

March 1981), and this distinction is made by the situational reasoning that establishes it. In fact, since decisions are only known after the fact and these must be known only as they are accounted for or legitimated, the management function cannot be known outside the accounts provided or the tales told for the decisions they take.

The nature of the referents of various expressions and contents, i.e., the extent to which a reality is "out there" to be captured, is always difficult to answer. Phenomenologists focus on the social construction of meaning. Weick, however, firmly believes that a causally articulated world exists. This world *is differentially perceived (enacted) and selected by organizations*. Luhmann (1986) argues that internal communication has little relation to the nature and quality of the communicational inputs. In order to sustain its boundaries, organizations maintain the nature of the communicational units and reproduce them. This is a kind of hybrid rationalism shared with systems theory and information theory because it presumes that "meaning" is a function of the "prior setting" (MacKay 1969) of the organization's receptors (essentially, in MacKay's view, a function of organizational capacity to reproduce itself, or engage in *autopoesis*). Somewhere in the middle of these views are those who see the organization as mediating material, technological, and social constraints in large part by communicating about them in a sanctioned fashion, and through use of routines.

The position adopted here is that the study of organizational culture and external communication must be cast in dialectic form and based on noted "differences." A study of the dialectics of organizational communication must include a form of self-reference in which terms contain their own opposites and thus refuse a singular grasp of their meanings. Dialectical reasoning relies on differences. "Difference is thus a unity which is at the same time divided from itself . . . and is intrinsic to all social forms" (Cooper and Burrell 1988:98). Difference, or what one might call "desire" or passion, the wish for the absent, grapples with formal organization, and is beyond full rational human control.

The summaries of organizational theories and paradigms of communicational research in Chapter 3 slide by the question of the *purpose of organizations* using the gloss of rationality. Formal organization is not just a means to "get things done" or to produce efficiently: rational organization is a format for denying passion, uncertainty, ambiguity, and seeking control over determinate forces knowingly beyond direct individual control (Cooper and Burrell 1988:99). In part, these "uncontrolled forces" are implicit in all meanings and actions, and contain "reflexive allusions to what has remained unstated" (Habermas 1972:168). The control of organizations by artificial mechanisms, technology, formal discourse derived from the language of computer engineers, and "adaptation" serves not only to deny the humanity of individuals, but the central themes of organization—negation of passions, feelings, and personhood.

These themes, taken from Derrida, Lyotard, and in the most exemplary form Foucault's *Discipline and Punish* (1977), place organizational communication in a new bifocal context. What is said and expressed is contrasted with what is not said and only implied. The complex triad of knowledge, feeling, and action is dramatically illustrated in organizational life situations.

The equally misleading distinction between expressive and rational or instrumental action crumbles on close examination. It is a function of a pseudorationality that overvalues instrumental and pragmatic actions, and the authority to define the differences between "moral" or "expressive" actions and others. Thus, Wuthnow (1987:66) defines a "moral code" as a set of cultural elements that define the nature of commitment to a particular course of behavior. But this definition begs the question of the particular line of action that authoritative structures constrain. They may deny many commitments, and are the source of the rituals and ceremonies that affirm some aspects of the narrative structure of communication and not others. As we will see in the examination of the police funeral, themes in the ceremony deny passion, commitment, purpose, and meaning to those excluded from the structure of the game (Lyotard 1984; Lyotard and Thébaud 1985).

Conclusions

This chapter outlines some of the problems associated with anomalous communications, and how from the range of stimuli, a sensible array is picked, honored, and ordered. It is suggested that the occupational culture serves as a "buffer" that absorbs and differentially amplifies some anomalies; thus an ethnographic analysis of occupational culture is essential to an analysis of patterns of internal paradox and resolution. The role of information in organizations is a variable, and the role it plays in enstructuring organizations varies as well (Stinchcombe 1990).

The next two chapters examine external communication in routine and crisis with materials from studies of American community policing and the NII.

External Communication I: Crisis, Routine, and Program in American Policing

Introduction

This chapter uses material taken from studies of the American urban police to illustrate types of external communication by organizations. Using the dramaturgical frame of reference will allow the problematics of policing, its dilemmas, to be identified and the communicational solutions police have devised to be considered. After characterizing the American police and their dilemmas, the chapter outlines with examples the rhetoric of the American police that is intended to persuade their many relevant publics of the legitimate authority, credibility, and power of the police organization. In order to maintain their public mandate and authority, the police routinely communicate with publics and attempt to develop proactive plans to enhance their image and authority. At times, they must respond to internal scandals and externally created crises. They employ what is termed "strategic communication" when faced with an innovation or reform that they see as essential to expanding their mandate.

These three types of external communication are illustrated here with examples adopted from American policing. Many of these problems are characteristic of "corporate discourse" generally (Jackall 1988; Cheney and Vibbert 1988). The first, *crisis communication*, arises as a result of threatening immediate events, such as a corruption scandal, allegations of excessive violence, or the slaying of a police officer. The second, *routine communication*, arises as police answer queries about their operations, activities, and motives in regard to pursuing criminal cases, case-processing, and responding to telephone calls for service from the public. The third type of external communication, *strategic communication*, is intended to package, present, and "sell" police programs and innovations in strategy to the publics. In this case, the most likely targeted audience is the elite members of the community. To discuss in further detail this typology of external communication, it is necessary to characterize sociologically American policing and its dilemmas, and then review key concepts used in dramaturgical analysis.

American Policing and Its Dilemmas

The most salient and distinguishing features of American policing are closely related to its characteristic dilemmas. A "dilemma" is a contradiction that does not yield readily to solution or even management. Given the perspective discussed in the preface and Chapter 1, it should be clear that these basic dilemmas are inherent in any social institution and are therefore not unique to policing. It is the manner in which the dilemmas are publicly managed that differs, as well as the local circumstances of politics, culture, and history, that shapes the particular manifestations of police strategies and tactics.

It is merely a truism to state that policing always in some respects reflects the social structure, history, and culture of the nation in which it resides. American policing is one example of Anglo-American policing, and it most resembles the police systems of India, Australia, New Zealand, England, and Canada.[1] American policing shares with these countries many of the following features, but the United States remains unique in other ways, the primary ones, in my view, being the pervasive ideology of radical individualism and pragmatism (the flip side of an antistate and antigovernmental ideology) combined with enormous affluence. It is this combination of pragmatism and individualism that makes American policing subject to wide variations in local acceptance. It also explains American policing's increasing dependence on formalized public relations, campaigns for public support, cycles of corruption and reform, and the characteristic budget cuts, hiring freezes, and hiring frenzies, differences based in city governmental response to economic fluctuations. Let us review in somewhat more detail these features of American policing.[2]

American policing must operate in the context of a very violent, ethnically heterogeneous, individualistically oriented *frontier* society. The rates of violent crime, including murder, place the United States in the top five most violent nations in the world.

American policing is *local* and decentralized in nature; few federal laws or procedures govern police performance. Policing reflects the local statutes of a collection of diverse states, and must cope with a maze of overlapping local, state, and federal laws, as well as governmental conventions that govern police accountability. Police are dependent upon the somewhat uncertain pattern of local politics and funding. Police are found at some *five levels of authority* ranging from local to federal (Bayley 1985:238). Although subject to debate, it is assumed that there are some 25,000 police agencies in the United States, distributed among local, county, township, sheriffs', state, and special police forces. The federal government alone employs agents in 113 agencies. The largest of these are the FBI, the Drug Enforcement Agency, the Bureau of Alcohol, Firearms and Tobacco, and the Secret Service. American police work in rather *small forces*. More than 90 percent of all munici- palities over 2,500 people have a police force, and a force of around 5 officers is modal for the country as a whole (Reiss 1974:681). (The largest urban forces, those in Los Angeles, New York, and Chicago, are dispro- portionately covered in the media.)

This localism and local control is in part a result of the ethnic diversity of American life and the tradition of local competition over political control of patronage (hiring of officers), the local-democratic ethos, and constitutional restrictions on a national police force. There is no central- ized recruitment, national performance standards, or a generally ac- cepted level of training or required training procedures. Although the FBI performs many national police functions almost by default, the United States lacks a fully developed, staffed, and supervised police college. Diverse uniforms are worn and a wide variety of weapons and ammunition—from the .357 Magnum load weapons to semiautomatic 9 mm—are acceptable to carry.

Organizationally, the American police are characterized by a tradition- al flat pyramid structure with the largest number of officers at the bottom. All officers enter at the bottom, and typically a chief "works his way to the top," serving in the lower ranks of some force somewhere for some period of time. There is little task specialization, little trans- ferability of skills, and 80–90 percent budget allocations are concentrated in personnel, benefits, and entitlements. Police operate primarily on a case-by-case, reactive basis, leaving the direct guidance of action and mobilization to the choices of individual officers (Reiss and Bordua 1967).

American policing has a *low ratio* of officers to people. Although estimates vary, there are some 480 people per police officer in the United States. During the period 1976–1986, the average was about 2.0–2.1 officers per thousand (Department of Justice 1987, 1988). Debate contin- ues about the actual number of officers.

Not all important American police organizations are public. It is esti- mated that there are some one million private police and their numbers are growing (Michalowski 1985:176). It is claimed that the growing number of private police exceeds the publicly employed police, and that private and public police are becoming increasingly interdependent (see Stenning and Shearing 1987; Marx 1988).

Dilemmas of American Policing

These characteristics of American policing affect the shaping, expansion, and contraction of the American police mandate and its communicational dilemmas. American police share features of these problems with other occupations. All occupations and organizations maintain fronts and seek to expand and defend their mandates. Agencies in the social-control domain seek systematically to mark norms or rules, and respond to their violation [either under- or overconformity (see Clark and Gibbs 1965:401)]. The *mandate* of an occupation both constrains and frees occupational action. It can be summarized as the degree of deference granted to an occupation by the publics, given a claim (Hughes 1958). The mandate is a *collective representation* (Durkheim 1964); it stands as a symbol of the whole. A mandate is in some sense transactional, in that repeated routine exchanges of information and meaning sustain the publics' confidence. The occupation's capacity to sustain publicly its credibility and legitimacy through direct action gives it additional power. Clearly, in industrial societies, the degree of authority and control a given named occupation maintains over the areas implied or specified in a mandate and license is frequently in flux and being challenged by new occupations and political changes; it expands and contracts, and is a flexible and symbolic construction. One source of this fluctuation is the dilemmas faced by the occupation and its attempts to cope with them. Since part of this coping involves developing and maintaining positive public perceptions and public trust, the management of appearances and the manipulation of symbols are an essential means of maintaining authority.

The police in the United States repeatedly face a set of vexing dramatic dilemmas (Manning 1977:17–20). (A dilemma is a contradiction between two sets of facts that will not yield to easy solution, and a paradox is a more extreme version of the same, which appears irresolvable.) Dramatic dilemmas of an occupation are those requiring systematic public or front stage displays of the capacity and will to overcome or manage them.

Some dilemmas of the police arise as a result of their role within the criminal justice system as officers of the court and its investigative arm, and some from other sources. Because of their role in the criminal justice system, the American police strive to balance their moral judgments and goals with their information-processing functions. In their role as law enforcement officers, and in their relations with various publics (some of whom are outside the criminal justice system itself), other dilemmas of interest arise. These are in part problems faced by all organizations.

Another set of dilemmas arises for the police because their claimed mandate includes notional responsibility for controlling all social events for which intervention might require violence (Bittner 1970,1974). The police are assigned a difficult role or granted a role (mandate) within the moral division of labor, and they struggle to maintain their position of moral and legal authority by dramaturgical management of appearances. This does not mean that technological, material, behavioral, or other factors do not shape the pattern of policing. The police are also shaped by structural differentiation, budgetary variations, and relative personnel distribution. Size and historical forces shape the mandate as do local political decisions (Langworthy 1986; Slovak 1986). However, an inextricable connection remains, on the one hand, between action and symbolization, especially images, and, on the other, the primacy of symbols that express power, rank, and authority in mass, complex, and media-mediated societies.

How do the police manage to maintain their power, authority, and credibility in an increasingly fragmented and heterogeneous society? Effective external communication is one answer to this question: The American police seek, via communication about their strategies and tactics, to dramatize the appearance of control of crime and maintenance of social order. Clearly, the active attempt to shape public opinion includes more than this theme, the appearance of control; furthermore, any organization will choose a variety of themes, subthemes, and even counterthemes to influence external environments. Given that resources and external constraints are many and determinantal of the range of themes possible, the active management of symbols and symbolic management of communication are critical to organizational function (Pfeffer 1981). Let us first review in more detail some of the dilemmas that underlie American urban policing. The contrasts are produced by comparing police claims with research evidence accumulated in the last 25 years or so (for a summary of these findings, see Mastrofski 1990).

These dilemmas have been discussed elsewhere (Manning 1977) and can be easily summarized or conflated as the "crime control" dilemma: The police claim the capacity to control crime fully but are, in fact, unable to do more than shape it, displace it, or alter the rates of types of crime. Most of their effects are brief, local, and transitory (Sherman 1992). This is the fundamental anvil on which the police have been hammered since the first wave of police reform took place in the 1930s

(Stead 1977). The recent moral panic concerning drugs, with the escalation of police rhetoric in terms of the metaphor of "war" or absolute, unconditional "victory" defined in terms of the eradication of the drug market, is a striking example of a claim for public trust that is certain to fail. Even defined in the narrowest possible terms of "demand reduction," police have only marginal measurable effects.

Policing is a traditional occupation with connections to sacred values such as honor, valor, and duty, yet police have a conditional obligation to intervene in whatever requires it (Bittner 1970). As a result, they have what might be called the "honor dilemma" insofar as they want to be known to (or claim to) be performing honorable and respectable work, yet must carry out potentially dishonorable, diverse unpleasant and "dirty work." For example, police in many cities are required to remove dead dogs and human bodies from houses, streets, and rivers; transport drunks and the homeless to shelters; respond to false alarms; and mediate family disputes. When honor fades, the resultant violent action also draws media attention and may be a source of criticism.

Police work is teamwork, from "the partnership convention" that police officers work in pairs, to the collective identification with social order. Teamwork suggests a respect for honoring shared fronts, strategies, and tactics. Police observe the "act concertedly" rule, and seek to display publicly, whenever possible, a unity of appearance and purpose. The police also attempt to display or to establish the unity of their more specific organizational goals and objectives, e.g., "fighting crime" or "protecting property," with their politically significant audiences (the "respectable majority" and local elites). Yet, their work is diverse, distributed in time and space, and filled with uncertainty. Although they patrol in quite visible vehicles and uniforms, their daily rounds and duties are rarely closely observed by respectable citizens.

The police attempt to create a sense of connection between the public's interests, values, and beliefs and their own publicly espoused values. Yet, they remain at the heart of social-conflict management with the middle classes, and the handling of disputes often results in conflict with many segments of society. They also are in less divisive conflict with lawbreakers and those who disrupt the police sense of order and propriety.

Police face the "efficiency dilemma." They tend not to be efficient for the reasons listed above, but moreover there may be very sound reasons why they are not and should not be expected to be "too efficient" in a democracy that values individual civil liberties and freedoms so highly (Laurie 1971). Nevertheless, the police wish to symbolize efficiency and efficacy, as well as to put a "high-tech" face on their work. However, the extraordinary concentration of police budget costs in salaries (about 90 percent) indicates that with respect to their central problem, "people management," the police cannot rely on any single technology but must rely on systematic "common sense." Police tasks are not guided by theoretic premises, a theory of abstract professional conduct, or clear standards and values rooted in law or traditions. Because they eschew theory and are subject to reactive mobilization, there are enormous variations in individual officer performance, in organizational performance, and in supervision and control.

Policing involves very complex decisions made in the immediate circumstances about the fates of individuals. It is "people work" that is carried out on the edge of organizational controls.

These dilemmas will surface as themes at various points in police rhetoric, in crisis management, in routine communications, and in strategic communication, and resolutions of these basic dilemmas will animate the surface changes in policing claimed by the police to be basic reforms.

The Drama of Control

The concept of the drama of control refers to the selective display of symbols that serve to draw and mark the bounds of the permissible, the possible, and the deviant (see Becker 1963; Goffman 1959; Gusfield 1981). When this drama is enacted by those with authority, the drama of control celebrates and marks the limits of informal social control and the borders of the law. Presenting strategically the contours and consequences of the enactment of the drama of control is the essence of external police communication when police are communicating about their role as a collective entity.

As noted in Chapter 1, the *dramaturgical perspective* on social life attempts to elucidate by revealing contrasts, showing how these contrasts are differentially perceived and acted upon, and how a potentially wide range or multiplicity of meanings is made coherent and unitary for social purposes (Goffman 1959; Gusfield 1981; Manning 1977). The dilemmas of the police listed above illustrate the persisting and underlying problems of maintaining the political front or mandate that is claimed. *Front* is defined by Erving Goffman as "that part of an individual's performance which regularly functions in a routine and fixed fashion to define the situation for those who observe the performance . . . expressive equipment of a standard kind intentionally or unwittingly employed by the individual during his performance" (1959:22). Front involves the *settings* routinely occupied and in which the performances occur; personal front includes costumes, uniforms, props, and the appearance and manner used to express the front (pp. 22–30). In Burke's (1962) terms, actors act using fronts in settings with some expressed purpose or agency. Thus, some coherence between setting, appearance, and manner is expected and its absence is an occasion for response to maintain the consistent front. This "response" can be called "front work." These concepts also help explain organizational actions.

Police do many things, but they certainly must engage in successful front work. The concept of front can be applied to the analysis of organizations and occupations: "actors" or "individuals" who "define the situation for those who observe the "performance." In a sense, what is outlined here is a view of paradox and its resolution at the occupational level that parallels the paradox resolution that takes place among organization members when confronted with paradoxical messages.

Understanding the uses and exploitation of symbolism (or the manipulation of signifiers) is essential to understanding the workings of dramaturgy. Police work, although visible, is known to most people at a second- or thirdhand level as a result of reading, watching television or films, or tales told by others of their experience with the police. Police symbolism produces images and narratives about events with which most people have little direct personal experience. The dramaturgical perspective recognizes that organizations use a slogan, a few words, or brief, almost encoded messages to convey to the relevant publics the complex, multifaceted events and social processes with which they cope. Thus, the police are "fighting a war on drugs," serve to "preserve and protect" (life and property), and are "handcuffed by laws." Labels such as these are used by the police with the complicity of the media to perpetuate stereotypes and favorable organizational images. Any general image projected and maintained by an organization is an attempt to gain the complicity of an audience with its own position or claims, especially those that express, mark, or celebrate a value such as "crime threatens us all."

Symbols organize experience. They serve dramaturgical ends. In arguing that symbols serve the dramaturgical purposes of the police it is claimed that by their displays of symbols such as the flag, slogans invoking duty, honor, and service, and the tools of authority and violence in the form of guns, nightsticks, and ammunition, the police indicate their connection with social order and their willingness to use legitimate violence. Insofar as the police become a part of the ongoing sense of community life and evoke that sense of mutual shared fate with community members to strengthen and make vibrant their position in the community, the police will maintain power and authority. The continued deference of citizens to the police in advance of the application of violence and in the absence of specific demands, commands, or laws designed to produce compliance or punish its absence, is the ultimate source of police power.

The media play an important role in maintaining and eroding police authority. People generally rely on and trust the image work of the police. The police, in turn, are "good sources" for the media, supplying them with facts, press releases, interviews, and advance "tips" (Ericson, Baranek, and Chan 1987). In fact, police and media people are one part of the same transactional exchange of information, favors, and tips, and reporters and officers, especially detectives, in the United States are boundary linkage people tying sources and media (see Hall et al. 1978; Fishman 1980; Ericson, Baranek, and Chan 1987; Ericson 1989, 1991). Rarely do the media assemble independent information on events that differs from the police perspective. A *media event* is an event created, amplified, and projected by the media and subsequently reported by media as real. The creation of a media event is an exercise in the construction of *hyperreality*, or images about images (Eco 1986). Examples of the creation of media images are stories done by media about other media people, media interviews based on an assumed and unproven thesis: "why our kids don't learn," reconstructions and recreations, fictional films based on "true stories," and investigative journalism generally. Television best reflects itself in an ongoing iteration of its own premises about itself and the society. Television simulates, over and over, the reality of itself. Media events are seen as real; yet they are a creation of media technologies, narratives, and agendas as well as "media logic" (Altheide 1979). Media people generalize without systematic evidence, often using frames like "people are wondering here if this will ever end," and creating moral panics by stringing together crimes to form "crime waves" and "rape epidemics." As a result of media actions, police are constantly responding to a mixture of actual incidents, incidents created, defined, and amplified by police or citizens, and media events. It is not surprising that police see themselves in part as media do, and tell stories about watching "Hill Street Blues" and reruns of "Hawaii 5-0" (see Vandenberg and Trujillo 1989).

The overall aim of the selective display of symbols by social-control agencies, what can be considered the performance of a drama, is to maintain their ecological niche in an environment and to sustain the appearance of control. The police, as a formal agency of control, cannot create social integration; they are at best able to sustain selectively, and on an ad hoc basis, aspects of their ordering actions. The informal and traditional sources of social control are more powerful than secondary patterns of social integration such as law or governmental social control (Black 1976). Nevertheless, symbolic sources of power are essential to agencies of formal social control such as the police, as they claim to act neutrally as third parties on behalf of the state. The power and public legitimacy of the police are integral to their survival as an organization, and thus they stand ready to adapt new tools of persuasion as organizational "weapons" when required (Selznick 1952).

If social consensus is more apparent than real, another way of describing police dramaturgy is to emphasize that essential to the maintenance of political power in a mass society is the active and visible *display* of (dramaturgical) control. Some opportunities for exercising the dramaturgical prerogative are a result of features of social structure, while others are rationally created by organizations as instrumentalities. Dramaturgical control, which results from deference and honoring of values and activities, can be displayed in public or ceremonial affirmations such as parades, funerals, and memorial services. It can also be seen in the deference and respect paid to police during their routines and everyday activities. The police who work in patrol, it is clear, are distinctive in appearance as well as quite visible. The police have an ample supply of costumes, props, and equipment (helicopters, guns, radios, cars) as well as a symbolic repertoire including symbols such as the flag, the city or state seal, slogans often borrowed from the government by which they are employed, and shorthand or "recipe" knowledge of the law. They are often the most strident voices of conventional morality as an occupation, even though as a group they are as diverse morally as they are intellectually.

Ceremonies, visible daily activities, props and symbols, and special knowledge and techniques constitute *resources* by which police can mark, claim, display, defend, and reaffirm their mandate. Insofar as one accepts the moral mandate of the police, the truthfulness of their communications is enhanced: the public accepts as credible versions of events produced by powerful and authoritative social institutions. Rather than viewing these as static "possessions," or obvious in some sense, it is useful to see them as resources variously available for managing the appearance of control and maintaining the integrity of the mandate. Although credibility and legitimacy may result from association with government, and are in that sense passive accoutrements, public relations and publicity efforts are also used by police actively to create and sustain a better public image. Let us now examine the active, rational police manipulation of symbols that serve to maintain a mandate and front. These efforts include strategy and tactics and programmatic attempts at self-promotion or persuasion of the worth of new ideas in policing.

Strategy, although it has several meanings, will be used here to indicate the allocation of resources to persuade, mark, claim, or show a version of events consistent with an overall goal or mandate. The police use a variety of strategies to assert and maintain their superordinate social position and to induce and reinforce public support (Beare 1987).[3] These include the rhetorical strategies used in public announcements and appearances (such as announcing a new neighborhood watch program), political strategies employed in gaining and maintaining power in the local political system (arguing that rises in crime require additional personnel), and ideological strategies, which serve to align their actions with superordinate "truths" and "realities" ("preserve and protect").

Although these strategies are an important aspect of front work and mandate management, operational strategies and "tactics" also serve to cope with these dilemmas and their uncertain appearance. (see Manning 1980:Ch. 5). *Tactics* is a relative term; tactics are a means to carry out or execute a given operational strategy. If one seeks to implement a community policing program, foot patrol is one tactic, decentralized ministations is another, and "Officer Friendly" appearances in primary schools is yet another. Tactics may require *subtactics* for their execution, such as requiring foot officers to call in at each business or neighborhood mall in their area.

The police seek to implement information control by means of lies, disinformation, misinformation, and propaganda. This is in part a result of their structurally determined incapacity to control the many and complex causes of crime directly, and partially a result of their self-serving claims or attempts to manage their dilemmas by public communications. As outlined above, the police cannot fully control events, even media-inspired events, or constrain all public knowledge about activities over which they claim control. Their information control and communicational strategies periodically fail. There are numerous sources of such failed front work and performance flaws, some of which are related to the dilemmas noted previously. Untoward events occur or information is received by the public: officers are shot, people defy police authority, crime continues to rise in official terms, and drug use and selling flourishes. As a result of public knowledge of these relevatory events, something like a *dialectic* develops between the dramatic claims and front of the police and ongoing, particularly media-shaped or -created events.

These dilemmas are indicative of fundamental dynamics of policing in Anglo-American societies. The dilemmas and their ineluctable quality are the root cause of the nature and kinds of dramaturgical appearance management of the police, to a lesser degree, their strategies and tactics, and finally at least to some degree, some features of their operations.

Types of External Police Communication: Crisis

Three types of external police communication, mentioned above, are important. The first is communication in crisis. Crisis-producing events include the shooting of an officer, a series of rapes, or a corruption scandal, and they serve to mobilize the community in defense of or in opposition to the police. The second type of communication, routine processing of calls to the police, is discussed in several places in this volume and is not discussed further in this chapter. The third type of communication, strategic communication, may take the form of introducing a program or new policy directed to long-standing problems or issues in a community such as crime prevention, juvenile delinquency, or "crime." Strategic communication is designed to increase public trust and confidence, or to focus public attention on a new approach to a problem so that the unaddressed root causes are not examined.

The three types of external communication have a number of relevant correlates, as shown in Table 7.1.

Note that in the case of *crisis communication* (column 1), the first three rows of the table display the groups most likely to support the police and their mandate, the target groups of interest in that modality of external communication, and the role of the media. In part because it is seen as being of short duration and in part because the event stimulating its appearance symbolizes a threat to the community at large, a *crisis* mode of communicating draws community support. During the course of response to the event, the media are likely to be supportive. This may change as protests and objections erode support and these events become the "news" to be covered and amplified. In the case of police work, events often contain rich and useful dramatic materials present in the form of a sacrifice made, a villain defeated, a symbol of honor or loss created, and a resolution of the situation. Such matters draw and hold media and public attention. Well-known people speak for the police and are accountable to political bodies (e.g., city council, county board, the mayor). Their response is to an external, unplanned event or series of events that are seen as unexpected, accidental, or unforeseen. The question of whether such an event is predictable and whether, therefore, someone is responsible for culpable for a failure to act in advance may itself be a focus of debates. The course of events in a crisis is by definition unpredictable and many aleatory features may cause reversals of the position of the organization—alleged "cover-ups," "restatements," and "clarifications."

In the case of *routine communication* (column 2), the public is dealt with in aggregate, one at a time as they call, and responses to events and individual calls are the focus of police attention. There are no specific

Table 7.1. Characteristics of Modes of External Communication

Crisis	Routine	Strategic
1. Consensus among the relevant publics, general support for police actions	1. Less visible consensus among relevant publics	1. Aim is to develop consensus
2. Targets are all community groups	2. Individual acts and events are focus of action and response	2. Problem oriented
3. Media in complicity, but support may be volatile	3. Media only aware of foul-ups, scandals, and egregious errors	3. Media complicity
4. Short duration	4. Ongoing activity of processing communications to and from the police	4. Future orientation
5. Concrete event(s) or villains precipitate responses	5. Multiple events with unrelated and complex meanings	5. Unfolding and complex relationship between events and programs
6. Spokespeople are known and identified	6. Many conflicts represented, no single spokesperson	6. Usually a senior officer
7. Unplanned and spontaneous response to external events	7. Reactive response to ordinary events	7. Enacting an environment
8. Tighter coupling evolves during crisis	8. Loose coupling maintained	8. Planned attempts to cope in advance with anticipated events by program, policy, or strategy (-ies)

target groups, only individuals. The media become aware of the problematic nature of "routine communication" only as a result of errors in judgment or accidents. Public awareness of police decisions is low. The many communicational channels in and out of the organization are handled by a routinized technology, sets of tasks and roles, and known modes of classification and interpretation. The result is maintenance of loose coupling with the environment (Manning 1982b).

In *strategic communication* (column 3), the aim is to develop a consensus in advance among the relevant target groups, and to use the media as a source of publicity. Police may call press conferences, issue press releases, and make a series of public announcements about the planned program. [Many researchers have noted that, typically, the police make these announcements confident that the program will work, but rarely call press conferences to present evidence of outcomes and results of programs (see Wetheritt 1988).] The ostensible stimulus for the program is the emergence of a type of community problem, e.g., drugs, an increasing burglary rate, or citizen concern about children's safety after school. The aim is to reduce the problem in the future by allocating resources and enacting a scenario, policy, or plan. Such programs, since they are police initiated, controlled, and funded, maintain police autonomy and the causal indeterminacy of the environment.

In summary, then, these three types of communication differ in the degree of consensus extant and anticipated, the target groups involved, the role of the media, the duration of the event(s), and the orientation of the responses to it (or them), the complexity of the meanings involved in the communication, the number of channels in and out utilized by the organization, and the degree to which the response to the events is planned or reactive and spontaneous. While routine and strategic communications intend to maintain the current level of loose coupling, crisis events tend to reduce looseness and to tighten the coupling between organization and environment. Both tight and loose coupling coexist under these circumstances.

Let us now turn to an example of crisis communication produced by one recurring dramatic dilemma, the death of an officer, which demonstrates the vulnerability and riskiness of policing and follow that with a discussion of a strategic rhetorical strategy, community policing.

External Communication in Crises

It is quite clear that police and crime news are media staples. A majority of all news and media coverage focuses on various forms of deviance and crime. When a single event or small but important series of events erupts, a few themes are developed, the threat is seen as external (e.g., "cop killers," "freeway murderers," a war on "crack" cocaine), the audience is general, and divisions in social values, if present, are obscured or ignored. The police front suggests maximal identification with the community represented by the individual victims. There may be specific villains of potential targets for police action. Policy issues may or may not arise in this context. Crisis communication seems to be centered by the media on statements of authorities and powerful leaders of the dominant groups (Molotch and Lester 1974, 1975). As a result, there are few cries for fundamental change, but an emphasis on "more of the same."

The police funeral is a vehicle for examining some of the more salient dramatic dilemmas of policing and how the police, in complicity with the mass media, use communication to create positive images of policing. These images circumvent and depress the dilemmas as well as reveal them. Let us first review the reported events associated with the recent killing of a police officer in Dallas.

The Events

On January 16, 1988, Dallas officer John Glenn Chase, 25, accosted while writing a traffic ticket, was distracted, shouted at, and punched by a homeless, perhaps mentally deranged, black "street person," Carl Williams. Williams and Chase then wrestled, and while a crowd watched, Williams shot Officer Chase point-blank with the officer's own .44. Some early reports (*Detroit News*, January 25, 1988) claimed that the watching citizens urged the killer on with cries of "Shoot him," (these reports proved to be unfounded). In the event, bystanders did little to prevent the shooting. The shooting had connotations of an assassination because it was public, was done with the officer's own gun, and was amplified by almost immediate police and community response. Two important reactions were communicated publicly almost immediately.

The police acted within a few minutes of hearing of the shooting, hunting down and killing Williams. According to news reports, off-duty officers heard about the murder on the radio, and encountered and killed the suspect nearby. Thus, two murders were carried out in the space of less than an hour, one in the name of the other, and by extension, in the name of the higher morality the police claim to represent.

Political officials also acted, communicating their outrage publicly. Officials, including the mayor, members of the city council, and the chief of police, made inflammatory public statements. Some members of the city council claimed that others on the city council (the black members), by being "antipolice," i.e., criticizing past police actions (see below), had had a hand (metaphorically) in the officer's killing.

These actions by the police and politicians, along with the murder of a police officer in Dallas in the previous week, marked the event publicly and associated the powerful white ruling elites of the city and the predominantly white police as representatives of "the community" in Dallas. Together, the killings and response dramatized an organizational communication of the events. The conjunction of event, definition, and response was seen by many as a reflection upon the viability of the central moral values of the city. The events and the response of the police and the political leaders of Dallas mobilized community opinion both for and against the police and their actions. These responses were but one set within an ongoing history of racial violence by the police and by blacks.

The media had an important role in defining the "causes" of the events and what they represented about the city of Dallas. The killing was taken very seriously as synecdochical of the social fabric of the city, in short, *not* seen as a "random" or "mysterious" happening. Shortly later, in mid-January 1988, CBS "Sunday Evening News" showed scenes from the funeral of Officer Chase. The funeral was attended by a large number of officers from the local area, and officers in uniform delivered homilies and tributes to their fallen fellow. CBS showed portions of a uniformed sergeant's speech in the church, which emphasized the tragic loss to the community that the killing represented and expressed the hope that this would never again happen. *The New York Times* reported that Dallas was "in an uproar" as a result of the slaying, and that "Dallas may now be paying the price for the quiescent 40 year period in which Dallas was run more like a corporation than a city" (January 1988). The *Times* went on to quote the Dallas chief of police, who said that the city council had contributed to the death of Officer Chase, presented a summary of changes in minority power in city government (although minorities constitute 50 percent of the population, they hold only two seats on the city council), and published a letter to the editor that read in part "No winner. Two cops dead. Citizens dead. A little bit of each of us has died. Peace died a little bit more." A picture of two officers in a police car was printed with the caption explaining that Dallas had "adopted two officer patrols after an officer was killed and racial tensions worsened." *Newsweek* (April 18, 1988) included a story, "Goodbye to the 'Dallas Way'," on the shooting and speculated on its significance for the changed nature of the Dallas community and its ethnic integration, morality, integrity, and future. *Insight*, a national news magazine published in Washington, featured a detailed story (August 29, 1988) and on the cover showed a picture of female officers crying near a flag-draped coffin. The murder of the officer was seen not just as a murder, but as an important, evocative symbol of a continuing threat to the moral integrity of one of America's largest cities. How does such a sequence of events speak to the dramatic dilemmas of the police?

An Analysis of the Communication of Community-Police Solidarity

Funerals in every known society are a celebration of the *sacred*. The sacred, the mysterious, powerful, and distant that arouses feelings of awe and worship, is found in some form in all societies. How does a funeral function to mark social values?

The funeral ceremony for a dead police officer underscores society's response to a very serious crime, murder, made more serious because the victim was a representative of central social values for which government and its agents are surrogates or proximal symbols. The funeral is an occasion for a public, collective display of society's views of itself; it is essentially *self-affirmational* from society's point of view. The funeral also symbolizes the authority of the state (and local authority), the coherence and importance of the police as an occupational group of singular significance and importance within the society, and their mutual identification. Not only does a religious funeral celebrate the place of God and of religious beliefs (or ideology), more generally, it conflates or makes equivalent the values, uniforms, and practices of the police with those of other sacred/religious entities and with the worthy citizens who support the police.

The funeral sets out for public appreciation what Durkheim (1964) calls "social facts": social matters such as social values, symbols, beliefs, and norms that are seen as external, constraining, and "real" in their consequences. All social facts are abstractions that find their evidence variously: in beliefs, values, assumptions, and the like. Social facts possess power and authority insofar as people believe in their importance and persistent presence in communal life. Durkheim believed that agreement on social facts, especially those which become recognized as essential to communal life, is the essence of social and moral integration. Crime is a primary example of a vehicle or event for mobilizing community sentiments.

The problem presented by analyzing the police as a modern complex or formal organization communicating to its publics is that increasingly fewer social values are widely shared. Even those shared may be defined variously by ethnic, class, or regional groups. Conversely, think of the importance in a postmodern society of the creation and construction of events to symbolize, suggest, or merely index consensus, rather than actually to sustain a viable, known, and shared moral order. Imagery and image manipulation may substitute for value consensus (Lukes 1975).

Mass societies contain vast, conflicting rules, standards, and beliefs; and the media homogenizes and flattens experience. Social facts do not possess the centrality they did for Durkheim at the beginning of the twentieth century. However, the display of images of control, the legitimation of events, and their selective distribution, all indicate important manifestations of social power and of conventional authority. Whether the celebration of these values is an indication of social consensus is not clear. However, the funeral does function to mark a number of matters linked closely to legitimate political authority.

The Dallas funeral of Officer Chase provides examples of these general points. The funeral was converted into a national media event, held in a large church, and attended by a collection of formally uniformed officers from all over the state of Texas. It displays aspects of unity of values and social solidarity. The funeral and officers' representation in it asserts the current status quo—serving to mark and maintain the relative position of groups in a moral hierarchy. The funeral marks the significance of a police death and represents it as a threat to the moral and social continuity of the community. The death of an officer is seen as if it were a threat to a critical segment of a much larger and invisible moral whole. The funeral celebrates violence; both as a source of control over crime and deviance, and as a right and authority of the state. It should be emphasized that sacrifice and hierarchy are linked, so that giving a life in public service sustains the social values of those in power. The murder of a police officer has political meanings: it is an assassination.

The funeral serves a reassuring function for those in power. The funeral bespeaks the *values held by those in power* (see Lukes 1975). These values assert the continuity of the society as well as other values, the ultimate sanctification of these values by policing, and reassurance to the police of the worth and virtue of their activities, even up to and including dying in the service of a city. The service offers the opportunity for reflexive reassurance: officers and others can see themselves engaging in the ceremony, honoring and being honored, and so they continue to see themselves seeing themselves in such an elevated moral position. Finally, the funeral symbolizes racial and gender unity within the police. The appearance of black officers in uniform at the funeral, on the other hand, speaks to the unity of interests of racial groups in support of the conventional forces of authority, as does the picture of crying female officers displaying gender unity on the cover of *Insight*.

However, the control of the definition of values by the media and the police means that although some values will be visibly marked, others are kept out of sight, are depressed in salience. It is good to review some of these invisible matters. This shooting of an officer by a black person was one of a series of known incidents of shooting involving black citizens and officers in Dallas from 1970, including the shooting of seven innocent youths in 1970, the 1973 murder of a 12-year-old by an officer (he was sentenced to five years), the killing of 70-year-old crippled Etta Collins by two officers in 1986, a shoot-out that led to the death of Officer Blair in March 1986, a November shooting of a bootlegger by shotgun, and the shooting of a black officer, James Joe, nine days before the Chase shooting (*Insight*, August 29, 1988). Conflict between black and white citizens in Dallas was expressed in this well-known series of violent encounters and in the "antipolice" remarks attributed to the (black) members of the city council.

Subsequent news articles reflected on the dubious or volatile current state of what used to be called "race relations," the integration of blacks and whites in Dallas. In spite of the unity produced by media versions of events displayed on such public occasions, the police cannot always conceal conflict or dilemmas: they are lightning rods for all forms of social conflict as well as for those of integration and unity. They manage and symbolize uncertainty.

This funeral is a scene, a front-stage occasion for the polishing and renewing of conventional values, yet it was also a facet of an ongoing struggle for community control and political power by ritualized communication. It is a case in point of response to an immediate crisis that displays the public association and identification with the police as symbolizing the community as a whole. On the other hand, the ongoing attempts by the police to manage the appearance of control and service are driven by the same growth in diversity, conflict, and ethnic/class divisions found in all urban American communities. The most important of these rhetorical strategies is "community policing."

Strategic External Communication: Community Policing

The image of policing is a dramatic one. This rich and evocative imagery sets the police organization in context, defining it as an essential part of a well-integrated communal whole. The police play a role in larger political dramas (see Wagner-Pacifici 1986), but are essentially the most powerful and authoritative source of definitions of crime and deviance in local communities. In the past, the American police have distanced themselves from communities by an emphasis upon rational crime-fighting and "professionalism," and by maintaining an aloof attitude to problems of local communities that were not, strictly speaking, matters of crime. As Fogelson (1977), among others, has noted, this positioning was in part an attempt to create the perception that the police were an apolitical force that might better withstand local pressures for corruption and in part an attempt on the part of senior members of the occupation to arrogate greater respect and deference to the occupation and its practitioners. With the appearance of the work of August Vollmer and O. W. Wilson in the late thirties, scientifically based crime fighting and administration became thematic of modern professional policing [see Stead (1977) for a review of this transformation]. The police, with some increasing skill, have been engaged in the management of public impressions of their power, efficacy, and impact for at least the last 30 years.

Once set apart from communities in order to decrease corruption and increase good government, the police suffered a new malaise—they lost contact with the local politics that sustained their previous authority. This required new forms of organizational communication and new forms of organizational innovation.[4] The police sought this new power source as the local base of authority rapidly shifted, and a low-level crisis of authority resulted. Indicative of this are turnovers in chiefs, low morale, strikes, and an increase in police labor-management disputes. New kinds of crises emerged. The "normal state of events" in policing seems to be a constant low-level crisis. The punctuation of routine by a shooting or a public crisis in crime control, e.g., a string of murders or rapes, is feared, but uncommon in most forces. What has become a more common problem for police is legitimacy and political authority.

Several structural factors have reduced police support and consensus about the quality and performance of the modern urban police. In spite of the continued use of the "crime-fighting" and professional models— and there is no perceptible diminution of these themes in modern policing—large minority populations in urban areas, excluded from opportunities, have become a permanent underclass. The problems of urban crime, social order, and integration were transformed into the practical problem of rationing and distributing urban services. Styles of policing the urban underclass changed little, and minority populations continued to be observed and policed closely, with resultant high rates of arrest. Urban budgets were strained and police were laid off. Services of all kinds were reduced, and private policing grew in numbers and influence. With the loss of the Law Enforcement Assistance Administration support in the late seventies, subsidies for various programs and equipment were lost and the programs were either dropped or supported from other budget categories. Retirement and overtime costs grew as a proportion of police budgets.

In the past, the urban police could segregate audiences and messages, and send the message of "service" to the middle classes implying their control of the "criminal classes" and the message of service to lower-class communities. Businesses were viewed as the primary clients in inner cities, but as businesses moved to shopping malls and hired private police, the service base for the inner city diminished. Violent crime increased. It was less easy to segregate audiences and appeal to majority sentiments with a crime control strategy while seeking to appeal to minority and lower-class groups with a service strategy.

Some social-psychological consequences of these changes were felt by the police. Although identification with the police for many groups reproduces the response that identification with a community in general might produce, this appeal to general community loyalty became increasingly problematic. Police could expect to benefit less from their association with symbols of community integration and appeals to commitment to the moral order. Public support for the police was more and more patterned by race, class, and age. Recent events, especially the riots of the sixties and the growing number of large cities with black politicians in positions of authority, reduced the viability of conventional police strategies. Urban diversity is now sought and politically acceptable.

While community identification and the symbolic authority of the police and other American institutions is declining, a new ideological theme has been emerging in police rhetoric in the last five to ten years: *community policing*. Rather than a new rhetorical strategy that replaces the crime control–professionalism strategy, which produced social distance, it is a contrapuntal theme: a harmony for the old melody. It now seeks control of the public by a reduction in social distance, a merging of communal and police interests, and a service and crime control isomorphism. Clearly, as in the past, the symbols created, organized, and displayed by police are ways of shaping thinking, focusing attention, and defining the meaning of situations. Community policing, which is both a rhetoric and an operational strategy adopting many tactical forms, is a relatively new tool in the drama of control. It is different, however, in the important sense that unlike the crisis appeal for unity in the face of the killing of an officer, this new rhetorical strategy is a long-term management approach to organizational communication.

This kind of strategic communication might be called "ideological work." A sociologist, Margaret Beare (1987), in an analysis based on news coverage of police activities in Toronto, has suggested that police carry out "ideological work" by producing and maintaining programs and policies that are publicly advanced and advertised by announcements, television advertisement campaigns (such as Operation Identification, Neighborhood Watch programs, and McGruff, the crime prevention dog-cop), or statements of specific foci and targets of their efforts. The newspaper coverage of policing includes stories on police ideology, including their views of the law and police professionalism, crime fighting, differential policing, isolation of dangerous class(es), and maintenance of a proactive police presence. These themes are "sold" to society in annual reports as well as newspapers. Beare documented changes (increases) in the extent of newspaper coverage of community policing in Toronto as an example of a campaign of external communication to "sell" an idea (community policing) to the local community.

Analysis of these kinds of public campaigns, like community policing, which is discussed below, suggests that they address unfolding issues, have set programmatic or policy themes, appeal to respectable audiences in particular, and have generalized targets. The articles vary in citing internal and external sources of police difficulties. Because they are public policy–shaped, such campaigns, like media-produced crime waves, may surface public dissent and disagreement about facets of the policy. There is an ironic sting potential in media campaigns because they highlight and educate people to the nature of police problems. Perhaps the most pertinent recent example of this sort of police communication is the media attention, partially police created, surrounding the growing fad of "community policing."

The rhetoric of community policing, a fairly recent appeal to the community for support and claimed legitimacy, is a powerful tool for shaping public opinion. Nevertheless, since public opinion is divided on the approval of police practices, many unanticipated and negative consequences result from the appeal to audiences on different grounds, and the use of complementary strategies of community control. What role does community policing play in the drama of control? What are its claims?

Assumptions about the Problem: Four Facets

Community policing, a loose collection of program elements, is based upon a set of unexamined *ideological assumptions* (see Manning 1984:212–13). These assumptions link the police as an organization to the local community and the community to the police. The assumptions have currency among police administrators, politicians, and social researchers. Community policing appeals to police administrators as well as to politicians and community members. Police administrators have long been wed to the notion of a rational-bureaucratic policing that would both permit greater control over discretion and new sources of internal control, evaluation, supervision, and promotion. Administrators are inclined to justify the idea with reference to assumptions about the needs of the community rather than their own administrative needs. These posited assumptions about community needs are not formally written in programs, found in police rules and regulations, or implied by the stated operational objectives of the programs. They are, like social life itself, rather unclear, unfolding, indeterminate, and subject to redefinition. Nevertheless, such ideas are quite powerful in shaping police community programs.

Four kinds of assumptions about the targets and aims of the communication lie behind the community-policing rhetoric. The first assumptions are general, about the nature of social order and social control and the police role in urban areas.[5] These general beliefs about the nature of the community and its needs are complemented by other assumptions about the nature of public demand for policing, the role of the police, and the consequences of community policing for police morale. These assumptions constitute bases for communicating.

1. Assumptions are made about *public order in urban areas*. There is an assumption that the public (undefined) yearns for order (undefined), community (undefined), and reduced crime, and that the police should and will quench this nostalgic thirst with increased community policing.[6] It is assumed that there is sufficient public consensus about the "desirable" and the good in respect of the quality of urban life and that notions like "order" and "disorder" share agreed-upon referents. This imagined order is seen as created or at least facilitated by police actions with, for, and by "communities." There is a sense in which police seek the paradoxical job of assisting a community to create a new order for itself.

2. Police administrators and politicians also entertain assumptions, perhaps necessarily, about *the nature of public needs and demands* to which they are responding (Manning 1984). These assumptions serve as a tacit justification or rationale for community policing and for persuasively "selling" to the public and politicians the community policing "package." These include the notion that the public is currently dissatisfied with present police practices, and that previous police approaches are seen as failed or have been demonstrated to have failed. People like seeing officers on foot and in and around places of business, and support the core police function, patrol.

3. A further set of assumptions bears on *the role of the police*. The presumed decline or erosion of the binding power of informal bases of social control in communities can be restored by police action to renew and reinforce these eroded patterns. The envisioned community police will be efficient, courteous, and accessible, and combine, within current budget limitations, both specialist and generalist functions. Community policing enacts the ever-viable continuing quest for a form of policing capable of controlling urban crime. Since it is assumed that people wish to see and be in routine personal contact with police officers in their neighborhoods and places of business, the more police seen, the more satisfaction with policing. Patrol remains a central feature of community policing although the tactical nature of patrol is modified in community policing since officers on foot rather than in cars carry out patrol activities. The key idea is that officers walking in an assigned area for at least some time during their tour of duty will increase the quality and quantity of contact between the police and public. This contact, in turn, will

have the anticipated consequences with respect to reduced fear of crime, increased security, better perceived quality of the urban environment, and so on.[7]

4.   Assumptions are made about the *consequences of community policing for police morale*. Morale and generalized police functions will be enhanced as a result of the success of community policing. This "spin-off" of freedom and job satisfaction produces a kind of "halo effect' for many officers and may have a general positive consequence (Wycoff 1988).

In sum, these four assumptions lead to the conclusion that community policing will better meet the stated needs than previous approaches.[8] This makes real both the problem to be addressed and the solutions advanced. Community policing is a solution seeking a problem as well as a solution to a problem. When implemented, community policing is a kind of police-cast drama or rhetoric in which police produce the script and players, cast the roles, and also serve as critical judges of the performance. The rhetorical reality of community policing is unquestioned, but the organizational infrastructure of policing has little changed. In order to understand the nature of the rhetoric of external communication, we have to examine closely the constraints on police action that arise directly from organizational structure. Let us now briefly examine the organizational context of policing and how it affects the rhetoric of policing.

Organizational Contexts and Rhetorical Strategies

In the past, it appeared that there were two principal imageries or metaphors used to describe Anglo-American policing. A third has arisen, brought into life by massive public relations efforts and federal and foundation funding. These distinctive images of the social organization of policing are found in the research literature, in textbooks, and in the popular press. Each image deserves some discussion; each is a dramaturgical "face" or metaphor used by the police selectively to display symbols and meanings to their advantage at given times with given audiences. The metaphors retain life in part because police researchers, textbook writers, and the media have often uncritically amplified elements of such "faces" and contributed to their lasting epistemological status as social realities. They remain in tension with each other and with observable facts; yet, there are truths about the practice and organization of large police organizations captured in these metaphors. All are ideal types and do not exist empirically. They are conceptual fictions used to explain aspects of police behavior and structure. They all contain some insights and truths and conceal others—all metaphors are partially blind.

The first metaphor for police organization is the view of policing as a *paramilitary or bureaucratic form* characterized by invisible, indirectly available, impersonal, specialist officers. They are armed Weberian bureaucrats. They focus on crime as a legal infraction, and are disinterested in "community work" because it is not truly "police work." Bureaucratic police are hierarchically and strategically organized to produce a response that is rational and appropriate to the scale, severity, and potential for development of a given problem. They are centrally commanded and owe allegiance to the commander and carry out orders that originate above. Although dispersed ecologically, they are allocated and directed from a central communications center, which stands as a surrogate for the orders of the chief. Certain tensions exist as a result, and are resolved by working agreements that generate apparent consensus and the common-sense reality of policing.[9]

The second metaphor for police organization might be called the view of policing as *public service*. It contains an implicit critique of the rational-bureaucratic model of policing and suggests the need for democratic leadership, human relations training, and officer education. When first publicized, its advocates claimed it to be a solution to problems of police morale and divided internal efforts as well as better suited to controlling and serving communities. It stands as something of a contrasting conception to the first type, police organization as a crime-fighting, rationally administered tool. The officer is to be an autonomous, well-educated civil servant who serves the public, is led and disciplined in a democratic fashion, and is sensitive to the differential requirements of the social groups and areas served (Angell 1971). Goals, objectives, and programs are decided by dispassionate professional administrators and managers who take well-considered decisions about the nature of the problems and the needed solution in consultation with other responsible figures such as civic leaders and elected politicians.

A third metaphor for policing has emerged in the last ten years. It might be termed the *economic-liberalist* view of policing. The driving, root metaphor here is economic and urges one to think in terms of supply and demand, and in market terms. Policing is a service, a distributional activity, that serves to reallocate collective goods (Feeley 1970). Yet, "police services" are not fully expansive, and citizen demand, although elastic, is not permitted to expand beyond set, police-based limits. On the other hand, somewhat in the same sense that one is required as a patriotic duty to buy an American car every two or three years, citizens must provide demand guidance to the police, and indicate what they will "buy" or what they will pay for, and the extent to which they take responsibility for their own problems. At the margins, then, the citizenry must decide collectively what they are willing to do, to pay for, and to support. Responsibility is shifted from the police to the public for "buying" in good faith, with tax dollars, and participating in police service. The economic-liberalist view of policing is well illustrated by many themes in the rhetoric of community policing. The officer envisioned by this view will act within the outlines of a community-policing strategy or program staffed by visible, available, and even personable officers. The officers are *demand managers*: often stationed nominally in a neighborhood school, storefront, or ministation, when not out earnestly serving the public on foot, they represent an active form of dedifferentiated social control. They pose as members of the community and are expected to act as moralists-in-residence. The officer represents an individual symbol for the community and stands in contrast to the stereotypic crime-focused specialist, entailed in the first and second metaphors. The organization serves general community needs. It is focused on diverse disorder and on building markets for service and increasing buying power in an enhanced quality of life. There are intimations that such a force will also be more democratic and concerned with the quality of the officers' lives. It will increase morale and loyalty to the organization and its mission. The community will be expected to exchange information, rewards, and support for the services they receive. *Caveat emptor* reigns. The economic-liberalist view of policing, when combined with a community policing program, is expected to offer solutions in the form of integrated crime-fighting tactics as well as the maintenance of community well-being insofar as the community demands and is willing to pay for these commodities (see Moore and Trojanowicz 1988).

These images or metaphors of policing contain an implicit basis for authority. The bureaucratic type tends to base authority in the position or office, the service model locates it in skill, and the economic-liberalist type sees it in demand management. Within any type of policing, authority can be based upon an office, the domains of which are spatial and temporal. This is the traditional authority of the patrol officer. A second form of authority is expert based, and inheres in specialist groups and units such as juvenile bureaus, detective divisions, and tactical squads (see Gouldner 1954), while the authority of the officer in the economic-liberalist model relies on creating, sustaining, and satisfying public demand. The result of this tension within police is that patrol and specialized units cooperate only when necessary to maintain their own autonomy and control. These forms of authority and procedurally based modes of case-processing conflict in practice, and any innovative program, such as community policing, will encounter tensions between bases of skill, authority, and public satisfaction. Demand managers differ in this type from the other two in terms of their authority bases. They are interested in controlling the demand in their local area, either raising it or lowering it, depending on what is required by local definitions of need. They derive support from "the community" and seek their legitimation in community satisfaction. They are dependent for legitimation on external audiences. This makes the role of the libertarian police officer something akin to the medical "quack"—a doctor who is somewhat overly sensitive to the assessments and opinions of the client rather than of colleagues (Hughes 1958).

There is an irony here, since as long as police exercise authority and violence in the name of the state they will be feared and loathed by some segments of the community, and will represent this violence potential to all segments of the community. The fact is, police exercise violence and will be periodically unpopular, the target of protest, and viewed ambivalently. Traditionally, of course, since the introduction of the police in London in 1829, the public has had little use for the police unless it is in trouble (Reith 1938; Miller 1977). Police presence is not reassuring unless one wants reassurance. Public attitudes to police remain deeply ambivalent and doubtless will, given the police's powers and potential.

It is important to note that these metaphors are drawn from police research and media coverage of policing, and they are thus encapsulated summaries of police rhetorical strategies. Like all forms of communication designed to overcome dilemmas, these rhetorics contain internal contradictions. The police strive to increase morale and bureaucratic administration while better serving "the community," yet there are quite different conceptions of the nature of the police mandate, police function, and the police role held by police officers, police administrators, police reformers, and politicians.

The actual operation of policing has changed little. Tensions remain in American policing that rhetoric cannot suppress. In many respects, all American policing relies heavily on radio-based patrol, specialized detective investigative units, and vice units that create their own work. Functional differences exist in role definition, sources of authority, and the focus of patrol. In the emerging economic-liberalist metaphor, the officer is often on foot rather than in a vehicle, and is guided and directed by programmatic interests toward certain tasks and duties. The unsolved question of how to guide and constrain discretion in patrol remains. The relatively unchanged nature of the underlying pattern of policing, and its traditional organizational form, suggests that any effects of a community-policing program would be revealed in the impact(s) it might have on the community, not on the practice of policing.

Community Policing as a Form of Strategic Organizational Communication

The strategic aims of this form of organizational communication are perhaps worthwhile noting. They are restatements at a lower level of generality of the broader ideological assumptions and claims outlined above. The communication is a kind of dramaturgical "sizing up" of the target groups, their putative needs, and hypothecated goals and consequences of policing. The rhetoric focuses on a set of *targets*; what people are presumed to want or *need*, the *consequences* of police activities, and *goals* of community policing. These will be discussed in order.

First, the communications assume that people desire more *information*, in particular about the status and outcomes of their own cases, wherever the case may be located in the criminal justice system, about victimization in their own "community," and about the quality of life within their community. Rather than specific concerns about crime and how it affects them, most people view dirt and disorder (undefined) as "signs of crime." If the police work to reduce such signs they will have a role in increasing the perceived quality of life in a community. Removing or altering these will decrease perceptions of fear. This assumes a naive and rationalistic notion of the relationships between information, social integration and the quality of life.

Second, claims are also made in these writings about the presumed *consequences of some kinds of police activities* for other forms of policing: Police activities in the community (various programs are included in this generalization) increase police job satisfaction. Community policing reduces demand upon police time as indicated by changes in the number of calls made to the police. Community policing facilitates police information-gathering. Community-policing officers develop new skills and roles (for example, they serve as mediators of disputes as well as being channels through which citizens can contact schools, local social services, and government). Community policing reduces posited psychological distance between the police and the public. This indicates a new form of personal rather than organizational authority is being nurtured. The police foot officer is seen as a surrogate for the community at large, functioning as eyes and ears, and acting as a moral and political force on behalf of the community.

Third, a series of *goals* for community policing is stated, based on assumptions about the nature of the impact of policing on communities. Consider the following statements, assuming each one is preceded by the phrase "community policing."

- The programs aim to increase citizens' perception of their personal safety and to decrease the amount of actual or perceived criminal activity.

- The programs aim to create community awareness of crime problems and methods of increasing law enforcement's ability to deal with actual or potential criminal activity effectively.
- They seek to develop citizen volunteer actions aimed at target crimes in support of and under the direction of the police department, and to eliminate citizen apathy about reporting crimes to the police.
- Visible foot officers doing community policing will provide reassurance to citizens.
- Increased access to police and "personal" contact with police increases citizen satisfaction.
- The programs will reduce the fear of crime, especially among the young, the old, and the weak or incapacitated, as well as reducing physical disorder (dirt, abandoned cars, etc.).

This list of goals and imputed consequences arose from interaction between police administrators, police researchers, and politicians, and is a heady mixture of hopes, proscriptions, prescriptions, and empirical inferences. The strategic communication used to sell the idea of community policing to communities is no different from other police strategies aimed at shaping and manipulating public opinion. Communicational strategies are also limited in their effectiveness. These strategies work best when they work least: when they are invisible, played out to segregated audiences so that potential contradictions are not apparent, and when other complementary strategies are also employed.[10]

Conclusions

This chapter on organizational communication provides evidence of how the modern police have become not only a physical presence in everyday life, but a symbolic presence ingratiating themselves into wider arenas of social action. They do so not only by political action, occupational routines, and "public relations," but by communicating in crisis and expressing their policy intentions. They maintain their symbolic, political, and physical presence in the community through these means.

To argue that the police engage the world dramatically is merely to extend to analysis of policing a perspective relevant for the analysis of all collective actions. The drama of policing, however, takes many forms, uses emergent and changing symbols, tactics, and rhetorics, and is flexible enough to meet emerging needs. It works with essentially dramatic stuff, the rise and fall of reputations, of good and evil, of individual morality. It possesses abundant traditions and conventions and participates in important community celebrations. The moral drama and the police role in it remains a vibrant and engaging spectacle, and each new mask is greeted with anticipation and has emotional potential. Police rhetoric remains a flexible and innovative tool.

Police communication in crisis is ironically much to their advantage. The media response to killings of police (not police killings of citizens) demonstrates that mobilization of strong community sentiments in support of the police can occur spontaneously. Police deaths become icons of moral solidarity. Those who do not celebrate and morne these deaths are marginal to such a consensus or are excluded from media comment. In this way, the conventional wisdom, as Baudrillard (1988) calls it, the *simulacrum*, or image of community integration, maintains its salience and, indeed, its hyperreality (Eco 1986). Ritual conceals as well as reveals, as does organizational communication.

On the other hand, community policing is a preplanned strategy, an idea whose rhetorical time has come. It serves broader community aims and entails an unfolding scenario. Community policing in its most ambitious forms seeks to reduce the costs of policing, increase the crime control capacity of policing, renew and restore the morality and integrity of communities, and even increase morale and decrease rates of turn-over within police organizations. It claims, in the long run, to reduce the fear of crime as well as the actual level of crime, and restore urban government to its proper role in maintaining community well-being (Greene and Mastrofski 1988).

It perhaps matters little that these goals may be mutually exclusive or conflicting. Communicative strategies are a symbolic management function (Pfeffer 1981), and speak to the expressive and ill-formed sense of what serves to reassure the public. The programs are part of the rhetoric of governmental symbolic action (Edelman 1964, 1977), and as a part of local government, they are one facet of cumbersome and awkward machinery. The police are only facet of social control, including informal as well as other formal agencies of control. As such, it is difficult, if not impossible, to examine the claims and aims of community policing as a communicational strategy outside the context of changes in social control and of a larger political reform movement (Mastrofski 1988).

External Communication II: Safety Discourse

Introduction

This chapter explores yet another type of external communication. It draws on several rather disparate ideas from the sociology of regulation, semiotics, and discourse analysis in order to illuminate the kinds of knowledge relevant to the study of external organizational communication as well as of risk and safety. In particular, the chapter explores how the denotative and connotative meanings of the concepts of "safety" and "risk" illustrated in guidance documents published by the NII and used to supervise the industry are embedded in paradigms or associative contexts.[1] Thus, a distinctive notion of safety is communicated that artfully conceals and reveals aspects of the concept of safety. In this sense, the inspectorate defines and manages the concepts central to the maintenance of its own mandate. To understand how this discourse is constructed and how the risks inherent in generation of electrical power by nuclear reactors are defined, two things are needed: an overview of discourse analysis and the range of meanings of the concept of risk.

At this point, a brief reprise of the argument about the centrality of language and semiotic analyses may be useful, because the assumptions underlying the arguments of this book differ from those of much quantitative research, and of non–linguistically oriented qualitative studies.

Focus: Discourse

The fieldwork model presented here is based on fundamental assumptions about language and discourse, and their role in shaping and sensitizing the research enterprise. Although discourse is variously defined, it refers generally to "forms of interaction, formal and informal, and written texts of all kinds" (Potter and Wetherell 1987:7). Discourse analysis is a method for studying organizational communication, communicational forms, and external and internal foci of organizational communication, and attempts to link discourse to meaning, to information, and to the patterning of social relations.

Humans are symbol-using animals whose language capacity virtually compels them to communicate, process meaning, and use information to organize and coordinate mutual lines of action. Language, both written and spoken, is the primary vehicle in organizational communication. This formulation does not omit the important contributions of nonverbal communication, but any analysis of nonverbal communication, or communication using other sign systems, is based upon the linguistic model. In any case, the integration of communication and collective action generally must occur through and by language.

As Barthes (1970:9–11) points out, language is the dominant mode of communication that shapes, channels, and makes meaningful all other forms of communication. Language shapes thought, thought images, and actions; language also is thought, produces images, and is action. A simple thesis that should guide a language-sensitive project is that language, the system from which signs are given their meaning, is not simply a tool, but something that constructs and maintains being and beings and maintains their significant grounding in social worlds. How is this grounding created and maintained in organizations by language?

Language is "doubly articulated" in the sense that it communicates about itself as well as "creates" multiple social worlds. Language constrains choices. Words, as signs, have multiple references simultaneously, and social structures are at least partially a function of metaphors, tropes, and paradigms, captured in some set of codes. For example, messages communicate denotatively, connotatively, metaphorically, and within a given style or trope. Because all messages, indeed all forms of communication, communicate at several levels simultaneously, it is possible that the same message has different meanings to different people, but more importantly for purposes of this discussion, that it communicates mutually contradictory actions (or thoughts) within itself. It cannot be easily fragmented, analyzed, or taken apart, bit by bit, because its central features are expressive and symbolic rather than conveying information. We return to these themes.

Meaning, of central interest here, is a function of content, context, and an interpretant. *Organization*, we have attempted to demonstrate, can be seen as referring to a collocation of codes, interpretants, and the loci of perspectives. Or it can be a function of these, when seen as a result of a perspective, or interpretant. These organizational codes, interpretants, and perspectives help to pin down communicated meaning and guide collective actions. To the extent that a given set of meanings is *dramatized*, other meanings are obviated, obscured, or obfuscated. This is true for research perspectives as well. Ideas that drive attitude research (based on the notion that people possess a constant propensity to act toward a designated object) are highly misleading insofar as they overlook the contextual aspects of language and even of naming (Potter and Wetherell 1987:35ff). No study can reduce the ambiguity of language, or finally establish a meaning, set of meanings, or "function" of discourse. These general axioms about language, meaning, and action have implication for fieldwork. This discourse-based model informs the following analysis of risk.

Communicating Risks Through Organizational Discourse

Literature on the conceptual analysis of risk and safety, even when carefully and systematically produced (Heimer 1988; Freudenberg 1989), amply illustrates the great difficulties involved in integrating an analysis of the social-organizational features of risk, especially those derived from subjective preferences, with institutional values and the social and political ideologies shaping these preferences (see Clarke 1988). It seems that statistically based arguments about choice, uncertainty, and even subjective matters associated with the concept of risk are limited in their capacity to illuminate organizational decisions and actions when these organizationally shaped and produced decisions are based on preferences, assessments, and routine procedures, rather than on statistically produced data. Models of decision-making and risk assessment that are psychologically derived, individualistic, and reductionistic lack descriptions of the constraints intrinsic to organizational context. Even descriptions of decision-making based on the somewhat special case of "reactive risk" (Heimer 1985a,b), in which both objective (known odds attached to outcomes) and subjective (sense of risk) aspects of decision-making interact to produce a series of changing consequences or "payoffs," are limited because the nature of the feedback and judgments made are institutionalized and conventionalized so that participants agree on the meaning of an outcome.

Heimer's analysis of reactive risk is suggestive, however, of analogous situations in which the regulators are dependent upon the industry for information, as is the case in nuclear safety regulation. However, the conventions in nuclear regulation are emergent, having been developed and formally approved slightly more than ten years ago in Britain (see below), and a negotiated information order is now being shaped. Thus, the guidance documents issued by the inspectorate are valuable sources of the ongoing enstructuration of the meanings of *risk, safety,* and *policy.*

Such models do not exhaust the sociologically relevant conceptions of risk and uncertainty, for the phenomenological and naturalistic study of the management of risk complements the positivistic modes of analysis. The naturalistic study of decisions in organizations is based in part on an analysis of discourse, and conceptual distinctions concerning how risk is defined and acted upon organizationally are required. These have been developed in other publications (Manning 1987b,1989a).

First, although the items of concern may be mechanical or technological, the decisions to be made always lie in *fields.* The fields within which assessments are cast and made are often collective; and definitions of risks and their consequences are organizational as well as personal (Clarke 1988). To understand, for example, regulatory decisions, one requires a socially located concept of acceptable risk or safety (Lowrance 1976) that states a level or value of safety, not of risk. The risk of driving can be seen in figures showing the rate of auto accidents (500,000 people a year die in them), but the value that is placed on preserving human life by requiring airbags, larger bumpers, and heavier chassis is based on political decisions.

Second, there exist many ways to calculate a risk and its consequences; multiple or even *pluralistic rationalities* (Douglas 1986) may obtain within any organization or within the negotiational context of regulator and regulatee. That is, mechanical aspects of the safety of the turbines, pressure vessel, and plumbing and electrical systems are assessed differently than the risks of exposure to radioactivity of workers on the site or nearby residents, and then the risks of terrorism or civil defense procedures.

Third, the political and organizational aspects of risk may be seen in the views the organization holds of its *mandate* and mission, and that are symbolized in its discourse. The mandate includes many kinds of risks assessed in quite diverse ways, and in the end is dependent on the legitimacy of the organization's claims with the political structure and the publics it encounters.

Fourth, "acceptable risks," when explained in writing, are cast in *forms of discourse* such as public relations pamphlets, guidance documents issued to the industry, and formal testimony prepared for and presented to royal commissions in England or House and Senate committees in the United States. These forms provide different *contexts* that transform the meaning of key terms. Lengthy narratives, or explanations sometimes called accounts (Scott and Lyman 1968), can be analyzed for their structure and elements and linked to structural conditions of regulation and institutional bias or preferences for examining certain kinds of risks and not others (Douglas 1986).

Fifth, discourse has *action* implications and is a form of symbolic action itself. Discourse frames action choices on the one hand, and reflects the pattern of institutional biases or value premises on the other. A concept of organizational discourse allows the analyst to link the concept of "routine" (Feldman 1988a) and institutional biases to provide an articulated mapping of discourse on action. The task at hand is to weave together the material in Chapter 5 on organizational structure and themes with the following material on safety discourse. To speak metaphorically, the discourse displays the organization.

Sixth, whatever conceptions of risk are employed by institutions are negotiated within a regulatory framework of *constraints*, real and material as well as symbolic, and these risks and acceptable risks must be communicated to audiences and legitimated. Risk is as much a matter of what the public accepts, once the issue is raised, as what the objective levels of risk might be.

The nature of organizational knowledge and discourse sets the terms for further discussion of the external communication that is employed by the NII. The guidance documents issued by the NII are a form of governmental social control and have a lawlike capacity to shape decisions.[2] It is important to pin down further the organizational discourse of interest.

Organizational Discourse

A fundamental focus of studies of organizational communication is the forms of discourse used to convey to external audiences the nature of the organizational mandate. Discourse serves to *translate* scientific, legal, and administrative rules into everyday knowledge. Since there are many possible narratives based on some version of ideal practice in manuals and the like, narratives-in-process and ideal codes may have to be mapped on each other. By examining the metaphors used to organize external communication in manuals, corporate reports, and the like (Filol 1989), one gets clues to the nature of a corporate audience and assembles the necessary front work to engage it in credible and sustaining communication.

Several additional features of organizational discourse are important in defining the field study of organizational communication. (see Manning 1989a). Clearly, some features of the analysis are implicit in the formulation of the focus of this theoretical domain. A linguistic or semiotic model of organization is a framework or heuristic for discovering differences by which utterances are defined and selected (Lemert 1979b:86). Explanations based on semiotics would seek to discover the principles that organize previously encoded values and signs about signs, or social organization and differentiation (Lemert 1979c, MacCannell and MacCanell 1982). Reasoning employs tokens of problems located in semantic or discourse fields. Key concepts, once elicited from interviewed organization members or publications, can be linked to semantic fields, roles and tasks, and the organizational mandate and the ideologies of the organization (Barley 1983a; Manning 1987a). The relevant kinds of meanings will include denotative, connotative, and ideological-mythological.

Recall the discussion in Chapter 3 concerning the role of discourse analysis in the study of organizational communication. It was noted there that organizational discourse includes in its focal concerns a view of resource base, the location or mapping of problematics, and trust in the environment as well as a set of techniques or modes of assessing that environment. It also contains stated (official) aims. Discourse includes and is based on a set of codes (implicit and explicit), which include ways of interpreting and sharing these interpretations and for organizing responses to alterations in both the physical and social world.

Organizational discourse also contains clusters of problematic paradigms, and ideological or connotative metaframes for stabilizing the world in counterfactual terms (Weick 1979; Luhmann 1985). These paradigms are signified by key selected terms that stand in part:whole relationship to the set of indicated terms. Organizational discourse frames reality (it provides rules for deciding, What is going on here?) and sets out the units (culturally defined and carried by sign vehicles) possessing the force to enact a role (Greimas 1966). Discourse produces means by which "new data" are selectively perceived, retained, and believed (Weick 1979:135). It contains explicitly stated biases that stratify preferences among types of risks internally and externally, enhancing some modes of uncertainty (information absence or overload) and depressing others. Plural rationalities, or multiple social worlds, will emerge and persist in organizations, especially within organizational segments, and are a basis for coping with forms and kinds of uncertainty (see Fischoff et al. 1981). Discourse serves to map ideas, symbols, and chunks of meaning upon nature, creating emergent ideas about nature, or "cultural bias" (Douglas 1986). The analysis of cultural bias is important in understanding how conceptions of the nature of the world are transposed into "facts" and practices in organizations. Cultural bias is the authority that defines the relevant facts or information and is the basis for assumptions underpinning those facts. It both constitutes and sets out the nature of organizational problems. Bias is distributed within organizations as well as across organizations.

Nuclear Discourse

The data used are primarily taken from the manuals used by the NII to guide its licensees. These manuals set out and communicate the nature of risk. This written material is interesting in part because it shows how the internal biases and institutionalized notions about risk are articulated with (or seen as governing) the external world of industry, management, nuclear power stations, and their reactors. This discourse constitutes the authoritative map of the territory.

The Nuclear Installations Inspectorate

As reviewed in Chapter 5, the NII has responsibility for ensuring the safety of the operations of some 18 civilian nuclear installations in England, Scotland, and Wales. It operates on the basis of an inspectorial model that values compliance and negotiation, and is focused on licensing and maintaining a safe operating condition or state. It employs about 103 civil servants, trained in mathematics, sciences, and engineering (applied and academically trained). It is divided into five branches, each with several sections, and maintains an inspectorial schedule for operating plants, surveillance of fuel reprocessing, policy-planning, and consulting the industry in creating in-process and future installations. The development of the NII was shaped by three acts of Parliament: the Electric Lighting Act of 1909, which concerns siting and planning consent for building electricity-generating installations; the Nuclear Installations (NI) Act of 1965; and the Health and Safety at Work Act of 1974. The latter extends the responsibility of the NII to the conditions of work with reference to both general and nuclear safety. The duty of the inspectorate is to ". . . see that the appropriate standards are developed and achieved and maintained by the licensee, to ensure that the necessary safety precautions are taken and to monitor and regulate the plant by means of its powers under the license" (NII 1982a:1). The NI Act of 1965 places an absolute liability upon the licensee with respect to injury to persons and damage to property. In addition, the licensees are responsible under the act for the safe design and operation of nuclear power stations so as to ensure the health and safety of their employees and other persons (*ibid.*).

Guidance Documents and Definitions

In 1982, two major guidance documents were written by NII and subsequently published: *The Work of HM Nuclear Installations Inspectorate* (NII 1982a) and *Nuclear Safety: HM Nuclear Installations Inspectorate Safety*

Assessment Principles for Nuclear Power Reactors (NII 1982b). In NII (1982b), for example, guidance is given to both the industry and the inspectors concerning the fundamental principles NII observes, the basic principles of safety, and the radiological and engineering principles said to underlie inspection and licensing.[3]

Several definitions are central to the regulatory activity of the NII (see NII 1982b:29, Glossary of Terms). These will be discussed in more detail following the narrative analysis below.

1.   The term *accident* is any event arising from a fault that gives rise to exposure to radioactivity in excess of those anticipated for normal operation.

2.   The *design basis* (of a system) is a formal statement of intended physical performance, limitations, and working conditions for a component or system. Three facets of the sign "fault," after a general definition, are discussed in the manual.

3.   A *fault* is any unforeseen, unplanned departure from the specified operation of a mode of a system component because of a malfunction, maloperation, or defect in a system or component.

4.   A *postulated fault* is any discrete fault sequence considered in accident analysis, irrespective of its probability or consequences, which may be used to provide a basis for the design of the plant, in particular for the design of any protective feature, or which may be used as a basis for evaluating the response of the reactor plant to such fault conditions.

5.   A *specified fault* is any foreseen fault that is assumed to occur and that is analyzed with a view to demonstrating plant safety. It is assumed that a plant built to specifications is safe when completed.

6.   The terms *safe state and safe* refer to a plant or subordinate system of the plant. A plant, for the purpose of these principles, is considered to be safe or in a safe state when it is in all respects within those limits which have been identified and specified for the purpose of limiting the risk due to that plant, at any time.

7.   The term, or sign, *safe* is also used to qualify actions or measures that may be taken in design, construction, or operation. In these cases, it is intended to indicate a bias being introduced by the application of that measure, etc., toward a lower level of expected risk to the plant.

8.   The practice of *quality assurance* refers to all those planned and systematic actions necessary to provide adequate confidence that an item or a facility will perform satisfactorily in serve. Quality assurance is a process-oriented term, whereas most of the other terms refer to either temporary or steady system states.

These definitions are rather circular and are interdependent. For example, the plant is defined as a set of systems that as stated in the design are presumed safe. The design provides specified and postulated faults against which precautions can be taken, while "faults" are seen as "unforeseen, unplanned departures" from specified operation. Operations are "safe," or are defined as being within the specified (negotiated) limits of risk due to normal operations. "Safer" suggests only lowered risk. Performance and satisfactory performance are defined, in turn, as meeting design specifications, or refer, at least implicitly, to the definition of design basis. The process of quality assurance is designed to ensure that absolute design specifications are approximated in practice.

These definitions guide the design and building of the plant, but they are also a part, on the one hand, of the licensing narrative in general as shaped by the principles outlined below and, on the other, of the natural history of the licensing process at a given reactor site.

NII Discourse

We can take sections of NII (1982b) to serve as an outline for more detailed discussion. The categories or subheads found in the three broad heads are the basis for creating a further set of *semantic groupings* (Table 8.1) that can be rearranged (Table 8.2) into associative contexts or paradigms. The subpoints can be arrayed under categories other than those proposed in NII (1982b) (Table 8.3). This logical and semiotic analysis can be reworked into a *natural history* of licensing and decommissioning discussed below.

Principles. Four basic principles are used to outline the responsibilities of the licensee and the inspectorate (the number of sections contained in the principles are enclosed in parentheses): fundamental principles (1), basic principles (1), radiological principles (3), engineering principles (17). The purpose of this section is to outline the subheads of this manual as a basis for the semiotic analysis of the discourse of safety of the NII. The numbers in parentheses in Tables 8.1–8.3 indicate the page(s) on which the material is found; the numbers in brackets indicate the number of subheads listed under the heading.

Each grouping and subgrouping in Table 8.1 can be considered a paradigm or associative context within which are found items that can be substituted for each other but contrast within that context. What is not clear is the order of importance of the various paradigms and their interrelationship.

The five stated fundamental requirements of nuclear safety concern primarily exposure to greater radiation than is recommended or suggested by international bodies. British standards are higher than international standards. This concern is located in the community rather than in a workplace, although the general public is mentioned in the event of an accident. The more serious the (anticipated) accident, the more effort can be required by the NII of the licensee to make reasonable attempts to prevent failure, to reduce the chances of accident, and to defend against the charge that more precautions are not "reasonably practicable." The burden is with the licensee. Accidents of greatest concern are abrupt, detected "accidents" or releases. Therefore, the 24 *basic principles* listed are based on scientific radiological principles, conventions of radioactive waste control, and principles for evaluating fault conditions and normal operations. Engineering principles (some 278), found in 20 pages of text, are subdivided into 17 major categories, ranging from general to specifics concerning decommissioning of reactors no longer in service and with abnormal wind loading that might affect the spread of a radioactive release.

The rearrangement found in Table 8.2 is a modest reordering of elements, and contains only a few changes designed to cluster ideas like "reliability and quality assurance," and "input-output systems," and does not alter requirements and basic principles. A second regrouping is found in Table 8.3.

Metaphors of Safety

As a result of this exercise in metaphoric analysis, we can see that at least three broad metaphors organize the safety discourse in this manual. The first metaphorical arrangement captures movement from inside to outside the systems. This is a conversion of scientific principles into spatial arrangement. The focus resides in the first place "inside" the reactors and its systems, then moves to surrounding functions, and finally rests in the "death" and burial of the reactor in the form of decommissioning. Concern moves, metaphorically speaking, from (a) the stated general principles of radioactive protection, to (b) the reactor and its protective systems seen as central to reliability and the quality assurance of the building, to (c) operation of the installation, to (d) layout, and finally to (e) decommissioning. This metaphor is illustrated roughly in the alignment of categories A–E in Table 8.3. The second broad grouping is *reactor centered*. It moves from the safety concerns of the reactor to the faults question, accidents, and their consequences. This pattern involves grouping 2.1 and 3.1, then reactor and protection systems (under the first grouping), 3.9, 3.12, 3.11, the reliability cluster in the first grouping, and external hazards (3.15). Again, the logic moves attention from center to periphery of the technology. The third broad grouping concerns *design and faults* and moves from design (points 1 and 2 in the first grouping, 3.1, 3.2, through safe operation and guarantees

Table 8.1.   The Discourse

1.   Fundamental requirements and policy (3)[1–5]. This section states that the assessment of safety is based on the recommendations of the International Commission on Radiological Protection and the requirements of the Euratom directive on radiation protection with respect to the exposure of persons to radiation on site and the protection of members of the general public. "A similar approach is applied to the limitation of the likelihood and consequences of accidents" (p. 3). The notion is that "reasonable attempts" should be made to prevent failure and to reduce the chances of accidents and their consequences. One could say that the more serious the accident, the more onerous the task of demonstrating that further precautions are not reasonably practicable. Design, construction, and operation are key features in plant safety.

2.   Basic principles (4–7)[4–28]. Introduction.

2.1 Radiological principles (4–5). Introduction; normal operation (4–5) [6–12]; fault conditions [13–17].

2.2 Radioactive waste (5)[18–24].

2.3 Principles in the evaluation of fault conditions and protective systems (5–7). Introduction; principles [25–26]; special case procedure [27]; rules for the conduct of the basic fault sequence evaluation [28 plus subpoints].

3.   Engineering principles (8–28)[29–307]. Introduction.

3.1 General principles (8)[29–30]. Introduction; nuclear plant characteristics; nuclear plant design; protection; testing, inspection, and maintenance; data used in the design safety case.

3.2 Reactor core and fuel (10–11)[56–72]. Introduction; design; operation; monitoring.

3.3 Primary coolant circuits (11–12)[73–87]. Introduction; general safety.

3.4 Reactor heat transport systems (12–13)[88–106]. Introduction; system design; coolant.

3.5 Protection system (13–14)[107–131]. Introduction; principles for the protection system; instrumentation; special principles for shutdown systems.

3.6 Essential services (16)[148–151]. Introduction.

3.7 Containment systems (16–17)[152–161]. Introduction

3.8 Fuel and absorber handling (17–18)[162–173]. Introduction.

3.9 Radiological protection engineering (18–20)[174–192]. Introduction; general; direct radiation; contamination by radioactive materials; instrumentation.

3.10 Radioactive waste management engineering (20–21)[193–217]. Introduction; general; waste storage; handling and transport; gaseous waste; liquid waste; solid waste.

3.11 The analysis of plant faults, transients, and abnormal conditions (21–23)[218–230]. Introduction.

3.12 Operating conditions (23)[232–239]. Introduction.

3.13 Reliability analysis (23–24)[240–254]. Introduction.

3.14 Layout (24–25)[255–263].

3.15 External hazards (25–26)[264–284]. Introduction; abnormal wind loading; seismic effects; flood; fire, explosion, missiles, etc.; aircraft impact.

3.16 Decommissioning (26–27)[285–294]. Introduction.

3.17 Quality assurance (27–28)[295–307]. Introduction.

Table 8.2. First Regrouping of the Discourse

---

1.   Fundamental requirements and policy (3)[1–5]; and 2. Basic principles
       (4–7), with subpoints 2.1 and 2.2 remain as head terms (see Table 8.1).
3.   Engineering principles (8–28)[29–307]. Introduction.
3.1   General principles (8)[29–30]. Introduction; nuclear plant
       characteristics; nuclear plant design; protection; testing, inspection,
       and maintenance; data used in the design safety case.
Reactor
3.2   Reactor core and fuel (10–11)[56–72]. Introduction; design; operation;
       monitoring.
3.3   Primary coolant circuits (11–12)[73–87]. Introduction; general safety.
3.4   Reactor heat transport systems (12–13)[88–106]. Introduction; system
       design; coolant.
Protection system
3.5   Protection system (13–14)[107–131]. Introduction; principles for the
       protection system; instrumentation; special principles for shutdown
       systems.
3.6   Essential services (16)[148–151]. Introduction.
3.7   Containment systems (16–17)[152–161]. Introduction.
Input-output systems
3.8   Fuel and absorber handling (17–18)[162–173]. Introduction.
3.9   Radiological protection engineering (18–20)[174–192]. Introduction;
       general; direct radiation; contamination by radioactive materials;
       instrumentation.
3.10   Radioactive waste management engineering (20–21)[193–217].
       Introduction; general; waste storage; handling and transport; gaseous
       waste; liquid waste; solid waste.
Faults
3.11   The analysis of plant faults, transients, and abnormal conditions
       (21–23)[218–230]. Introduction.
Operating
3.12   Operating conditions (23)[232–239]. Introduction.
Reliability and quality assurance
3.13   Reliability analysis (23–24)[240–254]. Introduction.
3.17   Quality assurance (27–28)[295–307]. Introduction.
Layout
3.14   Layout (24–25)[255–263].
External hazards
3.15   External hazards (25–26)[264–284]. Introduction; abnormal wind
       loading; seismic effects; flood; fire, explosion, missiles, etc.; aircraft
       impact.
Decommissioning
3.16   Decommissioning (26–27)[285–294]. Introduction.

---

thereof to decommissioning. A fourth focus could be *safety* (3.1) and
operations (3.5, 3.6, 3.7) and techniques for the analysis of safety (2.3,
3.11, 3.13, 3.17).

These metaphors, it would appear, do not consider a number of
matters that may arise in general discussions of safety. They do not
include matters of public reassurance or collective risk, and narrowly

Table 8.3.   Second Regrouping of Discourse

A. Radiological grouping
    2.1   Radiological principles (4–5). Introduction; normal operation (4–5) [6–12]; fault conditions [13–17].
    2.2   Radioactive waste (5)[18–24].
    3.8   Fuel and absorber handling (17–18)[162–173]. Introduction.
    3.10   Radioactive waste management engineering (20–21)[193–217]. Introduction; general; waste storage; handling and transport; gaseous waste; liquid waste; solid waste.
B. Reactor and protection thereof
    3.2   Reactor core and fuel (10–11)[56–72]. Introduction; design; operation; monitoring.
    3.3   Primary coolant circuits (11–12)[73–87]. Introduction; general safety.
    3.4   Reactor heat transport systems (12–13)[88–106]. Introduction; system design; coolant.
    3.5   Protection system (13–14)[107–131]. Introduction; Principles for the protection system; instrumentation; special principles for shutdown systems.
    3.6   Essential services (16)[148–151]. Introduction.
    3.7   Containment systems (16–17)[152–161]. Introduction.
C. Reliability, faults, and quality control (techniques)
    2.3   Principles in the evaluation of fault conditions and protective systems (5–7). Introduction; principles [25–26]; special case procedure [27]; rules for the conduct of the basic fault sequence evaluation [28 plus subpoints].
    3.11   The analysis of plant faults, transients, and abnormal conditions (21–23)[218–230]. Introduction.
    3.13   Reliability analysis (23–24)[240–254]. Introduction.
    3.17   Quality assurance (27–28)[295–307]. Introduction.
D. General plant and operation layout [could also include here 2.2, 3.10]
    3.8   Fuel and absorber handling (17–18)[162–173]. Introduction.
    3.9   Radiological protection engineering (18–20)[174–192]. Introduction; general; direct radiation; contamination by radioactive materials; instrumentation.
    3.12   Operating conditions (23)[232–239]. Introduction.
    3.14   Layout (24–25)[255–263].
    3.15   External hazards (25–26)[264–284]. Introduction; abnormal wind loading; seismic effects; flood; fire, explosion, missiles, etc.; aircraft impact.
E. Decommissioning
    3.16   Decommissioning (26–27)[285–294]. Introduction.

focus on the technical (mainly the reactor and radioactivity) in a non-technical fashion. A very narrow notion of risk and fault, based on engineering notions of safe operations and safe design, is contained in the document. Unforeseen and extremely rare events are not considered. No formal modes of risk analysis, fault trees, or probability statements are used, although remote (10^{-6} probability of occurrence) accidents are mentioned. Costs-benefits or such economistic calculations are not referenced with respect to the way in which a licensee might determine what is practicable in seeking safety. Human error, and "man-machine" interactions, the basis for errors that were in part responsible for both the Chernobyl and Three Mile Island accidents, are not mentioned, nor is ergonomics. No mention is made of ensuring the security of plant against war, revolution, terrorism, or radical shifts in social expectations of publics, or social conditions.

Diversity and redundancy in protection systems are the key, with containment, for dealing with the untoward or unforeseen, but safety is assumed to be *built into the design* of reactors such that the principal task is one of monitoring adherence to design specifications. This focus echoes the view of members of the NII that reactors (of whatever sort) are intrinsically safe. The imagined faults vary, however. The readjustment of the work of the NII as a result of the permission to build a pressurized water reactor only required adjustment of technique rather than of full-scale rethinking (it was claimed; see, however, O'Riordian, Kemp, and Purdue 1985, 1988).

The Natural History of Licensing as a Metaphor for Safety

The discourse of safety contains in microcosm an implicit parallel across the independent groupings found in the above figures. The natural history of the licensing process contains and manifests these elements in parallel sequence as well as in forming logical groupings.

Thus, for example, (1) the waste fuel sequence, driven by radiological protection principles, proceeds apace, aside from the concern for (2) faults and fault consequences and protection; (3) radiological protection principles in general; (4) techniques for the analysis of safety and quality; (5) the reactor as a unit with its safety and protection/containment systems; and concern with (6) the input/output processes, operations and layout, external hazards, and decommissioning. However, the linear, logical-inductive form of the manual's outline of safety contrasts with the narrative or unfolding storylike character of the licensing process. The integration of forms of knowledge, scientific and everyday, and the practical knowledge of the inspectors, occurs as a result of pragmatic, joint collective action.

Any ex post facto knowledge of the law, and of legal reasoning, is ill-suited to capture this transformation of forms of knowledge. The transformation moves from the scientific to the everyday, and from the closed-system world of engineering with its categorical designation of possible faults and consequences with the aleatory and potentially interactive complexity of the operation of a nuclear reactor (Perrow 1984).

Thus, the routines of the inspectors, and routines within the branches of the NII, serve to make sense of emergent and changing complexity. Space does not permit a full analysis of this integration via routines and inspectorial functions (see Hawkins 1984).

When the outline of nuclear safety discourse is set out, the logic is clearly linear, but the negotiation of a license takes place in parallel with several of the relevant systems and functions being assessed and assembled simultaneously, and is context dependent (Reiss 1984). That is, negotiations are based on the features of a given site, with a given type of reactor, and a history of personal relations, and with the design and building of the type of reactor at issue well in mind. The organizational discourse that results requires the mapping of scientific discourse onto the narrative forms of nuclear safety and the everyday logic of the participants who compose the "safety case" that grows and eventually becomes the basis for the license. The safety case is the statement of the expected limits of performance and the ways in which the installation contains assurances for coping with the anticipated untoward.

Conclusions

Observation of the NII's guidance manuals produces a set of metaphors for communicating risk to external audiences, serving to reassure them, to map the complex world of reactors on the social world, and to maintain the central symbolic necessity of the operation of the agency. This discourse is a means of controlling, limiting, and dramatizing a rather complex and multifaceted view of safety, and to focus external audiences' on selected features of safety.

A few further points could be explored in additional research. A close analysis of day-to-day operations of regulation requires knowledge-in-action, or what might be termed socially sanctioned organizational *routines* (Feldman 1988a). These routines link generalized bodies of knowledge with practices and procedures. Routines are key to understanding the bases for organizational action. Routines may link segments within an organization as well as the organizations involved in the regulatory culture (Meidinger 1987). The study of organizational routines involves concatenation of everyday knowledge, what Schutz calls "in order to" knowledge, and ex post facto knowledge of outcomes, or "because" knowledge (Schutz 1962). "Everyday life" knowledge is imbedded, tacit, implicit, encoded, typified, and context dependent, and sharply contrasts with the features of legal knowledge as explicit, codified, written, conventionalized, and relatively context free.

Because the logic of the discourse is that of a closed, independent set of systems with consideration of known faults and consequences (sequelae), it conveys the false security of referential scientific discourse. But the metaphors shift and the assurances of safety change from scientific to engineering to political. What might be considered further is the relevance of postmodernist views of science and reasoning (Lyotard and Thébaud 1985; Baudrillard 1988) to the deconstruction of this material. How do the *simulacra* alter in reference and function in different groupings of official safety discourse?

III

INFERENCES AND DIRECTIONS

$$9$$

Lessons for the Field

Introduction

The basic approach to the analysis of message-processing, including information and those noninformational matters that affect organizing, has been inductive. The purpose is not theory-building, but remains sensitive to developing a perspective on emergent and developing aspects of organizing. Blumer's (1969) guiding suggestion, that investigators should remain true to the social world, is our rule. This book is based on sensitizing concepts and addresses a broad set of questions and problems. The argument thus far has provided examples and research intended to illustrate problems and challenges associated with studying organizational communication dramaturgically.

This chapter addresses the research implications of this dramaturgical approach and features a fieldwork-based model for designing and executing organizational communication studies. It builds upon examples in Chapters 5 through 8 as well as the distilled cumulative experience of field-workers. It discusses stages in field research, the foci of such research, writing up materials gathered, and guideposts to data analysis. Chapter 10 assesses the relevance of postmodernism for ethnographic work in communicational studies. We begin with a paradigm for fieldwork.

A Paradigm for Field Research

An open context of action (Eco 1979), or sensitivity to emergent collective lines of action, should be assumed in the initial stages of fieldwork. As Douglas (1976) has suggested, fieldwork should be *de-*

focused initially. Too tight a focus restricts the kinds of problems discovered and refined for further analysis. A defocused, open mode of operating must begin a study, especially one carried out in a complex organization. Various tools and techniques, such as interviews, observations, questionnaires, and records analysis, can be employed over the course of the study. Regardless, the meanings of interest and the precise foci of any study will shift over time. Often, the fieldworkers' retrospective interpretation of motives and of focus is a revision of a rather vague original mandate and purpose. This means that developing hypotheses in advance is to be discouraged, that concepts should develop during the course of the research, and that the final product, or result, should be variously imagined and will be shaped in the writing stage. Once the field study, or the "ethnographic moment," is completed, the narrative perspective of the researcher used during the writing, in other words, the "voice of the writer," will also vary (Richardson 1990; Van Maanen 1988). Every text, as a set of expressions framed within some communicational form, has various potential content referents. Texts are in part created by the context, or what the reader brings to them, as well as by what is written. Further, any field-based report will be a partial rendition of what was seen and heard. Much is taken by the reader on trust. Although there are many outlines for doing field research (see Lofland 1979), field research in organizational communication is different insofar as it is a study of forms of communication themselves, and is a kind of communication about communication, or metacommunication.

What follows are suggestions and might be seen as "rules of thumb" for carrying off good fieldwork. As research progresses, field-workers modify their tactics and strategies, and iterations and elaborations of these "rules" will emerge. I consider aspects of working in the field— roles, targets, settings, methods and techniques for data gathering, and data analysis. Then I outline the factors—personal, social, and structural—that influence organizational communication. The nature of the rules that govern message flow and the relationship between the message stream and flow are discussed in the next section of the chapter.

Working in the Field

Roles. The role(s) of the field researcher has been widely and even deeply discussed (Adler and Adler 1987). The purpose of discussing field roles in this context is more limited and serves to argue that the field-worker must be in a position to observe and record detailed observations about communications (messages of whatever sort) of interest (this refers to meanings that have been identified previously as relevant to the field problem). This focus on the social role of the field-worker is tactical and means that once the *target(s)* or objects of research are identified, and the organizational communication system (OCS) that is at the heart of the organization in question is identified, then one develops the field roles. The field-worker must ensure that he or she is (a) in constant contact with the OCS, (b) in oscillating context with the various segments of the OCS (to observe roles and tasks within each subsegment or subsystem), and (c) has a precise knowledge of the technology of the OCS and how it mediates communication at every level (horizontal and vertical) of the organization. Then, as a result, he or she should be able (d) to articulate the difference between the system of relations (the linguistic system) and the performances observed (the social relations shaped by the system) and (e) to capture in speech encounters the relevant information about the OCS. Then, the field-worker should seek to be positioned (f) to depict the dialectic between the formal or official system, its functions, stated purposes, official aims, or claimed accomplishments and practices, on the one hand, and informal accommodations, on the other. Studying and answering these six points will require a changing and adaptive set of field roles, rather than a single role.

Targets. Targets are in one sense points of interest in a field of meaning. The targets should be described in full so that readers can appreciate the setting as well as the activities and actors found there. First, one should ask very broadly *what* meanings *where* are to be precisely delineated in the study of a given organization. Recall, for example, that Barley (1986) began with the question of how the occupation's members managed problematic interactions with clients. This question directed his attention to discovering a set of meanings about the removal of a body, about the proper presentation and posing of the body in the funeral home, and about furnishing the setting in a fashion consistent with the purpose of the drama. Bennett and Feldman (1981), in another case, asked how stories provided order and coherence, and therefore were directed to examining not only the institutional structure of law and the courts, but the internal structure of the stories. Second, the *location* or the "where" of the meanings of greatest interest must be identified and understood. The institutional structure must be understood as well as any intrainstitutional variations, e.g., types of courts include small claims, criminal, traffic, appellate, etc. The institutional biases and rhetorics, internal and external, should be pinned down and analyzed.

Settings. Setting can be used to refer to a concrete place, i.e., a going concern of some kind, a police department, a court, a university, or a small shop. However, in communicational research, it is important to recall that setting is a standing pattern of behavior, and may be observed across organizations as well as within them. This suggests looking at front and backstage as settings, and at internal and external settings for communication. Are there setting-specific features of the communication as well as generalizable features? Why is this the case?

Methods and techniques.   No single technique or method will suffice to produce an adequate organizational field study. The examples in Chapter 4 included research using techniques of interviewing, eliciting, observation, records analysis, and discourse analysis. Some approaches have taken the logic of communication as central, and have used techniques close to classical rhetoric, while others have made very detailed analyses of talk and of written texts. In many respects, the techniques an individual is able to master will set the limits of the research, so the first question one might ask, after defining the problem, is, What do I do well? The how, or the techniques one uses to gather data, and the why, or the purpose, of a study often become entangled, and perhaps this is inevitable. On the other hand, if one is entirely technique driven in the field, especially in the early stages of research, rather than defocused and open, the complexity and richness of organizational communication may be lost unintentionally.

Analysis.   Analysis involves breaking the problem at hand into component parts on the basis of a predetermined theoretical scheme, or through the Glaser and Strauss (1967) method of constant comparison and theory-building. The focus in a field study of organizational communication will be the complex relationships between information, meaning (or semantics), and social organization. Several approaches to the semantic domain are illustrated in Manning's work described in Chapter 4. Pragmatics, and the relationships between rational a priori schema and actual communication, govern Cicourel's analyses. In discourse analysis, the narrative logic and form of stories is used as a tool. In organizational studies, the relations between talk and action will shift in and out of focus. Jackall's and Manning's organizational fieldwork suggest how social organization will shape communication, and how talk and actions are sometimes loosely linked as in the case of getting the right "spin" on a story, or the right lie, and are sometimes rather more tightly linked (relatively) as when "officer in trouble" calls are sent on the radio and produce a swarm of cars on the scene.

Field-Relevant Variables

Examination of field studies of organizational communication suggests that data on three kinds of variables are needed for a complete ethnographic study of organizational communication: those relevant to the *person/situation* of the recipient of the message(s); those bearing on the relational locus or the *system of meanings within which the person-recipient is embedded*; the *structural* features of the organization.

Let us consider these variables using my analysis of police communication systems prior to providing a detailed example of an analysis based on these ideas. In this police example, the formal message system is central, but the centrality of a message system to an organization is a variable. In the case of public bureaucracies, such as welfare offices, police, fire, and other state bureaucracies, the external communication system is fundamental, and both defines the problems of these bureaucracies (i.e., rational allocation or rationing of goods and services where demand always exceeds supply) and provides the ostensible solution. In other organizations, such as law firms, corporations, schools, and universities, the formal communications system is secondary to the informal network of communications, gossip, and meetings.

In the police:

1. *Person-focused factors.* There are at least three person-focused or situational influences on the interpretation of messages, and these are drawn to some extent from conventional social psychology, which focuses on attitudes, roles, and persons. Here, given a message within a message system or interactional encounter, variables (or signs) such as *ambiguity* (lack of clarity in message meaning), *equivocality* (average doubt about the sender or trust), and kinds of *noise* (communication unwanted at the time of receipt of the message) are critical.

2. *Context factors.* Four relational or context factors influence message-processing, once a system is identified: the *field of activities* within which the message is heard; the *surrounding understandings*, or matters potentially relevant to the interpretation of the message; *paradigms* and *syntagms* found in the organizational segment in which messages are observed to be processed; and the *interpretive practices* (in part based on the codes, classifications, and formats of the organization).

3. *Organizational structure.* Three structural factors shape message-processing: *technology*, or the means by which work is accomplished in the segment; *roles and tasks* of the actors (including the nature of the hierarchical and horizontal differentiation of the organization); and the *classification system* for messages employed by the organization.

STUDYING MESSAGES IN ORGANIZATIONAL CONTEXT

Rules, Messages, and Reality

To study communication naturalistically, messages should be tracked within a communicational system. Messages arise in a set of variously organized *networks* that send messages with various degrees of order or redundancy (this may involve an interaction of channel and network source since some social networks call on or use only some lines, for example, banks). The message stream then created can be seen only as analytically partitionable, because in practice it appears as a constant flow of ongoing, overlapping, simultaneously processed bits (organized both vertically and horizontally). The sign vehicles and codes employed, or the culturally sanctioned means by which the messages are converted from "nature" to "culture," are set within the organization.

At this point, the message stream is seen as a sequence of discernible, discrete units, or *messages* defined as a set of signs clustered in texts encoded and decoded by interpretations. Messages arrive in a field and carry associated socially defined noise, equivocality, and ambiguity. Messages move, they are distorted, compressed, lost, and the operation of these factors is assumed to be constant in organizations, subject to empirical establishment of their variations. Messages are horizontally and vertically differentiated, sorted into mental categories, and disposed of. Some of these messages are, strictly speaking, nonproblematic, and are routed, made routine, and sent out for further processing within the normal round of organizational activities. Others, more important as sources of data, are those in which there is an ambiguity or uncertainty, or where the surrounding understandings transform them. Thus, crises are very revealing windows into organizational communication.

Messages may be seen as equivocal anywhere in the processing stream, and as a result, some sorts of "assembly rules" (Weick 1979:138–139ff.) are evoked by members in various segments (they may not be the same rules, or resolve equivocality in the same manner) to reduce equivocality to sensible levels. These rules will be given flesh in the example provided below. The existence of the rules for reducing ambiguity, in turn, are evoked when other cues fail or are themselves ambiguous, thus suggesting the paradoxical cycle outlined by Putnam (1982) and discussed above. A revealed paradox will give raise to an *account* or verbal explanation, feeding back into the sociocybernetic process of amplification and reduction in the ambiguity of messages. Matters of perception, suppression of detail, compression, selective readings, and distortion are assumed to be working, but are not matters selected for study in this analysis (see Potter and Wetherell 1987:Ch. 2). They are important research topics, however. Finally, the paradox reduction cycle reproduces itself in that these accounts remain in the organizational memory and will have a role in future understanding. Every field-worker has been told stories that are viewed by organizational members as "representative anecdotes," stories that accurately and succinctly sum up a kind of problem within that organization.

Some further research points can be emphasized here. Because it is essential that organizations separate *signals*, or data seen as potential information, from *symbol* or meaning, or actually utile materials, accounts and explanations for the flow of messages and for errors and miscues are an essential focus for a field-worker's notebook. Organizations need predictability and recurrent modes of organizing, and these are linked mentally and revealed in practice in the characteristic routines of organization members. It should be underscored again that *routines, organizing, and accounts provide meaning to messages. Messages do not alone provide meanings to accounts, organizing activities, or routines*. To a striking degree, messages and meanings are reflexively related, and mutually refer to each other.

All messages are representations of refracted portions of social worlds; and all messages are synecdochical (part representing whole) of each other. Thus, they are laminations of textually organized signs, and laminations of laminations leading to the kind of layered reality Eco (1986) calls "hyperreality" or sets of signifiers that often pass for truth. Messages echo each other as much as they echo other social worlds outside an organization. There is and can be no "pure" or "true" meaning of any message, and the purpose of serious and focused field research is to trace out the traces (fragments of information and socio-emotional effects) remaining in or brought to the message, rather than to pin down or triangulate the truth(s) they represent, contain, elide, or connote. Message analysis is always a cycle of resolution and paradox, partial understanding and reiteration, accounts that refer in part to the personal situation, in part to the relational aspect of the message, and in part to the structural variables shaping the message.

Stream and Flow

Another way to conceptualize the field-worker's interest in the problem of message analysis is to imagine the movement of a message, and how it might be tracked using the person-centered, social, and structural factors shaping the message flow.

Consider the *person-focused factors* first (cf. Manning 1988: Fig. 2.2). This is a linear/logical flowchart approach to the various problematics arising at each point in the message production process:

1.   Messages arise about an event in the social world that becomes an object when someone identifies it against the background of other objects.

2.   Messages arise in social networks of interpersonal relations and facts that contain varying amounts of information.

3.   The communicational units of research interest (calls, memos, reports, books, etc.) each have various amounts of ambiguity associated with them and are sent by someone in whom trust varies. Noise also accompanies all messages, but may vary in level and quality.

4.   Conventions (stereotypes, typifications, and labels about how messages are to be understood) are used by the receivers to classify and place in a taxonomy the messages.

Thus, the event in the social world now becomes transformed into an object for organizational action and is usually described in a written *text* (a selected, formatted set of signs taken as coherent in a setting by recipients). Behind any organizational outcome is a social process.

Now, consider the *relational factors* that pattern message flow regardless of content:

1.   When a message is received, it is always received in a field of activities, tasks, and noises and in a particular setting.

2.   Characteristic paradigms and syntagms (associational contexts and culturally accepted units for ordering the content of the message) are identified (this is tacit and not cognitively active as a process).

3.   Surrounding understandings such as current political pressures on the organization, or media concern, may change the nature of the processing of the message.

4.   Interpretive practices are used to encode and decode messages. This work in part is based on the classification system or codes (formal or not) used as "folk taxonomies" within the organization, and in part of shared conventions that are segment specific.

Finally, consider how to study the *structural factors* in message processing such as the technology, the roles and tasks of the senders and receivers, and the classification system of the organization.

In process terms, messages at each point within the organization and at each analytic point listed above are sorted into categories: clear/unclear. These signal problematic situations to which field-workers must turn attention. At these crisis or turning points, variance must be compressed into organizationally acceptable routines. Rules, as well as the vague sense of the appropriate reading of the social, often quite setting specific, that which Giddens (1984) calls "knowledgeability," are used by actors to sort and filter messages within the organization. Clearly, at times, messages are paradoxical, and contain the paradoxes noted above.

At the point of paradox, at least two alternative processes can take place: (1) an account for the paradox can be called for, a clarification, or requests for reasons why may arise from somewhere in the organization, or (2) some shared confusion about the nature of the units used to analyze the problem themselves arises. Here, tacit meanings and background expectancies are questioned and confusion may begin. For the loss of a *sense* of the organizational grounds for routine action leads to "disorganization" (Garfinkel 1963), and often is not (or at least easily) verbally accountable (Rawls 1989).

These problems of explanation gloss the explanatory problem within sociology that results from the false distinction between agency and structure, micro vs. macro levels of explanation. The interaction order is an emergent pattern of action and meaning that cannot be predicted or understood from "norms" or "values" or preconstituted structures (Goffman 1983b). It may produce anomalies that are seen as structural or make reference to organizational rules and procedures, but questions concerning the grounds of interaction itself are not accountable, for once they are raised, some basic form of anomie is indicated. So, paradoxes remain.

Field Notes

Little space can be spared here for a discussion of field notes (see Jackson 1987; Jackson 1990), for they remain rather an esoteric matter, known only to the field-worker and perhaps a trusted colleague or supervisor, and used variously to document arguments and points of view. Very little is known about how field notes become texts, and even less is known about the relationships between the field, or the social events studied and observed, and the notes written about them. Virtually all field-workers draw on memory, their sense of the place or event, vague recollections of events, other people's remarks, tales of their informants that cannot be verified, and other talk, reports of social events seen only by the respondent and told to the field-worker, that cannot be directly verified by observation. Even interviews can be transcribed in various degrees of detail [compare the Jefferson orthographic conventions for transcribing speech into written text with those of Paget (1988) or Cicourel (1975)], videos and films can be edited, and written notes, no matter how detailed they might be, are always incomplete [see Garfinkel (1967) on the "etc." clause]. Furthermore, it is not possible to treat articles as other than trustworthy renditions of events, until evidence to the contrary appears. Science rests on a hierarchy of trust.

It is perhaps fair to say that only recently have serious questions been raised about how one transforms the field experience, perhaps even an epiphany, to a written text (see Needham 1986; Rosaldo 1986; Van Maanen 1988; Agar 1990).

Writing and Writing Up

Desk work, the final aspect of research, is qualitatively different from the others. The issues raised by current interest in narrative style are related to the issues of postmodernism above, and the claim that objective, neutral, scientific analysis and writing is not possible.

Writing up requires the choice of a narrative style and voice, often unreflective in character, for the presentation of field materials. Writing is also a reflection of perspective, or way of looking, but insofar as there are many perspectives, some of which are excluded by the words written, one can imagine other perspectives and question the universal truth of any given report or document. Writing is writing for an audience, and the more clear one's audience is to the writer, the more clarity in style and expression will result. Standards vary according to the audience one addresses (Lyotard and Thébaud 1985), and no fixed or universal principles govern what is good or clear communication.[1] All communication is situated and made sensible by the contexts or "game(s)" in which it is located. Furthermore, for most academic writers, training takes place informally in graduate school as they read and critique the best works in their field as failed, flawed, and inadequate. When they write their theses and dissertations, they must follow flawlessly the guide provided by the particular graduate school for style, format, and even to some degree the content of the work. A dissertation can be rejected because the margins are too wide, the paper is of incorrect standard, or the footnotes are in the wrong style as a result, few become creative scholars! The following section concerns metacommunication, or communication about studies of communication.

Survey research texts (Babbie 1990) traditionally provide lists of what ought be included in a final research report, and such lists ought to be used as an example of a paradigm for occupational communication: how social scientists communicate with themselves about the workings of research. Included in these formatted operations are such matters as the theories used, review of the literature, the definition of the research problem, the data used and how they were gathered and analyzed, findings, the limits of the study, conclusions, and implications for future research. These are helpful lists, but they better suit studies cast in the positivistic and quantitative modes than field or qualitative studies.

A long rhetorical tradition of writing is found in the social sciences (Gusfield 1976; Becker 1984; Richardson 1990), and within individual disciplines (McCloskey 1985). A set of tacit conventions guides writing up field studies, and these can be seen in journals such as the *Quarterly Journal of Speech Communication*, the *Journal of Contemporary Ethnography*, the *American Anthropologist*, and *Human Organization*. They are based on the background and tradition of field studies in sociology and anthropology in particular (see Strauss 1987; Lofland 1979; Manning 1987a; Rosaldo 1989; Van Maanen 1992).

Qualitative studies differ from positivistic studies in several important ways. They do not assume that the identity of the object in the social world is independent of the perceptions and recipes of the observer. Facts and values merge into perceptual frameworks that construe and construct meaning. Qualitative studies do not define the operations of research typically as capturing the precise nature of the social world: their work is not a reflection of reality, it is a creation of a narrative.

Fieldwork in sociology has been very much influenced by the positivistic model of data and analysis. Only a few important exceptions in the fieldwork tradition (Douglas 1976; Johnson 1975) argue against statistical enumeration and description and the associated positivism that entails an implicit model of disproving hypotheses. Qualitative work is not failed positivism or merely a preliminary attempt to gather background data for a hypothesis-testing study. Qualitative work should adopt a considered position that rejects positivism because, "To get the organization into countable, measurable form is to strip it of what made it worth counting in the first place" (Weick 1979:29). Although much of this argument has been outlined above, it is important to bear in mind that studying organizing, the imposition of order on the stream of experience (pp. 11–12), requires varying the perspective and voice of the observer. Since organizations contain multiple social realities, multiple causal maps, or imagined logical relations between social acts (and imagined acts) and responses and imagined responses of others, field methods must reflect and capture the central character of organizing. What is being argued here is that not only the operations of the research project, but report writing should mirror these assumptions.

Questions of the validity of the narrative perspective and forms of discourse used in writing research reports now are being addressed in several disciplines (Mastrofski and Parks, 1990). In the last ten years or so, partially as a result of postmodernist influences, many have argued that modifications in traditional styles of writing up field studies and in writing conventions themselves are necessary (Tyler 1987; Clifford 1988; Marcus and Fischer 1988; Clifford and Marcus 1986; Rosaldo 1989; Rose 1990). These new modes of writing up do not assume the world is the sort of reality that can be precisely mirrored (Van Maanen 1979, 1983, 1990; Louis 1986; Martin and Siehl 1988; Denzin 1989; Van Maanen 1990). These new modes of writing significantly affect at least a set of currently published qualitative studies. In the lead are the anthropologists, perhaps because their discipline is at risk, in part because its historical focus, "primitive peoples," is nearly extinct and under threat.[2] The discipline is turning inward, and it seems more and more inclined to substitute navel-gazing for native-observing. Anthropologists have raised the most serious questions about the functions and purpose of writing field reports, their validity, and the culturally and historically embedded nature of "truth."

Geertz Work

The most poetic of these critics is anthropologist Clifford Geertz. His recent book, *Works and Lives* (1988), contains several versions of this crisis in writing, and it is perhaps valuable to review his primary points.

Geertz claims that anthropological writing is a literary style, or a written mode of representing the self-representation of preliterate primitives to members of complex urban societies. This theme of Geertz's essays on the work and representational styles of anthropologists is an echo of Claude Lévi-Strauss's brilliant semiautobiographical work, *Tristes Tropiques* (1975). What is being represented in anthropologists' writing? Geertz asks. Is the observer's voice (the written word) all that remains of a complex social system? Let us take an example of Geertz's own work to see how conventions of writing gloss some underlying questions.

Geertz's (1973) paper on Balinese "deep play" is a rich and even paradigmatic tale, an elegantly polished and apparently detailed version of the relationships between action, language, and meaning. In this brilliant analysis of the role of fighting cocks and "cock fights" (pun on male genitals in English) in Balinese culture, Geertz argues that the fights between cocks represent in microcosm or symbolize a number of cultural themes: *status battles* (between groups of men aligned by kinship loyalties), *games with binary outcomes* (occasions for gambling—opportunities either to win or lose), a visit to some *secular version of heaven or hell* or good and evil, a kind of *inversion of the feared* (death, loss of control, shame), and an occasion for *focused* passion.

Each of these italicized clusters of meanings might be viewed as paradigms or metaphoric associational contexts within which cultural elements of the fight are variously ordered. "Cocks," and "cock fights," are at once denotative, connotative, metaphoric, and ideological signs. The paradigms within which the elements are placed are, variously, nature vs. culture, men/cocks/animals, status battles, gambling occasions, and so on (see Geertz 1973:447n.35).

In one sense, these themes set into paradigms are levels of analysis, but in another they are simultaneous conflations of perception (whose perceptions?), ordering (whose ordering?), and forms of collective social relations. Geertz claims that this is a model of actors' meanings, but it is not clear how that conclusion was arrived at. This view of Balinese culture in microcosm is esthetically pleasing, but is one of several possible readings, even of his formally stated scheme.

For example, the relationships between nature and culture, or men and animals, is mediated. Men are represented by a series of features (metonymically) as are the cocks (ambient genitals, pets, masturbatory foci, and narcissistically cathected) and are gathered at a higher level: both men and cocks are "heroes."But men also have selves, and these selves (in this sense) can be seen as standing between and mediating nature and culture. The opposition of nature and culture is bridged at the level of the self in culture. Nature and culture are opposed at a still higher level. "Nature" is seen as wild, clumsy, distant, feared, and animalistic, while "culture" is seen as tamed, close at hand, desired, and human. Heaven and hell are also oppositions in the fight, in that the elements are comparable in metonymical sets of elements, but set apart as mere secular manifestations and thus made manageable and controllable. Winning and losing in the gambling world is a binary situation, but Geertz shows that by separating the main or center bet from the side bets, people hedge against the potentially mortal consequences of the deep play. Socially consequential losses or gains are minimized and are narrowly circumscribed by rules of betting. Geertz lists (pp. 437–41) without attribution no less than 17 rules for betting on cocks.

But do these oppositions line up as neatly as suggested? Are there not different kinds of oppositions at different levels of analysis? Are the forms listed not different in content and detail? Are there "left" and "right" sides of his argument? (Geertz does not line up the materials in left and right oppositions, but he implies that they are oppositional without a clear discussion of what is meant by "oppositional" or discussing what the sides might mean.) By arguing that the kind of play described is merely playful and esthetic, not practical, he gathers the cock fight domains into the world of thought, seeing the fights as cultural texts used by Balinese "to read each other."But whose voice is speaking of these oppositions, these formal elements, these higher levels of connections? The anthropologist's. And, one might add, what about the views, perceptions, and so on of women? Do they not constitute part of "Balinese culture"? and do they not provide some central function as audience, affirming or denying some of the structural features of the cock fights?

If meaning comes from opposition and difference, are the differences that Geertz adumbrates on the surface or in some identifiable code? Clearly, he sees it as a matter of encoding and code-meaning, yet it is the code of the civilized structuralist that is used for male experience, and it is possible that several other types of codes might underlie the game, e.g., primitivism vs. nationalism, secular and sacred, a marxist code of exploitation and domination, or even alternative visions of the side play/ center play opposition. Perhaps a cockfight means something quite different to Balinese females.

Because all the cultural signs communicated as messages in the game are contextual, they are multiplex, or have many relationships one to the other, some of which will be contradictory. Structuralism assumes that a deep code for meaning exists that crosses (to some extent) domains of meaning at the denotative, connotative, and even the mythological level.

Recognition of the existence of varying modes of representing the voice of the observer raises and marks dramatically a metacommunicational question now troubling many researchers: How do communicational conventions or forms (narrative perspective, scope of facts to be included, and the role of the person or writer in the communication) affect or pattern communication about communication? Are anthropological works only a cultural or narrative form, like literature, with rather shaky claims to representational reality? Or are they only the container for the contained? Are types of tales merely variegated textual renditions of reality? These questions are specifically raised by postmodern views of communication outlined in Chapter 2 and developed further below.

Other Tales

Like Geertz's book, Van Maanen's *Tales of the Field* (1988) shifts attention to the varying narrative voices used in writing up field data. Various forms of presenting "tales of the field," in Van Maanen's terms, are available to the writer: one can write "realistic" tales, the traditional mode of reporting data in a neutral and depersonalized fashion as objective albeit esoteric fact; one can present "confessional tales," an emergent mode in which the writer's perspective and experience become a (central) feature of the narrative; and one can play out "impressionistic tales," a style more common of late in which the conventions are much freer in form, and the writing may resemble postmodern discourse. He suggests that there are some progressive or temporal aspects to the currency of these styles, with the impressionist now in vogue. Surely few impressionistic tales are found in anthropological journals. These remain safely realist in intention, style, and purpose, even when avowing a lust for postmodernism. Some of the essential features of these three genres are listed below.

Realist tales   assume a matter-of-fact, objective, theoretically informed, nonpersonal perspective in which the native's views are reported through the eyes of the reporter/anthropologist.

Confessional tales assume a dialectic between matter-of-fact and personal responses and out-of-scene (back- or off-stage action) events, treated as socially constructed events. Writers maintain a low level of theorizing and focus on the native's perspective and social reality. The theme of the writing is a counterpoint between the unrevealed personal context of the work and its role in shaping and constraining the reported (and unreported) facts.

Impressionist tales are presented in a style analogous to that of impressionist painting. They render or express something of a personal style, are in ways nonrepresentational, full of assorted bits and pieces of feelings, observations, changes in voice and perspective, and an active eschewal of scientific, objective reporting. They bear some resemblance to the "nonfictional fiction" of Joe McGinnis, Tom Wolff, and Truman Capote (see Agar 1990).

Van Maanen provides examples of each type of tale from recently published fieldwork. He provides in each of the three sections of the book rich and detailed examples that draw on his own fieldwork in a large West Coast, urban American police department. By casting long vignettes from his work in each of the three modes, he raises questions about the independent effects of writing style on conclusions and claims made by field-workers, suggesting that any version could have been different, as well as arguing that within a single work, style or tale form may vary. Voice, or the role of the writer (whether writing in the first-person singular, "I saw him crossing the field," in the first-person plural, "We could now see him crossing the field," or in the narrative voice, "The man crossed the field") shapes the perspective of the text for the reader. Perspective is an important consideration in writing because it not only reflects the field role of the observer (both as played and as remembered) and the later role of the writer, but how a text (and its subtexts or alternative readings) might be understood by a reader. These arguments move the question of validity and reliability of data and findings to an esthetic mode, or simply suggest the rule that if the story is a good one, it is believable. This might be called the principle of the "narrative truth test."

One of the most awkward features of the revision to narrative truth is that of identifying generalizable criteria by which one might evaluate reported findings. When the assumption of a constructed reality and rejection of classic questions of validity dominate, the role of a critic or evaluator becomes problematic, and many stories flower. There is a related irony. Virtually all studies of organizational communication take a realist pose, even those that develop subtle pictures of organizational or occupational communication, e.g., those reviewed in Chapter 4 (see however, Pacanowsky 1983). The ironic trope is favored in the social sciences. Whose truth, whose perspective, is displayed in organizational analysis based on an ironic trope?

Conclusions

The fieldwork model presented here presents a kind of mental checklist for the field researcher, and presents some examples of field research on communications. In the last half of the chapter, the question of how to transform field notes into a manuscript or report is raised, and the stylistic features of social science writing are noted. In the next chapter, questions about representation are again raised, this time in the context of postmodernism and postmodern ethnography.

Aspects of a Postmodern Ethnography
of Communication

Introduction

Reflection on the problems associated with studying organizational communication in differing cultural contexts is now possible. The influence of postmodernism on social science is rather recent, and this book contains glimpses of its influence. Let us review some of the points made, especially in Chapter 2, about the influence of postmodernism.

Chapters 2 and 9 suggest that a "crisis in representation" has emerged in the social sciences. This crisis includes issues of the proper "voice" (first person, third person, the voice of the observed) for storytelling, the role of values and ideology in representation, the appropriate narrative structure, genre, and style for a study, and the transformation of field data into a text. The examples in Chapters 4 and 9 also suggested that the process by which a field study is transformed into a text reflects a series of decisions and tacit assumptions. Writing, creating pictures of social reality such that readers can jointly imagine or "see for themselves" (see Atkinson 1991; 1992), reflects ideas about the nature of the representations current within the society in which writing is done. Thus, a view is always a view of and from a particular perspective and position.

As the chapters on organizational processing of messages showed, uncertainty about meaning is general. This point is consistent with the claim that a representational crisis exists in the social sciences (see Baudrillard 1988; Lyotard 1984; Featherstone 1988; Harvey 1989; Dickens and Fontana, forthcoming; Jameson 1991). This crisis is in part a product of the influence of social science writing. Social science rhetoric now shapes the matters on which it comments, e.g., social policies on homelessness, crime and health care (Giddens 1990). Conventional genres and modes of literary expression are being eroded, redefined, elided with each other, and deliberately confounded (Sypher 1963). The distinctions made in the past between "discourse," "politics," and "reality" are increasingly blurred because political rhetoric and imagery combine to shape all that is taken to be real (Gitlin 1980, 1983). Language can be used playfully to reconstruct and deconstruct reality, and this, in turn, can heighten awareness of the social-world-creating power of language. This focus is called the *linguistic turn* in social theory (Brown 1990).

Postmodernism brings these issues to the forefront of the social sciences, but unfortunately has supplied neither directions nor answers. What does the postmodernist attack on traditional forms of rationality leave as guidelines for research for the student of organizational communications? This chapter, influenced by postmodernism, contains some modest directions for a discourse-sensitive naturalistic study, a "postmodern ethnography" of organizational communication.

Postmodernism

Postmodernism raises fundamental questions about the epistemology and the research practices of modern social science. Consider several of these. Postmodernism questions the centrality of rational knowledge and representation by arguing that the "real world" is impossible to grasp fully. Postmodernism, influenced by semiotics, assumes that meaning arises from differences in context. It restricts itself to analyses of signs and *simulacra*, or representations, and their interrelationships. Reality, according to Baudrillard (1988:145), is that which can be reproduced. The quest for truth or reality is impossible, ill-fated, and naive. It may even be misleading and create false illusions. Inherited modes of representation (writing and other forms of symbolization) are questioned, in part because media-produced imagery prefigures and shapes experience and in part because linear representational texts seem less consistent with the fragmented, self-saturating, high-technology environment of modern communication. Words and texts of any kind fail to pin down meaning fully. Many interpretations, with tenacious but problematic validity, coexist. Postmodernism rejects a correspondence theory of truth—the notion that words accurately map reality—and distrusts grand theories such as science, religion, and economics. Postmodernism focuses attention away from the "average," "normal," or the "conventional," in part because such words are often used by those in power to dismiss ideas, persons, values, or politics viewed as "marginal." Diversity, chaos, excess, even the margins of experience, are to be appreciated and elevated as varieties of human being in the world. Fragmented experience is normal, and selves are seen as either nonexistent or saturated with information and multiple facets (Gergen 1991).

Postmodernism argues that philosophical analysis does not produce knowledge of the "true" or "just," but merely creates and obscures new disjunctions between signifiers and signifieds. It uncovers variations in context and interpretation that undercut the belief that language will produce a form of truth or viable solutions to political and social quandaries. Language is a problematic that undercuts its own veridicality and contains its own mine(d) fields. To convey the arbitrariness of language, Derrida (1976), Foucault, and Lyotard use words to suggest alternative or suppressed meanings, erode the carrying capacity of words by using extensive figurative language, and carry on extended book-length punning. They employ terms, even technical terms, in confusing ways to suggest the illusory character of society and the chimera of seeking a single and abiding truth.

This tradition of nominalism and surrealism has a long history in French letters. It is manifest in the masterworks of Kojève, Bataille, the surrealists, Beckett, Ionesco, Camus, and Sarraute. It resonates in the vexing writings of the *chosistes* (Sypher 1963). By effacing or decentering the self, making reality a function of a field of experience, and playing on surfaces, these writers disrupt basic assumptions about writing. Is writing a "translated" version of speech? Is speech more "accurate" than writing in revealing thought? How do authors "write" (describe, display) a "self," and create versions of objective reality "out there"? Most importantly for intellectuals, postmodernists question the capacity of words to represent reality firmly. Words cannot "mirror" nature, provide a "speaker's guide to the universe," or even capture, correspond to, or mirror the physical and social world (Rorty 1979).

The idea that discourse, especially scientific discourse, has a universal and transsituational meaning is also challenged by postmodernists. Forms of authoritative reasoning and logic, found in science (and traditional logic and classical rhetoric), are questioned. Rather than seeking to establish or legitimate by power or authority some set of universal meanings, while suppressing others, postmodern philosophers, especially pragmatists like Rorty and Lyotard, urge observers to confront and analyze how "gaps," or *differences* between what signs (signifiers or expressions) indicate and what is taken to be indicated (signifieds or contents), communicate. The gaps between ideas, the connections that link them, are tenuous and based on unstated philosophical assumptions. Gaps produce a profound and abiding sense of ambiguity and even loss (of connection to others) in communication. Postmodernists seek to explicate this abiding sense of difference and gap, waiting, and loss of the direct confirmatory aspects of communication.

Communication is not meaning. However, communication cannot fail to be meaningful. Even a "meaningless" sentence conveys the sense that it is meaningless! A scheme of discourse analysis is needed. Such a scheme might be called a perspective for analyzing metadiscourse, or models for the analysis of models of meaning or language (Potter and Wetherell 1987). Such a critique of conventional wisdom and writing is not nihilistic, nor is it anti-intellectual. It simply asks for different sorts of reflection on the writing practices and assumptions made by intellectuals.

Having located a problem in the nature and quality of the phenomenology that links signifiers and signifieds (what might be glossed with the term *culture*), postmodernists reject the universal validity of codes and voices that utter, often from an unexplicated social and political location or perspective, sanctioned "truths." If no position exists from which truth is unequivocally spoken, and no shared standards legitimate communicational discourse, varieties of equally discreditable discourse will flourish. This form of analysis, formalized as the process of deconstruction, is most associated with Jacques Derrida.

Deconstruction

Deconstruction is not mere nihilism. It is a patterned form of critique of writing and the assumptions of writers and readers (Norris 1982). Deconstruction takes several forms. Deconstruction is a means to see words in context and to examine the effects of changing contexts on meaning.

Deconstruction uses imaginative variation in figure and ground, idea and context, to discover the contextual influence on ideas. Old ideas may be placed in new contexts or vice versa (Martin 1990). What is said, as well as how it is said—for example, with gaps and unstated meanings, the metaphors used, disruptions in logic, and paradoxes in reasoning—signals ideological work that shapes meaning. Any work is set in a field of knowledge and events, most of which are not revealed in textual analysis. To say that there is nothing outside the text is merely to say that what is written is in fact a selective and partial representation and can be understood for what it says and does not reveal. There is always a "surplus" of meaning that is brought to a text by a reader, and understood. Finally, as has been implied in this argument, the logical, linear, and factual aspects of discourse are only an aspect of what is communicated, even in scientific work. The poetic, the political, and the ideologi-

cal are always present, even if apparently suppressed by a literary
rhetoric such as scientific rhetoric. Several examples of the work of
deconstruction may be useful.

Setting and scene influence the meaning of communication. Think of
Herr Dr. Sigmund Freud with a cigar, perched on his chair, occupying a
30-second interview "slot" on "Good Morning America." He might
wait, smiling, for the end of an excited presentation by a voluptuous
blond hostess on the consequences of the latest fad diet. Imagine the
beefy "Monday Night Football" announcers hosting an opera broadcast;
Virginia Woolf writing scripts for television shows such as "Roseanne"
or "Knots Landing"; or Robert Goulet and Luciano Pavarotti singing an
extended Wagnerian aria with country music star Dolly Parton.

Context may be revealed through a playful approach to a text. Celebration of the "tricks" possible with language (and with word pro-
cessors and desk-top printers!) is taken as a sign of cleverness or even
wisdom. Here are some. Linguistic tricks play on the reflexive (~~features~~)
properties of writing and discourse. By using the strikeover feature of
the word processor, I demonstrated a change of mind after I first wrote
"features." By showing that I had crossed it out, I suggested that other
sentences in this book could have been and *were* once otherwise. (They
certainly were!) These " " suggest that texts have self-erosive features.
The previous sentences, even as they appear in front of me, are only
partially satisfactory. I write then directly to the reader, to you, in order
to alert you: **Wait and see!** I could change my mind! I have before! Many
sentences were once otherwise. As I edit (reedit, and reedit yet again)
what I have written, I add this sentence and the sentence beginning
"Deconstruction . . ." in an attempt to clarify the above points (I went
back and reedited it).

The idea presented above is in part accomplished by violating the
accepted academic convention of avoiding the use of *I* and never ad-
dressing the reader directly. This convention which makes the writer
and reader invisible, resembles the convention that ignores the absent
presence of a camera (which one knows took the movie or television
pictures) while watching a movie or television. It partially reveals *how*
language produces imagery, shapes thought, and refers to itself.
Language has constitutive powers because it refers to itself (as does this
phrase and these parentheses) and to ideas and symbols it contains.
(The idea that language is reflexive allows one to read a sentence as
referring to itself.) Language refers also to ideas about other ideas. It has
an *assumed* reference to the physical and social world. Furthermore,
language speaks of users, of the social qualities of speakers and hearers,
as well as the pattern of their social relationships. There is much expressed that language merely stands for, rather than conveys. Deconstruction turns attention to how language creates some meanings, and

suppresses other meaning. Deconstruction alerts one to those things assumed or unsaid, that which language cannot convey.

Metaphoric language is often revealing, like treating business as a matter of "sport," diplomacy as a game, or academic life as a business. By asking both how something is like and not like something it resembles, one can reveal the double entendres of such language as well as the blindness it creates.

The power of language, when linked to authority and legitimating conventions, maintains the status quo and reduces awareness of existing alternative interpretations or "subtexts." These subtexts may be associated with the powerless, the inarticulate, the silenced. Can these points about language and deconstruction clarify doing a postmodern ethnography of communication?

Foci of Ethnography

Postmodernism alludes to, points out, and is emblematic of salient features of modern society. These features of modern society should guide fieldwork. The following ideas seem to capture aspects of the family of meanings that surround postmodernism and postmodern ethnography (see Baudrillard 1988; Lyotard 1984; Eco 1986; Featherstone 1988) and its depiction of society. Postmodern ethnography should reflect contingencies in postmodern societies.

Five essential features of postmodernism constitute an ideal type:

1.   Postmodern societies manifest in dramatic proportions visible, vast, and rapid changes in temporal and spatial relations.

2.   In postmodern societies, a high degree of mutual dependence develops between images, language, and action. Prefigurative images shape action choices and accounts of their meaning. There is a sense in which images of an actor's actions affect and are part of social action.

3.   "Reality" dances with *hyperreality*—signifiers are produced and consumed, but lack precise referential functions and easily identified signifieds that serve to complete the sign.

4.   History loses its relevance for understanding the present.

5.   The focus on consumption blurs differences and renders invisible patterns of inequality of races, classes, and gender groups.

What do these five trends signify for the ethnographic enterprise?

The essential features of the acutely self-conscious postmodern ethnography are not succinctly summarized in a single *locus classicus*.[1] To a striking degree, the critical writings in the postmodernist tradition concern matters of form and style, the representations of representations, rather more than the forms, genres, and validity or reliability of field data (Van Maanen 1989). The student who wishes to carry out a postmodern ethnography of organizational communication must act like the *bricoleur*, or modest collector (Lévi-Strauss 1966), assembling bits and pieces of information, and fragments from the handful of published postmodern ethnographies. The implicit tenets of postmodern ethnography are still embedded in the oral traditions and the semimystified "trade secrets" of the social sciences (Van Maanen 1990).[2]

There are, however, some clues to directions available to the scholar. Researchers are urged to innovate and experiment. Anthropologists George Marcus and M. J. J. Fischer, in *Anthropology as Cultural Critique: An Experimental Moment in the Human Sciences,* argue that "every individual project of ethnographic research and writing is potentially an experiment" (1986:ix). They encourage the "play of ideas, free of authoritative paradigms" *(ibid.)* The word *experimental* in this context implies several things about ethnographic work, it would appear. The authors suggest several characteristic features of this new, emergent literary form.

They argue that postmodern ethnography should be emergent, find various voices for expressing experience, draw on other disciplines and times, eschew imperialism of thought and perspective, even mixing various perspectives and times in writing styles, and reflect broader historical and economic forces. Postmodern ethnography should experiment with genres and styles, with matters suppressed or thought of as "unsayable," and reject simple causal models or prediction.

A fine example of postmodernist ethnography is John Dorst, *The Written Suburb: An American Site, An Ethnographic Dilemma* (1989). Dorst shows, in a very densely woven argument, how a suburb with historical roots "writes" or inscribes an ideology that provides a mythical history and an historical appearance for itself even as it eschews its actual rather messy and uneven past. Dorst calls the community of Chadd's Ford, Pennsylvania, a "self-writing suburb," for the community has consciously attempted to create its own ethnography and history by stitching together a quilt composed of fragments of its past, newly created celebrations and rituals, and a museum reflecting an art style. It has "self-inscribed" a past, created a visible culture, and made manifest a community where very little of this existed in any coherent form 20 years previously. Chadd's Ford does for itself, creates and writes a history, what ethnographers have claimed to do for years (p. 2)! The "ethnographic dilemma" of the book's subtitle is this: Dorst has written an ethnography of a community that has already done so rather well. Postmodern ethnography is writing about "writing" (in the metaphoric sense of creating a story) and so it is "writing itself."

Doing Postmodern Ethnography

Although it is not at all obvious what sort of ethnographic work is portended by postmodernist thinking, it is possible to review briefly themes in postmodernist ethnography and connect them explicitly to ethnographic work.

Understandings of social life should be represented using semiotic-influenced analyses (Manning 1987a), and eschew simple referential statements about the "real world." Even such distinctions may be misleading. Here the task is to show how differences in representation create realities and sustain assumptions (Jones et al. 1988). The use of the word *minority* is a good example. It implies that there is a binary division of society between majority and minority, and that "people of color" are minorities. The United States is a very complex, multiethnic society without a single majority. In Texas, California, and Florida "whites" are minorities, and in some parts of those states, English is the second language. Consider then in an organization how "minority" might or might not be described for communicational purposes: Females? People of African-American descent? Gays or lesbians? Asian-Americans? Jews? What "diversity" does each represent, and how does silencing criticism of such groups facilitate organizational communication?

Metanarratives are used to obscure complexity. Metanarratives such as positivism, economics, and religion long associated with the powerful—males, whites, Western Europeans, and members of other developed societies—sustain the fiction that scientific authority, when linked to governmental funding, provides objective facts. A study of local knowledge and community traditions, and personal narratives of persons with AIDS, may reveal a depth of understanding of the experience of AIDS, for example, that governmentally funded epidemiological studies will not uncover.

These two points imply that an ethnography of communication should study signwork, the production and use of signs in a system of relationships. Known sign systems should be studied as anchors in social reality. These may include such systems as those communicated by a television station, an occupational group such as the modern urban police, or governmental symbolization or ideologies. Think of the pictures of reality based on assumptions about connotative meanings stimulated by the phrase we are "protecting our life-style by sending troops to Saudi Arabia" (August 1990). The power to produce images grows from producing an unexplicated perspective and voice. For each reified concept and attribution used in communicative discourse, ask from whose perspective, or from the point of view of what audiences, is this imagery produced?

Increasingly, images are created and index other images. Ethnographic research should focus on identifying important signifiers left dangling and unconnected to signifieds, and assembling arbitrary points in fields of meaning that are often fragmented and disconnected from experience. Ethnography should identify the precise role of images (and metaphors) and sign functions in producing realities. These images change as the material world changes, as do the *(codes)*, or sets of rules and principles that organize the sign system by which the material world is understood.

One should be aware, in doing a postmodern ethnography, of the role of images of events, media-generated scenarios, and second- and third-hand notions about life in shaping meaning. They increasingly dominate everyday experience. Thus, communication about products, such as advertising, self-advertisements such as T-shirts, and group rituals and celebrations such as company picnics and games should be rich settings for studying how such things as "loyalty" and "success," both floating signifiers without obvious referents, are framed and "pinned down" in talk and in socially guided activities.

Postmodern ethnography will seek also to explicate the underlying codes, usually invisible to the outsider, that order organizational communication. For example, although a citizen may view a call to 911 as an "emergency" by definition, the police quickly sort out and refuse half the calls, categorize the remaining calls into three types ("rush," "later," and "maybe") and respond to calls in part as a result of these coding operations. It is not possible to predict what code will be used strictly from knowledge of the content or the official label ("burglary," "robbery," "rape") given to the call. Knowledge of the codes is essential, and detailed knowledge of the relationship between code, data, and coder is even more important.

Postmodern ethnography should seek the sources of organizational power and credibility. Organizations possess legitimate power, and grant credibility to some information and codes more than to others. How is symbolic credibility (trust in what is said) established by the police? How is it challenged? Is the hierarchy of credibility—the truth attributed to different socially valued sources of knowledge and of communicational forms (science, music, history, religion)—blurred? What resources are used to "sell" an idea? We have seen that corporate managers (Jackall 1988:Ch. 4) use lying, avoid blame, and assemble ad hoc justifications for their expedient actions. This style is possible because corporate executives are tied by a thin tissue of trust that enables them to communicate and work together in spite of their cynicism.

How is the present seen as containing the past and the future? In a sense, modern societies are writing their own history. They possess the capacity to symbolize, simulate, present, and represent themselves to themselves (Dorst 1989). In postmodernist views of contemporary society, time is no longer a linear matter shaped or directly constrained by past events. Symbols no longer stop time; they produce and reproduce it.

There are several implications of this formulation of time and history. Time is conflated in television advertisements. Fifties rock and soul songs are used to sell soft drinks; Patsy Cline's classic country song, "I Fall to Pieces," is used as an ironic background for the durability of racing cars, and a video shows a posing Madonna as Rita Hayworth, as Marilyn Monroe, and as "herself." Forms are also *intertextual* (Kristeva 1981): A video made to be seen as a song is played is shown on MTV to promote sales of Madonna's album based (partially) on a movie *(Dick Tracy)*. The movie loosely draws characters, both heroes and villains, from a cartoon. Time can become elastic, as in the film *Back to the Future*. The past can be heard now. Under the headline, "Tapes Add Life to Dunes" *(Lansing State Journal,* September 3, 1989), a story explained that a company in Ann Arbor, Michigan was marketing a tape to be played in your car as you drive through "one of the most scenic areas in Michigan. This cassette tour offers nature information, historical facts and Indian legends with sound effects that tell the story of the Sleeping Bear Dunes." Indian legends, with background musical sound effects, are told. Stories of past shipwrecks are included to be played while looking at Lake Michigan. The tape also includes "the famous Chippewa legend of Sleeping Bear. A haunting wood flute musical background takes you back in time and allows your imagination to take over." The symbolic line between past and present is erased as one "hears" the past while watching the present. You are taken back in time while your imagination takes over. (What it—or you—takes over is not clear.)

Ethnography must specify how the various forms and kinds of mass communication are used to persuade and sell, to generate desire, by using symbolic messages (Williamson 1976; Barthel 1988). How is the image of "desirability" created and sustained in spite of massive consumption? The introduction of minor body changes on cars called "new models" each year by American automakers is used to boost sales, just as changes in makeup maintain the image of a shifting and elusive beauty sought by all ensure that one is "attractive," "sexy," and "in style."

Ethnography should instruct about how symbolic boundaries or familiar social forms are questioned, blurred, played with, and reconstructed. Note the integration of commercials, information, and enter-

tainment on television, the spawning of "rockumentaries" and re-cre-
ations (often hypothetical) of news events. Witness the blur of feature
movies loosely based on books (many of them self-serving autobiogra-
phies) written about "real events." In these examples, the "real" events
are those that are reproducible. In "live" performance, rock performers
dance to taped background music and lip-sync to their own previously
recorded singing. In 1990, Hank Williams, Jr., recorded a duet with his
dead father. He mixed his own singing with a tape of his father's voice
to create a duet rendition of "I've Got Tears in My Beer." He also spliced
films of his father's performance with his own to create a timely video.

Naturalistic ethnography should examine carefully the extent to
which what is "real" becomes increasingly dubious while the notion of
the real is reduced to that which can be reproduced (Baudrillard
1988:145). For example, artificial windows, with scenes produced by
computer graphics, can be placed in otherwise windowless hospital
rooms to produce "a room with a view" (*Newsweek*, March 26, 1990). The
Detroit News (September 1, 1989) discussed the ethics of placing Ann
Margaret's body under Oprah Winfrey's head on the cover of *TV Guide*
(August 26, 1989). It was explained, under the headline "Strange Head-
fellows," that "composites are also used in advertising to create more
appealing images." In advertising, photographs are touched up, and
one baby's body will be used with another's head if one is better looking
than the other. "Composites" are used (a car actually photographed in
Detroit is shown with a San Francisco landscape behind it). *Entertainment Tonight* was quoted by the *News* writer as calling the practice
"Oprahgate," a pun on Watergate without the remotest relationship to
it (unless it is an ironic point about cover-up vs. cover-up!). The artist
who created this grotesquerie said he would have used "Flipper" (the
name of a dolphin TV star) if it would have served his purpose and was
completely unaware of the issues of fabrication and deception involved.
The reader, one assumes, would see almost any body beneath Oprah's
head as hers. The fact that body/head connections are seen as arbitrary
by the infrastructure of the media is yet another answer to the question:
What is a person? What is an identity and selfhood?

Signs that defer reflection should be examined. Control, often in the
form of media imagery, regulates the organization of cultural experience
(Ericson et al. 1988). "Deterrence" means a delay in understanding the
character of the sign vehicles and functions that create powerful social
institutions. The most fundamental matters are often obscured, or attention is displaced away from them. Thus, in a spectacular twist of logic,
Baudrillard argues (1989) that Disneyland is *not* simply a playground
that symbolizes America. Its existence deters Americans from examining
American life and from concluding that Disneyland is America. That is,

Americans are as fully preoccupied with buying and selling symbols, fantasies, images, and desires as is corporate Disneyland. Disneyland is not a caricature, or parody, it is America. Not surprisingly, even that most obvious undeniable, death, is signified in diverting ways and is turned into a commodity. "Death," i.e., the signifier, in the modern age is a product bought and sold. It is given a precise monetary value on a life insurance policy, in medicare entitlements, or in a public burial ceremony (how much the county will pay for the fiberboard casket). It is something to guard against, the anatomical equivalent of "history." It is a negation of the present, not a positive and ritualized social state.

New forms of ethnography that suit the postmodern world will seek to avoid the types of explanations and explanatory narratives found in standard social sciences research. Especially dubious, given the slippery nature of representation and "reality," are those patterned by the assumptions of positivism. For example, one should avoid causal and correlational explanations in preference to folktales, narratives, glimpses, fragments, and pastiche. A universal perspective is rejected. Stories from the perspective of the other or stories using several voices and told (perhaps simultaneously) from many perspectives should be sought. Accepted conventions used to establish proof are rejected for notions like "narrative integrity," "esthetic appeal," and "timeliness." Patterns of intentionality are neither sought nor reflected upon. Standard statistical data are eschewed as is binary logic (either/or, yes/no). The infrastructure of any argument need not be inductive or deductive, and may rely on modal or deontic logic.[3]

It is important to note that postmodernism differs from symbolic interactionism in that the self is not the central concept. The self, as located in an individual who speaks and writes, and who is the "author" of thoughts and feelings, is secondary to the system within which meanings lie, the codes used, and the voices available from which to speak or write. In some respects, the self vanishes. Often deconstruction serves to show that interests and power marginalize certain voices and efface certain selves. In this sense, then selves are merely a reflection of current political ideology, a field of forces, and history. The role of the self is debatable: "the concept of the self remains an ambiguous feature of postmodernism. It floats even without an established embodied place" (Lemert 1979b).

Having now presented a difficult and abstract research agenda, let us take a rather simple example of how meaning is conveyed in postmodern communication. This example will signal something of organizational communication as well as of aspects of postmodern ethnography: the wearing of a "baseball cap" in a university. This is organizational communication in the sense that in this ecologically bounded system of densely articulated interaction that is authoritatively constrained, these messages communicate both about function and style.

The Cap[4]

A cap takes meaning from the contexts in which it is worn (see Pitt-Rivers, 1967). The cap's meaning varies with the *interpretant*, or that which completes the sign. The cap is an iconic sign, but it stands for or indicates social roles, attitudes, and gender as well as other signs. Wearing the cap reflects changes in clothing form and function, i.e., differences, and is a unit in an ensemble and of the fashion system.

The baseball cap, our topic here, like other items of leisure wear, is a necessary but not sufficient standard requirement for male (and some female) undergraduate students at midwestern universities (and perhaps at other universities). Some of the principal features of the cap can be derived from semiotic analysis.

The baseball cap is identified in the first instance by its *shape*. Caps shaped like those worn traditionally by baseball players while playing to shade their eyes against the sun take their meaning from contrasts with other similarly shaped caps. They vary in the length and direction of the bill, in the surface covered by the oval-shaped top portion, and in size. Similar caps are worn as cycling hats, as beanies, as visors when open at the top and sides, and as hunting caps (with flaps turned up on the sides).

The cap has *instrumental and utility values*. It shades the eyes from the sun, it protects the head and keeps it warm, and it covers and conceals as well as protects hair, whether combed or not, from the wind and sun. It keeps unruly or long hair in place, especially when playing in active games. It can be used to cover something from sight.

Caps also indicate *social roles and group ties*. This results because when the cap communicates or indicates expectations of self or other it serves as a role sign. Wearing a baseball cap on campus indicates social roles and identities (who or what a person is in social terms). Caps indicate team membership, e.g., a local high school or intramural team, or semipro team. As in the past, caps are worn by members of the university baseball team when playing baseball and coaches of university baseball and football teams when coaching. Delivery people and other blue-collar workers on campus wear caps with the names of their businesses emblazoned on the front. Some Michigan State University workers wear caps with "MSU" on the front, but this is a choice, not part of a uniform. All these instances variously indicate membership, i.e., wearing the cap says, "I am a delivery person," "I am a coach," or "I am a

baseball player." The cap also communicates other modes of identification. The shape of the cap on a student conflates two signs: the working
man's hat in the same shape (semantically, this suggests *identification*
with the working class or at least a *disidentification* with the upper middle
class), and the baseball cap (suggesting play, leisure, and warm-weather
activities).

Caps *elicit and display imagery*. These functions of the cap are less
closely tied to specific social relationships, social structure, signs about
signs, or social organization. They say something generally about, communicate an attitude toward, or merely display generalized imagery.
The cap with "Budweiser" on the front communicates "trust" in a
brand, or brand "loyalty" as well as advertising the brand of beer. It may
also communicate a tentative social bond in the sense that it announces
an identity—"I am a fan of x"—with which others might also identify.
This offers a symbolic bond of support through claiming to be a fan and
identifying with other fans (of the same team, of basketball, or of
sports). It may announce vicarious identification with a team, e.g.,
"Detroit Tigers," "LA Dodgers," or "Detroit Pistons." The cap's em-
blem should be read as "I support the LA Lakers" (and implicitly, "Do
you?"). It asks, "Have we anything in common?" rather than saying "I
am a member of the LA Lakers basketball team." The aggregate "LA
Lakers fans" is, needless to say, not a social group with shared perspective, roles, norms, values, and beliefs.

Cap wearing has *syntactical meaning as part of a unit* or outfit. It occu-
pies a place within the structure of a clothing ensemble.

1.   The cap is generally non–occasion linked: it is associated with
nonformal wear on campus. On campus, the hat is worn with any
everyday clothes seen as nonformal. I have not seen it worn with a dress
and heels, or with a coat and tie. On an airplane flight from San
Francisco to Detroit, I sat next to a well-dressed man wearing a dark blue
blazer, white button-down "ivy league shirt" and tie, and a dark blue
University of Michigan baseball cap. I don't know why and did not ask
him. These seem to be the only clothes with which it is not worn.

2.   Cap-wearing indicates the loose linkage between type of dress
and occasion of varying degree of ostensible formality on the campus.
Caps are keyed to a wide range of settings and occasions in campus life.
One can wear (apparently) a baseball cap to any occasion or event where
one does not wear a coat and tie or dress and heels. Of course, as
mentioned above, one can wear it to play softball or baseball on the
campus.

3.   Caps indicate varying "quality" and/or "cost." About 15 years
ago, cheap polyester caps with adjustable backstraps became widely
available. These cheap caps were the most popular form, and soon were

made, like T-shirts, with beer and other advertising names on them. They were rarely worn on campus. Other people on campus wore caps in the older wool style, suggesting that they were or are baseball players (some of these are still seen).

4. Caps are worn to indicate participation in leisure activities or, as shown below, a leisurely attitude. In the last five years, the habit of wearing baseball caps for leisure rather than for actual play spread widely. They are now also worn for playing golf.

The cap is a part of fashion, a *fashion instrument* that signifies differences. It is an indication of fashion, or the creating and marketing of differences for a profit (Barthes 1983). The material used to make the cap indicates vertical differentiation ("quality") within the fashion world. As caps gained wide popularity, there was an attempt to differentiate them as commodities, and to create horizontal and vertical distinctions between types of caps. Caps can be divided now into "cheap" and "expensive" on the basis of the materials used. Caps made from fine wool were worn widely by baseball teams at many levels from little league to professional before the advent of cheap, widely available polyester caps. Polyester caps, with netting at the rear quadrant of the cap, an opening at the back, and an adjustable plastic strap, are still sold, as are corduroy caps with letters sewn on the front. Wool caps remain the most expensive and are sized according to conventional measures of head circumference (e.g., 7¼). (Both polyester and corduroy caps have the plastic adjustable backstrap with pegs and holes.) These distinctions, coded with a system of fashion, are rather weak and are easily changed, as is the case for all fashion, by commercial forces.

The cap, like all clothing, indicates a *mood* or generalized feelings or sentiment (Stone 1962). It can signal support of a team (the mood of sports enthusiasm), a feeling of self-confidence (it's "cool" when it's worn), a feeling ("good," "active," "sporty," or "insecure"), an attributed identity or trait (the person wearing the hat is a "slob," is "lazy," does not care for his or her hair, or "I am such a person"). The "mood" communicated is often gender-specific. Females wear caps less often than men. Females who wear baseball caps are seen as "sporty," "tomboyish," or "masculine." Caps on females are more often associated with style or fashion (as an accent). Because it connotes a game and game-playing, it is associated with male leisure pursuits and action. Males may be seen as having messy hair they want to conceal, or as seeking to be "macho."

The cap can convey an *attitude*, or tendency to act. In the context of a midwestern megaversity, the cap-as-sign connotes a youthful lack of interest in matters serious. It questions (even if slightly) the authority of classroom, teacher, and conventional dress codes. It signals at least an indifference to conventional manners and etiquette. Since it is worn not as a removable, but as a part of the head, it is not removed while attending lectures, eating, or conferring with professors during office hours. In this sense, baseball caps symbolize distance from a role, or "role distance" (Goffman 1961). Wearing of the baseball cap by non-employees (and those listed above) connotes the absence of serious business and authority.

The *position of the bill communicates or denotes the mood of the wearer.*

1.   When worn straight ahead, it tends to be seen as instrumental, group-based or "normal." It does not indicate a particular mood. When so worn by adults, the cap also denotes social relationships. Clues are given off by such signs as the name of a firm, a team, a university, or a school. Claims to group membership are also made.

2.   When the bill is worn sideways and down or backwards by students, it connotes leisure. So wearing the cap suggests more exotic leisure activities and is associated with skateboarding, surfing, and moped riding. Worn by adults, such a positioning signifies an identification with youth. Thus, to understand the meaning of a hat worn backwards (or askew), one has to see it encoded as "that which is worn backwards in windy, fast, or difficult activities in which the wind might lift the hat off the head." The lead singer of the rap group "2 Live Crew" wears a dark blue baseball cap backwards while singing, thus signaling the risk and danger of his dancing and singing. When my best friend, a full professor at a "major eastern university," appeared in his university office on a weekday morning wearing sandals, a Hawaiian shirt, and a reversed baseball cap, he was "making a statement." He was signaling an attitude toward conventional authority and associated dress codes.

3.   Fully reversed, of course, the hat denotes the position of catcher on a baseball team (he or she has to wear it reversed to accommodate the protective face mask), and also connotes "a fool." Baseball clowns, who performed at minor league parks many years ago, wore their hats reversed or sideways to convey comedy.

The cap *stands for a code* and the code affirms the cap's meaning. The cap indicates the relevance of the code. The cap as a sign in the context of playful activity connotes the code of leisure. Once one knows the code, cap-wearing is an instanciation of leisure. The code of leisure is connoted when the hat is worn either frontwards or backwards.

The cap has *gender-specific meanings.* Females wear the cap forward, bill ahead, and sitting on top of or raised in front to show the hair. Females may display some organizational identity such as "KAT" or "MSU." Such messages are ambiguous when a male wears a cap with "KAT" (a sorority) on it, or when a seven-year-old wears an MSU cap.

The baseball cap, because it serves as such an all-purpose sign vehicle, sending so many messages, contributes to, but does not erase, the blurring of class, race, and gender differences in dress. Let us examine a few of these functions.

The baseball cap *can pun.* As is true with T-shirts and other modern icons, the baseball hat can serve as a means to pun, to play with signs, to mislead, and to lie. In short, it can carry ambiguous status claims. Students who wear naval service caps, or police caps, groups of young men and women in casual dress seen on the street with "FBI," "Michigan State Police," or "USS Tigercat" on the front of their caps, further blur lines of authority and identity in postmodern society. Is the 14-year-old wearing a blue FBI cap really the special agent in Lansing? As one informant mentioned, the cap can tell you where a person (possibly) spent his or her vacation, has traveled or visited, or his or her home town.

The sign is *transformed into an index* when associated by context when worn by members of the FBI, DEA, and SWAT teams in local police departments. These icons are functional signs of authority, and the caps are emblazoned with very large initials of authority on the front. They may also contain an indication of rank, e.g., sergeant or lieutenant.

Time is irrelevant. The past, present, and future can be conflated in leisure wear. For example, one can buy an "authentic" Flying Tiger Leather Flight Jacket (L.L. Bean, fall 1990 catalog) and "old" caps as well. Brooklyn Dodgers (a team that no longer exists since the Brooklyn Dodgers are now the LA Dodgers), and New York Giants caps (worn by Spike Lee at a New York Knicks basketball game) display past and present conflated.

Caps have *cosmetic meanings.* The cap can be used by men and women to cover messy or dirty hair. It conceals carelessly done hair, a bald spot, or a bad haircut. In short, it not only announces, it conceals and covers.

Caps have *personal meanings* known only to the person and his or her best friends. These can be a result of a gift (it stands for the giver and the receiver), the special occasion on which the hat was obtained, or the other generalized personal attachments to an object of clothing. At times these are in tension, because the personal meanings may be more salient that the overt, signaled meanings that others observe. Wearing a Baltimore Orioles cap may be more important as a sign of visit for a wedding in the Washington area than as support for the Orioles team.

The cap worn (or not) *may mean nothing at all,* or possess no gender-specific meanings for the wearer. At the other extreme, one respondent ironically said about it, "The cap—American fashion at its pinnacle. Yuck." Presumably this means that the cap conveys in one compressed sign vehicle all that is wrong about American fashion.

This brief overview of the meanings of wearing a cap shaped like those worn by American baseball players, the "baseball cap," suggests that postmodern society blurs the functions of many sign vehicles that might once have differentiated social groups and roles. This suggests the need to study further the decline in using differences in ritualized activity to mark social boundaries. To what degree are clothes, decorum, nonverbal postures and gestures, and settings consistently signaled? How are the boundaries of events and settings made more porous and ambiguous? In a postmodern society, such cultural icons as hats and T-shirts become increasingly ambiguous signs. They refer to themselves, they serve as means to make puns, and they signal ambiguous gender claims and social relationships.

Comment

This series of observations suggests also how postmodern ethnography might work. The example of the cap is merely an exercise in ethnographic analysis that does not probe broader questions about fashion, power, class, and authority, all of which could be analyzed. The cap as an object for analysis can stand as a metaphor for any number of objects about which communication occurs and by which social organization is displayed. It is a way of talking to ourselves.

Postmodern social theory rejects totalities and totalizing explanations, especially those coming from outside individual experience, and rejects integration of the micro and macro, seeing these as just another artificial division—one read off the other. Hats, as Baudrillard might argue, "displace reality into another structure." What do they *not* mean? The above sketch is not intended as a full analysis and explanation. It looks more like the mapping of a kind of reality that exists only in this mapping process. Informational technologies define what is real in the postmodern world and create systems of meaning (public vs. private) that radically contrast. How are hats shown on television, on videos, on MTV, and in films? Are there folk narrative explanations for hat-wearing, and a folk etiquette? Finally, representation of hats in this way deters other meanings and an examination of the structural changes that lie behind the diffusion of the sign from that of a game player to everyday wear. Is life merely a game after all?

Conclusions

Among other things, a postmodern ethnography should establish how what is taken to be socially significant is established and what constitutes the relevant differences between the multiple and various versions of a narrative, a code, or a policy. One may not seek the referential reality of the code, or its empirical utility for explaining other social action. One may only want to uncover what is concealed or revealed by a given code or paradigm. How are the oppositions between elements manifested in a discovered hierarchy reversible, or arbitrary? Do these differences, suppressed elements and oppositions, maintain a place in a larger political economy or circulation of images, signifiers, and material goods?

This chapter summarizes some of the problems in fieldwork in communication, and some of the unresolved epistemological questions that arise in making sense of field data derived from studies of organizational communication. The most sophisticated of the organizational studies maintain a sense of perspective, but the voice of the observer disappears in the report. In some, the self vanishes into performances or "double interacts." For example, the Burkean-dramaturgical approach illustrated in O'Donnell and Pacanowsky (1983) emphasizes perspective, or subjectively articulated meanings, while Weick and those influenced by him focus on interactions and couplings. It is clear that the implications of the problematic character of perspective, voice, and even the fact-value distinction, are being recognized. These questions continue to shape studies of organizational communication (Morgan 1986).

Postmodernism provides an opportunity for reinvigorating ethnographic research. The features of modern society associated with the postmodernist perspective resonate with many of the aims of ethnographic research since alterations in society alter the time and place assumptions made about culture and its description, the role of the observer and the subject in scientific observations, and the context-based nature of description and discourse.

Communications, anthropology, and sociology, admittedly, respond differentially to the challenge. Arguably, anthropology is neither as theoretically grounded nor as positivistic as sociology. It relies upon comparative ethnographic work. The anthropologist Paul Stoller observes, accurately I think, "Anthropology has one strength: ethnography, the original, albeit imperfect product of our discipline. Despite its taken for granted status, ethnography . . . has been and will continue to be our core contribution" (1989:13). On the other hand, the very fundamental presumptions of positivistic sociology deny the emergent, fragile, and reflexive character of modern life, and they do so by clinging to the putative methodological center of the paradigm.

Communications seem increasingly influenced by interpretive work and paradigms. Yet, as Goffman continued to argue, without close and detailed descriptions of social life, the social sciences are in danger of becoming an empty, technocratic enterprise. Postmodernism represents a transdisciplinary challenge. Ethnography is one sure way of understanding the other that connects the social sciences to their humanistic mandates (Van Maanen 1989: xiv).

Notes

Chapter 2

1.   The broad theme advanced by the knowledge society advocates is challenging and well illustrated in a recent collection of conference papers edited by Bohme and Stehr (1986). The following pages are adopted from my review of that book (Manning 1987c).

2.   This assessment of the postindustrial-society thesis or the knowledge society notion is colored by my sympathy with the postmodernist perspective.

3.   The thesis of an inevitable drift toward a knowledge society is an analog to the discredited "end of ideology" thesis (Bell 1962), a gloss on the deterioration of knowledge standards and the massification and erosion of scholarly controls upon scientific work.

Chapter 3

1.   Originally used by a systems theorist W. R. Ashby (1956) and subsequently by Herbert Simon (1969), Glassman's work is cited as "the first systematic exploration of loose coupling (Weick 1976:13). Weick (p.3) cites Glassman's definition of loose coupling as being present when weak variables are shared by two systems and/or when two systems have few variables in common. As a result, the two systems "are independent of each other" *(ibid.)*. This is the first version of the concept, but others can be found. In a second rendition of the concept, Weick (1976:3) claims that observation of *events* rather than variables may serve as surrogates or perhaps as indices of loose coupling. He states that when using loose coupling he wishes to convey an image of a kind of relationship between events such that even though events are responsive to each other, each event also preserves its own identity and evidences some physical or logical separateness.

2.   Weick does not accept this logic (1976:5).

3.   The most important overview, concept, and perspective is *The Social Psychology of Organizing* (Weick 1979; see also Orton and Weick 1990), where the concept is not defined. It is discussed, exemplified by stories, anecdotes, jokes, poems, and cartoons, and illustrated by quotes from other scholars. The examples provided, usually anecdotal, and used in explication of the theory or the

metaphoric paradigm, vary in their level, complexity, and substance. This is quite intentional, I assume, as is Weick's statement about scope and domain assumptions of the idea. He argues that one has to find the time and place where one's theories hold (1979:38; see also Weick 1991).

4. Research based on loose coupling, according to Orton and Weick (1990), lacks specificity or ties to known bodies of other theories, uses few rigorous empirical testing procedures, is disciplinary in focus, and lacks specified practical relevance.

5. The perspective contains an explicit critique of formal theories of deciding based on information and schemes linking ends and means theoretically. In this sense, it builds on and shares the March/Simon/Olsen/Cohen vision of social integration produced by action and routines, interlocking sequences driven by nonlogical forces outside the immediate context of deciding (see also March and Olsen 1976). Deciding takes place in socially constructed environments that exist "in the eye of the beholder" and are shared subjective constructions that emerge and evolve, break, and are reassembled (paraphrasing Weick 1979:168). Rigid heuristics and decision rules may exist only in some segments of an organization, for a period of time, or with respect to certain kinds of decisions (Feldman 1988a).

Chapter 4

1. Several features of the organizations in which case-processing occurs are noteworthy. No rules firmly omit certain choices in the settings studied. Specific directions about working cases are not provided, e.g., what must be done about the case, how much time should be spent on it, what resources can be expended to pursue it, and how it should be resolved. Such guidelines as are provided do not consider content and quality, but merely seek to increase the chance of achieving an acceptable paper outcome. There is little monitoring or supervision in the process of police cases, as has been noted by others (Chatterton 1983; Van Maanen 1983; Manning 1980).

2. These comments are adopted from Waegel (1981) and Sudnow (1965).

3. Sudnow emphasizes that these "working typifications" do not apply in serious or infrequently seen crimes in this office and that there are recalcitrant defendants and crimes that are not typically bargained in this way, even if they are viewed as typical for this area. However, the overall picture is one of easing and guiding complex organizational decisions by shorthand recipes, typifications, and chunked and coded depictions of events and persons.

4. The attorneys are, in Galanter's (1974) terms, "repeat players," those who are part of the court team, which excludes only the defendant in the unfolding drama [see Blumberg (1967) and Casper (1973) on the views of those who have pleaded guilty]. Two features of the organizational context bear on the processing of the cases. The first is the degree of media or public attention on the case and how exceptional it is within the organization. The more unusual and public the case, Waegel argues, the easier it is to solve because the perpetrator is known. The second feature of context is the amount and kind of information available.

5. Think of an example that is not occupational, but illustrates ambiguity. As I write this, I am listening to Bruce Springsteen, the poet of the working class, singing "Glory Days." I recall another of his songs on the same album, "Your

Home Town." As I listen, I think of my own father, of my son and my brother, and about their glory days. I vaguely consider what might be called mine. Personal associations and symbolizations, as Freud repeatedly demonstrated, embed dreams, tales, stories, and the like and cannot be removed totally from the meanings that are taken from them. Self-meanings are an important part of the fieldwork context, and one strives to know one's self and how that self-knowledge patterns understandings, data, and records gathered in the course of fieldwork. Context is partially a function of one's taken for granted understandings and projections, and understanding these is primary in the interpretive quest. What the song means is a combination of what I personally bring to the experience, as well as the narrative structure and content of the song.

6. I draw here on published reviews of Jackall's work by Van Maanen (1989) and Calhoun (1989).

7. If one sees ethnographic research as based on a model of interrelated subjective meanings as features of the setting, and the ways they are pinned down, then developing a positivistic model of variables set in formal statistical models of empirical relations (nature, strength, direction, and robustness) is premature at this point in the development of *loose coupling*.

Chapter 5

1. This paper was originally presented to meetings of the Law and Society Association, Madison, Wisconsin, June 1989. The fieldwork included historical research on the origins of nuclear power in Britain and, more specifically, the growth of the regulatory structure for the production of nuclear-generated energy, and a comparative analysis of nuclear safety policies and approaches in France, the United States, and Britain. Newspaper clippings from newspapers published in Britain and the United States on nuclear power and related issues such as waste disposal, fuel-reprocessing, the economics of power production, and international developments in the nuclear power have been collected and filed since 1982. I have had access to some documents and records and transcripts of the Sizewell Inquiry (1983–1985) and the subsequent summary, the *Layfield Report* (1987). Fieldwork was undertaken in three of the four branches of the inspectorate. (Branch three, fuel-reprocessing located at Bootle, was omitted from the study.) This included attendance at meetings; joint conferences with the licensees who produce power, Central Electricity Generating Board (CEGB) and two others, and plant management; a site visit to a power station on an inspection; and 21 interviews with NII members, including the chief inspector, Mr. Anthony, deputy chief inspectors, section heads, and inspectors. Field notes were gathered during two periods of intensive fieldwork.

2. The following few paragraphs are adopted from Manning (1989a).

3. Details of the organizations and the communities are found in Manning (1988a: Ch. 4).

4. Always, fatefully and ominously, lurks the smoking desecration, images of death and destruction, represented by the smoking and scarred grounds surrounding Chernobyl, the steam and smoke rising from the two stacks of Three Mile Island, and the floating clouds of radioactive steam polluting the air and fields of rural Windscale in England. These are mere icons, minirehearsals perhaps for the dreadful and almost unimaginable consequences of nuclear war, holocausts, or large-scale accidents.

Chapter 6

1.   The internal differentiation of the police is detailed elsewhere (Manning 1977, 1979a, 1990a).

2.   Some general points can be made about the relationships between information, organization, and ritual. With respect to more specialized work, such as that of detectives and vice/drug work, the job of dramaturgical presentation is more complex and subtle. It is also community or context specific to a marked degree. The less the public knows about day-to-day operations, the better; major events, such as "busts" of large numbers of "dealers" and seizures of drugs, are highly publicized. Routine figures on arrests are issued, but most of these are made by patrol officers, and (varying from city to city) many cases are never brought to trial because the arrestee is "turned" to make cases on other users/ dealers. If one looks at the dramaturgical potential of detective work, one sees quickly that detectives are not Sherlock Holmes in modern dress, but are clerks. They are in fact primarily "paper pushers," who take advantage of available information rather than creating new information or following leads. When they make an arrest, it is often with information obtained by patrol officers from witnesses at the scene (see Greenwood, Chaiken, and Petersilia 1977). Much of their important work is "cooling out the mark," explaining to the public why it is impossible for overworked detectives to make arrests and why the victims or complainants should consider their case unsolvable. Detectives elevate the rare arrest of a famous case, or solution based on diligent pursuit of evidence and witnesses, and depress the tiresome, boring, and unrewarding task of simply filing the vast majority of crime complaints for which no witness or forensic evidence is available (see Waegel 1981).

3.   The police everywhere are "information workers" (Ericson and Shearing, 1986) who gather and process information, and in so doing display the power and legitimacy of the state. As societies become more complex, and judgments about morality and standards of decency diversify, the police find their moral ground somewhat undercut.

4.   It is perhaps likely that a number of types of social integration and command authority exist in urban departments (see Wilson 1968; Bordua and Reiss 1967; Reppetto 1978). Rubinstein's work (1973) is a limited picture, despite its detail, because it omits discussion of police authority and decisions above the level of the street. Ethnographies based solely upon observation of discretion by uniformed patrol officers are an inadequate basis for generalization about policing. Interactional studies are valuable and among these the careful and comprehensive works of Sykes and Brent (1983) and Brown (1981) stand out. Brown's is important because it details policy differences and attempts comparative analysis of patterns of discretion among patrol officers in several southern California cities. Issues arising from the comparative study of policing are well illustrated by the work of David Bayley (1975, 1979), especially his internationally focused *Patterns of Policing* (1985).

5.   This summary is taken in part from Manning (1989b).

Chapter 7

1.   Types of policing may be found worldwide, but comparative analysis is still very limited in its grasp of such variations (see Bayley 1975, 1979, 1985).

There does appear to be an Anglo-American type of policing (Bayley 1979). The Anglo-American societies are a group of nation-states and cultural regions that share a number of features derived from their British heritage and the common-law tradition so central to it. Included in this category are Australia, Canada, New Zealand, Great Britain, and to a lesser degree, India and Northern Ireland (see Bayley 1979). Clearly, further features would be required to differentiate American policing from policing in Anglo-American societies as well as from other societies. Using such types highlights the need for research employing the ideal types to focus inquiries. There is much to be discovered yet about the types and kinds of policing practiced in urban United States, and much of this work should be historical, if not historical and comparative cross-cultural.

2. Some of these points were published in Manning (1988b).

3. Such random alternation in strategies and tactics may be of considerable benefit to the police as well as the public. Police may benefit through the development and execution of large operations, shifting resources, mounting evaluations, and engaging in political dialogue. They may continue to redefine themselves to themselves and, as a result, begin to see themselves in a new light. They may continue to examine the nature of their role, the rewards associated with it, the limits of the crime-fighting rhetoric, and the challenges of urban diversity.

4. Mastrofski (1988) argues that community policing should be seen as part of an ongoing reform movement that includes various foundations, educational institutions, urban politicians in nonmachine cities, and criminal justice educa-tors. It cannot be seen independently of other movements that stress the unity of life, the wholeness of experience, and current American ideologies concerning the "good."

5. These assumptions are gathered from the publications listed in the bibli-ography found in Greene and Mastrofski, editors, 1988, especially the works of Kelling, Trojanowicz, and the authors of the articles of the special issue of *Crime and Delinquency* (1987), which was devoted to community policing (see also Reichers and Roberg 1990).

6. The concept of order in some sense implies a crime-free environment, although several urban ethnographies have described the extent to which many urban areas are crime dependent and noted that order is in fact integrally related to criminal activities (see Suttles 1968; Horowitz 1984).

7. This proposition was examined by experiments done in the early 1980s by the Police Foundation (1981) in Newark. Evidence does not consistently support the claims.

8. Unfortunately, the evidence available to authors of early critical reviews of studies of community policing was limited. See several of the chapters in Greene and Mastrofski (1988), e.g., Mastrofski, Taylor and Greene, Klockars and Cordner. It was possible later to consider the raw data and full technical reports. Untested and unproven assumptions were made about the impact and conse-quences of community-policing programs, and the ideologies invoked to ratio-nalize community-policing programs (however defined; cf. Manning 1984: 207–11) were tacit and unexplicated. Furthermore, the links between the as-sumptions, ideologies, programs, operational tactics, and strategies were even more opaque. Some of the most telling problems surfaced in early evaluations and in later work because key concepts were neither theoretically deduced or derived, nor operationally defined. Evidence bearing directly upon assump-tions, promised outcomes, or programs was uneven and difficult to interpret.

9. See for example, McNamara's (1967) exposition of the contradictions

between the paramilitary bureaucracy of the police and policing in action (Manning 1977; Jermeir and Berkes 1979).

   10.   A number of questions might be asked about the implicit, unintended consequences of community policing, whether seen as an ideology, program, tactic, or passing historical moment. These issues include such matters as the increasing dependence of the community upon the police for ordering social relations, and increasing use of the media to influence public opinion. The notion that the police defend and advance their own interests, which may or may not coincide with the hypothetical "greatest good" argument, even with the apparent decline of the police unionization movement, remains. A continuing issue is the potential that more sophisticated, electronically equipped police with greater legal and social power of surveillance have for penetrating private spheres even further (see Stinchcombe 1964; Ericson and Shearing 1986; Marx 1988).

Chapter 8

   1.   Data are drawn from a two-year study of the NII (see ch. 5, note 1). The principal source of materials for this chapter is a manual used to guide inspection and licensing of nuclear installations by the NII.
   2.   Thus, the reasoning employed resembles legal reasoning. Knowledge, especially the character and presence or absence of anticipatory knowledge, when contrasted with actual or claimed events, is the heart of legal reasoning. This is especially true in the case of criminal and tort law. This assumption about the sort of knowledge relevant to legal decision-making frames the objects of concern within a sanctioned field of observations. It creates "facts" on which decisions will be based.
   A logical model of legal reasoning would suggest that legal reasoning seeks precisely to define (1) events and (2) their consequentiality (Scheppele 1989). However, legal knowledge is applied ex post facto and then becomes a basis for deciding forms of corrective legal action, remedies, and punishments, and is the basis for regulatory activity. Administrative law governing state-based service provision is a special case of regulation. Although regulation concerns the establishing of a "safe state" of operations (or the primary state set by governmental rules), it must also attend, on a day-to-day basis, to alterations in this state-sanctioned primary "safe state," and accidents and their consequences.
   3.   My knowledge of current practices is limited. I cannot say whether and to what degree these principles are practiced now, and how they will be and are being modified as a result of the planned building of a pressurized water reactor in Essex. The most current assessment is found in O'Riordian, Kemp, and Purdue (1988).

Chapter 9

   1.   See Richardson (1990) and Becker (1984) on writing for different audiences.
   2.   Geertz's *Works and Lives* (1988) focuses on this theme. The book is "primarily concerned with 'how anthropologists write'—that is, it is textually-oriented" (p. vi).

Chapter 10

1.   There are a number of ethnographies that claim to be written in this style and writers who claim to know what this style ought to be, but few books, in my judgment, qualify (see, however, Dorst 1989; Rose 1986, 1990; and Stoller 1989).

2.   Because many postmodern writers are profoundly ignorant of the sociological tradition and often eschew or ignore sociological writing, their works appear ahistorical and sometimes naive. Nevertheless, a distinctive set of ideational themes in French social thought connects postmodernism directly to the current preoccupations of ethnographers. A useful example of this is the golden thread of continuity found running between the French "Durkheimian school" of sociology (Lévi-Strauss, 1945) with its affinity for artistic ethnography, expressionism, and experimentalism, and postmodernism. The influence of the phenomenological reading of Hegel introduced to France by Alexandre Kojève upon Aron, Bataille, and Callois was also enormous. Ethnographic work in Africa by Leiris, Griaule, and Rouch, and the rich and challenging experimental writings of *College de France* members, such as Bataille and Callois, encouraged by Mauss, also indirectly inspired current postmodernist ethnography (Clifford 1988; Hollier 1988).

3.   These points, taken together, suggest that the process of doing ethnography will involve a principle derived from semiotics, what Barthes calls "the commutative test" (1983:27). The test can be used once a structure of relations is identified. Given an identified structure of relations, an element is altered and the consequences examined. The interpretive task is to determine whether this change alters the reading or usage of the structure that results. By looking at alterations in small units or elements of a structure in conjunction or separately, one can identify a general inventory of "concomitant variations . . . and consequently to determine a certain number of commutative classes in the ensemble of a given structure" (pp. 19–20). This procedure best begins with a careful description of a structure, its units, relations, and codes.

4.   I am grateful to Professor Juniper Wiley, of California State University, Long Beach, for administering a brief questionnaire on the cap on my behalf. As I write this, I am wearing a corduroy baseball cap given to me by my son, who was attending the University of Michigan Law School at the time. "Michigan" is inscribed on its front. The bill is straight forward.

References

Adler, P., and P. Adler (1987). *Membership Roles in Field Research*. Newbury Park, CA: Sage.

Agar, M. (1990). "Text and Field: Exploring the Excluded Middle." *Journal of Contemporary Ethnography* 19 (April):73–88.

Agger, B. (1989). *Fast Capitalism*. Urbana: University of Illinois Press.

Altheide, D. (1979). *Media Reality*. Newbury Park, CA: Sage.

Altheide, D., and J. Johnson (1977). *Bureaucratic Propaganda*. Boston: Allyn and Bacon.

Angell, J. (1971). "An Alternative to the Classic Police Organizational Arrangements: A Democratic Model." *Criminology* (August/November):185–206.

Ashby, E. (1956). *Design for a Brain*. New York: Wiley.

Ashmore, M. (1987). *The Reflexive Thesis*. Chicago: University of Chicago Press.

Atkinson, P. (1990). *The Ethnographic Imagination*. London: Routledge.

Atkinson, P. (1992). *Ethnographic Authors and Audiences*. Newbury Park, CA: Sage.

Babbie, E. (1990). *Survey Research*. 2d ed. Belmont, CA: Wadsworth.

Barley, S. (1983a). "Semiotics and the Study of Occupational and Organizational Cultures." *Administrative Science Quarterly* 23:383–413.

Barley, S. (1983b). "Codes of the Dead: The Semiotics of Funeral Work." *Urban Life* 10:459–61.

Barley, S. (1986). "Technology as an Occasion for Structuring." *Administrative Science Quarterly* 31:78–108.

Barnard, C. (1938). *The Functions of the Executive*. Cambridge, MA: Harvard University Press.

Barthel, D. (1988). *Putting on Appearances*. Philadelphia: Temple University Press.

Barthes, R. (1970). *Writing Degree Zero and Elements of Semiology*. Boston: Beacon.

Barthes, R. (1983). *The Fashion System*. New York: Hill and Wang.

Bateson, G. (1972). *Steps toward an Ecology of Mind*. New York: Ballantine.

Baudrillard, J. (1988). *Jean Baudrillard: Selected Writings*. Edited by Mark Poster. Stanford: Stanford University Press.

Baudrillard, J. (1989). *America*. Translated by Chris Turner. London: Verso.

Bayley, D. (1975). "The Police and Political Development in Europe." Pp. 1328–79 in *The Formation of National States in Europe*, edited by C. Tilly. Princeton, NJ: Princeton University Press.

Bayley, D. (1979). "Police Function, Structure and Control in Western Europe." Pp. 109–44 in *Crime and Justice: An Annual Review of Research*, edited by Norval Morris and Michael Tonry. Chicago: University of Chicago Press.

Bayley, D. (1985). *Patterns of Policing*. New Brunswick, NJ: Rutgers University Press.

Beare, M. (1987). "The Police and Ideological Work." Paper presented to the ASC, Montreal.

Becker, H. S. (1963). *Outsiders*. Glencoe, IL: Free Press.

Becker, H. S. (1984). *Writing for Social Scientists*. Chicago: University of Chicago Press.

Bell, D. (1962). *The End of Ideology*. New York: Free Press.

Bell, D. (1973). *The Coming of Post-Industrial Society*. New York: Basic Books.

Bennett, W. L., and M. S. Feldman (1981). *Reconstructing Reality in the Courtroom*. New Brunswick, NJ: Rutgers University Press.

Bentz, V. M. (1989). *Becoming Mature*. Hawthorne, NY: Aldine/deGruyter.

Berman, M. (1988). *All That Is Solid Melts into Air*. New York: Penguin.

Birdwhistell, R. (1970). *Kinesics and Context*. Philadelphia: University of Pennsylvania Press.

Bittner, E. (1970). *The Functions of Police in Urban Society*. Bethesda, MD: NIMH.

Bittner, E. (1974). "A Theory of Police: Florence Nightingale in Pursuit of Willie Sutton." Pp. 17–44 in *The Potential for Reform of Criminal Justice*, edited by H. Jacob. Newbury Park, CA: Sage.

Black, D. J. (1976). *The Behavior of Law*. New York: Academic Press.

Black, D. J. (1983). "Crime as Social Control." *American Sociological Review* 48 (February):34–45.

Blau, P. (1960). *Dynamics of Bureaucracy*. Chicago: University of Chicago Press.

Blumberg, A. (1967). *Criminal Justice*. New York: Quadrangle.

Blumer, H. (1969). *Symbolic Interactionism*. Englewood Cliffs, NJ: Prentice-Hall.

Blumer, H. (1990). *Industrialization and Social Order*. Edited with an introduction by T. Morrione and D. Maines. Hawthorne, NY: Aldine/deGruyter.

Bohme, G., and N. Stehr, eds. (1986). *The Knowledge Society*. Dordrecht: Reidel.

Boje, D. (1991). "The Storytelling Organization: A Study of Story Performance in an Office-Supply Firm." *Administrative Science Quarterly* 36:106–126.

Bordua, D., and A. J. Reiss, Jr. (1967). "Law Enforcement." Pp. 375–303 in *The Uses of Sociology*, edited by P. Lazarsfeld, W. Sewell, and H. Wilensky. New York: Basic Books.

Bottomley, K., and C. Coleman (1980). *Understanding Crime Rates*. Farnworth, UK: Gower.

Bourdieu, P. (1977). *Outline of a Theory of Practice*. Cambridge: Cambridge University Press.

Bourdieu, P. (1983). *Homo Academicus*. Cambridge: Harvard University Press.

Broms, H., and H. Gahmberg (1983). "Communications to Self in Organizations and Cultures." *Administrative Science Quarterly* 28 (September):482–95.

Brown, M. (1981). *Working the Street*. New York: Russell Sage.

Brown, M. H. (1990). "Defining Stories in Organizations." Pp. 162–90 in *Communication Yearbook* 13, edited by J. A. Anderson. Newbury Park, CA: Sage.

Brown, R. (1977). *A Poetic for Sociology*. New York: Cambridge University Press.

Brown, R. (1990). "Rhetoric, Textuality, and the Postmodern Turn in Sociological Theory." *Sociological Theory* 8 (Fall):188–97.

Burke, K. (1962). *A Grammar of Motives and a Rhetoric of Motives.* Cleveland: World Publishing.

Burke, K. (1965). *Permanence and Change.* Indianapolis: Bobbs-Merrill.

Burns, T., and G. Stalker (1960). *The Management of Innovation.* London: Tavistock.

Burrell, G., and G. Morgan (1979). *Sociological Paradigms and Organizational Analysis.* London: Heinemann.

Calhoun, C. (1989). "Review of R. Jackall's *Moral Mazes.*" *Contemporary Sociology* 18 (July):542–45.

Casper, J. (1973). *American Criminal Justice: The Defendant's Perspective.* Englewood Cliffs, NJ: Prentice-Hall.

Chatterton, M. (1983). "Police Work and Assault Charges." Pp. 194–222 in *Control in the Police Organization,* edited by M. Punch. Cambridge, MA: MIT Press.

Cheney, D., and S. Vibbert (1987). "Corporate Discourse." in *Handbook of Organizational Communication,* Newbury Park, CA: Sage.

Cicourel, A. (1966). *Method and Measurement in Sociology.* Glencoe, IL: Free Press.

Cicourel, A. (1970). *The Social Organization of Juvenile Justice.* London: Heinemann.

Cicourel, A. (1973). *Cognitive Sociology.* New York: Free Press.

Cicourel, A. (1975). "Discourse and Text: Cognitive and Linguistic Process in Studies of Social Structure." *Versus* 12 (Sept./Dec.):33–84.

Cicourel, A. (1976). "Discourse, Autonomous Grammars and Contextualized Processing of Information." Paper presented to conference at the University of Bonn, West Germany.

Cicourel, A. (1981). "Language and Belief in a Medical Setting." Pp. 48–78 in *Contemporary Perceptions of Language: Interdisciplinary Dimensions,* edited by H. Brynes. Washington: Georgetown University Press.

Cicourel, A. (1985). "Text and Discourse." Pp. 159–85 in *Annual Review of Anthropology* edited by B. Siegel, 14. Palo Alto, CA: Annual Reviews Press.

Cicourel, A. (1986). "Social Measurement as the Creation of Expert Systems." Pp. 246–70 in *Metatheory in Social Science* edited by D. Fiske and R. A. Schweder, Chicago: University of Chicago Press.

Clark, A. L., and J. Gibbs (1965). "Social Control: A Reformulation." *Social Problems* 12 (Spring):398–415.

Clarke, L. (1988). *Acceptable Risk?* Berkeley: University of California Press.

Clifford, J. (1988). *The Predicament of Culture.* Cambridge, MA: Harvard University Press.

Clifford, J., and G. Marcus (eds.) (1986). *Writing Culture: The Poetics and Politics of Ethnography.* Berkeley: University of California Press.

Cohen, M., and J. March (1974). *Leadership and Ambiguity.* New York: McGraw-Hill.

Cohen, S. (1979). *Folk Devils and Moral Panics.* 2d ed. London: Paladin.

Conrad, C. (1989). *Organizational Communication.* 2d ed. New York: McGraw-Hill.

Cooper, R., and G. Burrell (1988). "Modernism, Postmodernism and Organizational Analysis: An Introduction." *Organization Studies* 9(1):91–112.

Crime and Delinquency (1987). Special issue on community policing. Vol. 33, no. 1.

Crozier, M. (1964). *The Bureaucratic Phenomenon*. Chicago: University of Chicago Press.

Culler, J. (1975). *Structuralist Poetics*. Ithaca, NY: Cornell University Press.

Dance, F. X. (1982). *Human Communication Theory*. New York: Harper and Row.

Davis, S. (1983). "Restoring the Semblance of Order: Police Strategies in the Domestic Dispute." *Symbolic Interaction* 6(2):261–78.

Deleuze, J., and F. Guattauri (1976). *Anti-Oedipus*. Minneapolis: University of Minnesota Press.

Denzin, N. (1986). "Postmodern Social Theory." *Sociological Theory* 4 (Fall): 194–204.

Denzin, N. (forthcoming) "Deconstruction." In *Postmodernism and Social Science*, edited by D. Dickens and A. Fontana. Chicago: University of Chicago Press.

Department of Justice (1987). *Criminal Statistics*. Washington: USGPO.

Department of Justice (1988). *Criminal Statistics*. Washington: USGPO.

Derrida, J. (1976). *On Grammatology*. Translated with a preface by Gayatri Chakravorty Spivak. Baltimore, MD: Johns Hopkins University Press.

Dickens, D., and A. Fontana (eds.) (1992). *Postmodernism and Social Science*. Chicago: University of Chicago Press.

Dingwall, R., and P. M. Strong (1982). "The Interactional Study of Organizations: A Critique and Reformulation." *Urban Life* 14 (July):205–31.

Dorst, J. (1989). *The Written Suburb*. Philadelphia, PA: University of Pennsylvania Press.

Douglas, J. (1976). *Investigative Social Research*. Beverly Hills, CA: Sage.

Douglas, M. (1986). *Risk Analysis According to the Social Sciences*. New York: Russell Sage.

Douglas, M. (1987). *How Institutions Think*. Syracuse, NY: Syracuse University Press.

Duncan, H. (1968). *Symbols in Society*. New York: Oxford University Press.

Duncan, H. (1969). *Symbols in Sociological Theory*. New York: Oxford University Press.

Duncan, H. (1985 [1962]). *Communication and Social Order*. New Brunswick, NJ: Transaction Books.

Durkheim, E. (1964). *Rules of Sociological Method*. Glencoe, IL: Free Press.

Eco, U. (1976). *A Theory of Semiotics*. Bloomington: University of Indiana Press.

Eco, U. (1979). *The Role of the Reader*. Bloomington: University of Indiana Press.

Eco, U. (1986). *Travels in Hyperreality*. New York: Harcourt Brace Jovanovich.

Edelman, M. (1964). *Symbolic Uses of Politics*. Urbana: University of Illinois Press.

Edelman, M. (1971). *Politics as Symbolic Action*. Chicago: Markham.

Edelman, M. (1977). *Political Language*. Chicago: Markham.

Edelman, M. (1987). *Constructing the Political Spectacle*. Chicago: University of Chicago Press.

Elster, J. (1985). *Sour Grapes*. Cambridge: Cambridge University Press.

Emerson, R. (1983). "Holistic Effects in Social Control Decision-Making." *Law and Society Review* 17 (December):425–55.

Ericson, R. V. (1989). "Patrolling the Facts: Secrecy and Publicity in Policework" *British Journal of Sociology* 40 (June):205–226.

Ericson, R. V. (1991). "Mass Media, Crime, Law, and Justice." *The British Journal of Criminology* 31 (Summer):219–249.

Ericson, R. V., and C. D. Shearing (1986). "The Scientification of Police Work." Pp. 129–59 in *The Knowledge Society*, edited by G. Bohme and N. Stehr. Dordrecht: Reidel.

Ericson, R., J. Baranek, and J. Chan (1987). *Visualizing Deviance*. Toronto: University of Toronto Press.

Ericson, R., et al. (1988). *Negotiating Control*. Toronto: University of Toronto Press.

Etzioni, A. (1975). *Complex Organizations*. New York: Free Press.

Featherstone, M. (ed.) (1988). *Postmodernism*. London: Sage.

Feeley, M. (1970). "Coercion and Compliance: A New Look at an Old Problem." *Law and Society Review* 4 (May):505–19.

Feldman, M. S. (1988a). "Understanding Organizational Routines: Stability and Change." Working paper #88/35, Norwegian Research Center in Organization and Management, University of Bergen, Norway.

Feldman, M. S. (1988b). "Coping with Ambiguity." Unpublished working paper, IPPS, University of Michigan, Ann Arbor.

Feldman, M. S. (1988c). "Studying Change in Organizational Routines." Unpublished working paper, IPPS, University of Michigan, Ann Arbor.

Feldman, M. S. (1988d). "Organizational Goals and the Use of Analysis." Working paper.

Feldman, M. S. (1989). *Order without Design*. Stanford: Stanford University Press.

Feldman, M. S., and J. March (1981). "Information in Organizations as Symbol and Signal." *Administrative Science Quarterly* 26:171–86.

Filol, C. M. (1989). "A Semiotic Analysis of Corporate Language: Organizational Boundaries and Joint Venturing." *Administrative Science Quarterly* 34:277–303.

Fischoff, B., et al. (1981). *Acceptable Risk*. New York: Cambridge University Press.

Fisher, B. A. (1978). *Perspectives on Human Communication*. New York: Macmillan.

Fishman, M. (1980). "Crime Waves as Ideology." *Social Problems* 25:531–43.

Fogelson, R. (1977). *Big City Police*. Cambridge, MA: Harvard University Press.

Foucault, M. (1977). *Discipline and Punish*. Translated by A. M. Smith. New York: Pantheon.

Freeman, J., and M. Hannan (1989). *Organizational Ecology*. Cambridge, MA: Harvard University Press.

Freudenberg, W. (1989). "Perceived Risk, Real Risk: Social Science and the Art of Probabilistic Risk Assessment." *Science* 242 (7 October):44–49.

Frost, B., et al. (eds.) (1985). *Organizational Culture*. Beverly Hills, CA: Sage.

Galanter, M. (1974). "Why the 'Haves' Come Out Ahead: Speculations on the Limits of Legal Change." *Law and Society Review* 9:95–160.

Garfinkel, H. (1963). "A Conception of, Experiments with, 'Trust' as a Condition of Stable, Concerted Actions." Pp. 187–238 in *Motivation and Social Interaction*, edited by O. J. Harvey. New York: Ronald Press.

Garfinkel, H. (1964). "The Routine Grounds of Everyday Activities. *Social Problems* (Winter):11:225–250.

Garfinkel, H. (ed.) (1967). *Studies in Ethnomethodology*. Englewood Cliffs, NJ: Prentice-Hall.

Geertz, C. (1973). *The Interpretation of Culture*. New York: Basic Books.

Geertz, C. (1988). *Works and Lives: The Anthropologist as Author*. Stanford: Stanford University Press.

Geiger, T. (1969). *Social Order and Mass Society*. Translated and edited by R. Mayentz. Chicago: University of Chicago Press.

Gergen, K. (1991). *The Saturated Self*. New York: Basic Books.

Giddens, A. (1984). *The Constitution of Society*. Berkeley: University of California Press.

Gitlin, T. (1980). *The Whole World Is Watching*. Berkeley: University of California Press.

Gitlin, T. (1983). *Inside "Prime Time."* New York: Pantheon.

Glaser, B., and A. Strauss (1967). *The Discovery of Grounded Theory*. Chicago: Aldine.

Glassman, R. B. (1973). "Persistence and Loose Coupling in Living Systems." *Behavioral Science* 18:83–98.

Goffman, E. (1959). *The Presentation of Self in Everyday Life*. New York: Doubleday Anchor.

Goffman, E. (1961). "Fun in Games." Pp. 17–81 in *Encounters*, Indianapolis, IN: Bobbs-Merrill.

Goffman, E. (1962). *Asylums*. Chicago: Aldine.

Goffman, E. (1969). *Strategic Interaction*. Philadelphia: University of Pennsylvania Press.

Goffman, E. (1974). *Frame Analysis*. Cambridge, MA: Harvard University Press.

Goffman, E. (1981). *Forms of Talk*. Oxford: Blackwell.

Goffman, E. (1983a). "Felicity's Condition." *American Journal of Sociology* 89 (July):1–53.

Goffman, E. (1983b). "The Interaction Order." *American Sociological Review* 48 (February):1–17.

Goodall, H. L. (1989). *Casing a Promised Land*. Carbondale: Southern Illinois University Press.

Gouldner, A. W. (1954). *Patterns of Industrial Bureaucracy*. Glencoe, IL: Free Press.

Gouldner, A. W. (1959). "Reciprocity and Autonomy in Functional Theory." Pp. 241–270 in *Symposium on Sociological Theory*, edited by L. Gross. Chicago: Row Peterson.

Greene, J., and S. Mastrofski (eds.) (1988). *Community Policing*. New York: Praeger.

Greenwood, P., J. Chaiken, and J. Petersilia (1977). *The Criminal Investigation Process*. Lexington, MA: Heath.

Greimas, A. J. (1966). *Sémantique Structurale*. Paris: Larousse.

Gronn, P. C. (1983). "Talk as Work." *Administrative Science Quarterly* 28:1–21.

Guiraud, P. (1975). *Semiology*. London: Routledge and Kegan Paul.

Gusfield, J. (1963). *Symbolic Crusade*. Urbana: University of Illinois Press.

Gusfield, J. (1976). "The Literary Rhetoric of Science." *Administrative Science Quarterly* 41 (February):16–34.

Gusfield, J. (1981). *The Culture of Public Problems.* Chicago: University of Chicago Press.

Gusfield, J. (ed.) (1989). *Kenneth Burke on Symbols and Society.* Chicago: University of Chicago Press.

Haas, J. E., and T. Drabek (1973). *Complex Organizations.* New York: Macmillan.

Habenstein, R. H. (1962). "The Funeral Director." Pp. 225–246 in *Human Behavior and Social Process,* edited by A. Rose. Boston: Houghton-Mifflin.

Habermas, J. (1972). *Knowledge and Human Interests.* Boston: Beacon.

Habermas, J. (1979). *Communication and the Evolution of Society.* Boston: Beacon.

Habermas, J. (1984). *The Theory of Communicative Action.* Vol. 1. Translated by T. McCarthy. Boston: Beacon.

Hall, P. (1972). "A Symbolic Interactionist Conception of Politics," *Sociological Inquiry* 42:35–75.

Hall, P. (1987). "Interactionism and the Study of Social Organization." *Sociological Quarterly* 28:1–22.

Hall, P., and D. A. Spencer Hall (1982). "The Social Conditions of Negotiated Order." *Urban Life* 11:328–49.

Hall, S., et al. (1978). *Policing the Crisis.* London: Macmillan.

Harvey, D. (1989). *The Condition of Postmodernity.* Oxford: Blackwell.

Hawkes, T. (1977). *Structuralism and Semiotics.* Berkley: University of California Press.

Hawkins, K. (1984). *Environment and Enforcement.* Oxford: Oxford University Press.

Heimer, C. (1985a). *Reactive Risk and Rational Action.* Berkeley: University of California Press.

Heimer, C. (1985b). "Allocating Information Costs in a Negotiated Information Order: Interorganizational Constraints on Decision-making in Norwegian Oil Insurance." *Administrative Science Quarterly* 30:395–417.

Heimer, C. (1988). "Social Structure, Psychology, and the Estimation of Risk." Pp. 491–519 in *Annual Review of Sociology.* Palo Alto, CA: Annual Reviews Press.

Heller, Joseph (1975). *Something Happened.* New York: Ballantine.

Hilgartner, S., and C. Bosk (1988). "The Rise and Fall of Social Problems." *American Journal of Sociology* 94 (June):53–78.

Hirschman, A. (1970). *Exit, Voice and Loyalty.* Cambridge, MA: Harvard University Press.

Hobbs, D. (1988). *Doing the Business: Entrepreneurship, the Working Class, and Detectives in the East End of London.* Oxford: Oxford University Press.

Holdaway, S. (1988). "Discovering Structure: Studies of the British Police Occupational Structure." Pp. 55–75 in *Police Research: Some Future Prospects,* edited by M. Weatheritt. Aldershot, UK: Avebury.

Hollier, D. (ed.) (1988). *The College of Sociology.* Minneapolis: University of Minnesota Press.

Horowitz, R. (1984). *Honor and the American Dream.* New Brunswick, NJ: Rutgers University Press.

Horowitz, R. *Identity and Cultural Commitment.* (forthcoming).

Hughes, E. C. (1958). *Men and Their Work.* Glencoe, IL: Free Press.

Hunt, J. (1989). *Psychoanalytic Aspects of Fieldwork*. Newbury Park, CA: Sage.

Hunt, J. C., and P. K. Manning (1991). "The Social Context of Police Lying." *Symbolic Interaction* Spring 14(1):51–70.

Ianni, E., and F. Ianni (1983). "Street Cops and Management Cops: Two Cultures of Policing." Pp. 251–74 in *Control in the Police Organization*, edited by M. Punch. Cambridge, MA: MIT Press.

Jackall, R. (1988). *Moral Mazes*. New York: Oxford University Press.

Jackson, Bruce (1987). *Fieldwork*. Urbana: University of Illinois Press.

Jackson, Jean (1990). " 'Deja entendu': The Liminal Quality of Anthropological Fieldnotes." *Journal of Contemporary Ethnography* 19 (April):8–43.

Jakobson, R. (1960). "Closing Statement." Pp. 350–77 in *The Uses of Language*, edited by T. Sebeok. Cambridge, MA: MIT Press.

Jameson, F. (1991). *Postmodernism, or the Logic of Late Capitalism*. Durham, NC: Duke University Press.

Jermeir, J., and L. Berkes (1979). "Leader Behavior in a Police Command Bureaucracy: A Closer Look at the Quasi-military Model." *Administrative Science Quarterly* 24 (March):1–23.

Johnson, J. (1975). *Doing Field Research*. New York: Free Press.

Johnson, J. (1989). "Lessons of Burography." *American Behavioral Scientist* 25 (4):439–450.

Jones, M., M. Moore, and R. Snyder (eds.) (1988). *Inside Organizations*. Newbury Park, CA: Sage.

Journal of Communication (1985). Special issue on narrative and storytelling. Volume 35, no. 4.

Katz, F. (1965). "Explaining Work Groups in Complex Organizations: The Case for Autonomy in Structure." *Administrative Science Quarterly* (September) 10:204–223.

Kay, P., and B. Berlin (1969). *Basic Color Terms*. Berkeley: University of California Press.

Kirk, J., and M. L. Miller (1985). *Reliability and Validity in Qualitative Research*. Newbury Park, CA: Sage.

Klapp, O. (1978). *Opening and Closing*. Cambridge: Cambridge University Press.

Klapp, O. (1986). *Overload and Boredom*. Westport, CT: Greenwood.

Kling, Robert, and E. Gerson (1978). "Patterns of Segmentation and Intersection in the Computing World." *Symbolic Interaction* 1:24–43.

Knorr-Cetina, K. (1981). *The Manufacture of Knowledge*. Oxford: Pergamon.

Kreps, G. L. (1990). *Organizational Communication*. 2d ed. New York: Longman.

Kristeva, J. (1981). *Desire in Language*. New York: Columbia University Press.

Krone, K. J., F. Jablin, and L. Putnam (1987). "Communication Theory and Organization Communication: Multiple Perspectives." Pp. 8–40 in *Handbook of Organizational Communication*, edited by F. Jablin, K. Roberts, and L. Porter. Newbury Park, CA: Sage.

Kuhn, T. (1970). *The Structure of Scientific Revolutions*. Chicago: University of Chicago Press.

Langer, S. (1951). *Philosophy in a New Key*. New York: Mentor Books.

Langworthy, D. (1986). *The Structure of Police Organizations*. New York: Praeger.

Larson, R. (1990). *Rapid Response and Community Policing: Are They Really in Conflict?* Community Policing Series #20, School of Criminal Justice, Michigan State University, E. Lansing.

LaTour, B., and S. Woolgar (1979). *Laboratory Life.* Newbury Park, CA: Sage.

Laurie, P. (1971). *Scotland Yard.* London: Penguin.

Layfield Report (1987). Report on the Siting of Sizewell 'b'. London: H.M. S.O.

Lemert, C. (1979a). *The Twilight of Man.* Carbondale: Southern Illinois University Press.

Lemert, C. (1979b). "Structuralist Semiotics." Pp. 96–111 in *Theoretical Perspectives in Sociology,* edited by S. McNall. New York: St. Martin's.

Lemert, C. (1979c). "Language, Structure and Measurement." *American Journal of Sociology* 84 (January):929–57.

Lemert, C. (1990). "The Uses of French Structuralisms in Sociology." Pp. 230–54 in *Frontiers of Social Theory,* edited by G. Ritzer. New York: Columbia University Press.

Lévi-Strauss, C. (1945). "French Sociology." Pp. 503–37 in *Twentieth Century Sociology,* edited by G. Gurvitch and W. Moore. New York: Philosophical Library.

Lévi-Strauss, C. (1963). *Structural Anthropology.* New York: Basic Books.

Lévi-Strauss, C. (1966). *The Savage Mind.* Chicago: University of Chicago Press.

Lévi-Strauss, C. (1975). *Tristes Tropiques.* Translated by J. Russell. New York: Atheneum.

Levinson, S. (1983). *Pragmatics.* Cambridge: Cambridge University Press.

Likert, R. (1961). *New Patterns of Management.* New York: McGraw-Hill.

Lindblom, C. and D. Cohen (1979). *Useful Knowledge.* New Haven, CT: Yale University Press.

Lipsky, M. (1982). *Street-Level Bureaucracy.* New York: Russell Sage.

Lofland, J. (1979). *Analyzing Social Settings.* Belmont, CA: Wadsworth.

Louis, M. L. (1986). "An Investigator's Guide to Workplace Culture." Pp. 73–93 in *Organizational Culture,* edited by B. Frost et al. Newbury Park, CA: Sage.

Lowrance, W. W. (1976). *Of Acceptable Risk.* Los Altos, CA: Kaufman.

Luhmann, N. (1985). *The Sociology of Law.* Translated by E. King-Utz and Martin Albrow. London: Routledge.

Luhmann, N. (1986). "The Autopoesis of Social Systems." Pp. 172–92 in *Sociocybernetic Paradoxes,* edited by F. Geyer and J. Van Der Zouwen. London: Sage.

Lukes, S. (1975). "Political Ritual and Social Integration." *Sociology* 9:289–308.

Lyotard, J. F. (1984). *The Postmodern Condition.* Foreword by F. Jameson. Minneapolis: University of Minnesota Press.

Lyotard, J. F., and F. Thébaud (1985). *Just Gaming.* Minneapolis: University of Minnesota Press.

MacCannell, D. and J. F. MacCannell. (1982). *The Time of the Sign.* Bloomington: University of Indiana Press.

McBarnett, D. (1981). *Conviction.* London: Macmillan.

McCloskey, R. (1985). *The Rhetoric of Economics.* Madison: University of Wisconsin Press.

McGregor, D. (1960). *The Human Side of Enterprise*. New York: McGraw-Hill.

Mackay, J. (1969). *Information, Mechanism and Meaning*. Cambridge, MA: MIT Press.

McNamara, J. (1967). "Uncertainties in Police Work: The Relevance of Recruits' Background and Training." Pp. 163–252 in *The Police*, edited by D. Bordua. New York: Wiley.

McPhee, R. (1988). "Argument Fields and Organizational Logics." Paper presented to the SCA, New Orleans.

McPhee, R. (1990). "Alternative Approaches to Integrating Longitudinal Case Studies." *Organizational Science* 1(4, November):393–405.

Maines, D. (1977). "Social Organization and Social Structure in Symbolic Interactionist Thought." Pp. 235–59 in *Annual Review of Sociology*. Palo Alto, CA: Annual Reviews Press.

Maines, D. (1988). "Myth, Text, and Interactionist Complicity in the Neglect of Blumer's Macrosociology." *Symbolic Interaction* 11:43–57.

Maines, D., and J. Charlton (1985). "The Negotiated Order Approach to the Analysis of Organizations." Pp. 271–308 in *Foundations of Interpretive Sociology*, edited by H. Faberman and R. Perinbanayagam. Greenwich, CT: JAI Press.

Mannheim, K. (1949). *Essays in the Sociology of Knowledge*. London: Routledge and Kegan Paul.

Manning, P. K. (1977). *Police Work*. Cambridge, MA: MIT Press.

Manning, P. K. (1979a). "The Social Control of Police Work." Pp. 41–65 in *The British Police*, edited by Simon Holdaway. London: Edward Arnold.

Manning, P. K. (1979b). "Metaphors of the Field." *Administrative Science Quarterly* 24 (December):660–71.

Manning, P. K. (1980). *Narcs' Game*. Cambridge, MA: MIT Press.

Manning, P. K. (1982a). "Organisational Work: Enstructuration of the Environment." *British Journal of Sociology* 33:118–39.

Manning, P. K. (1982b). "Producing Drama: Symbolic Communication and the Police." *Symbolic Interaction* 5 (Fall):223–41.

Manning, P. K. (1984). "Community Policing." *American Journal of Police* 3:205–27.

Manning, P. K. (1986). "Signwork." *Human Relations* 39:283–308.

Manning, P. K. (1987a). *Fieldwork and Semiotics*. Beverly Hills, CA: Sage.

Manning, P. K. (1987b). "The Ironies of Compliance." Pp. 293–316 in *Private Policing*, edited by C. Shearing and P. Stenning. Beverly Hills, CA: Sage.

Manning, P. K. (1987c). "Review of Bohme, G., and N. Stehr (eds.), *The Knowledge Society*." *Contemporary Sociology* 17 (July):519–21.

Manning, P. K. (1988a). *Symbolic Communication: Signifying Calls and the Police Response*. Cambridge, MA: MIT Press.

Manning, P. K. (1988b). "Organizational Beliefs and Uncertainty." Pp. 80–98 in *Actions and Beliefs*, edited by N. Fielding. Farnworth, UK: Gower.

Manning, P. K. (1989a). "Studying Policies in the Field." pp. 213–35 in *The Politics of Field Research*, edited by D. Silverman and J. Gubrium. London: Sage.

Manning, P. K. (1989b). "Review of Dick Hobbs, *Doing the Business.*" *American Journal of Sociology* 95 (3), November:779–80.

Manning, P. K. (1990a). "The Challenge of Postmodernism." Paper presented to ASA, Washington, D.C., August.

Manning, P. K. (1990b). "The Police." Pp. 337–57 in *Criminology,* edited by J. Sheley. Belmont, CA: Wadsworth.

Manning, P. K. (1990c). "Ethnographic Semiotic Research." *American Journal of Semiotics* 81/2:27–45.

Cullum-Swan, B., and Manning P. K. (1990). "Some Ethnographic Glimpses of Death." "Unpublished paper, Michigan State University. October.

March, J., and J. Olsen (1976). *Ambiguity and Choice in Organizations.* Bergen, Norway: Universitetsforlegat.

March, J., and H. Simon (1960). *Organizations.* New York: Wiley.

Marcus, G., and M. M. J. Fischer (1986). *Anthropology as Cultural Critique.* Berkeley: University of California Press.

Martin, J. (1990). "Deconstructing Organizational Taboos: The Suppression of Gender Conflict in Organizations." *Organizational Science* 1(4, November):339–59.

Martin, J., Martha S. Feldman, Mary Jo Hatch, and S. Sitkin (1983). "The Uniqueness Paradox in Organizational Stories." *Administrative Science Quarterly* 28:438–53.

Marx, G. (1988). *Undercover.* Berkeley: University of California Press.

Mastrofski, S. (1990). "The Prospects of Change in Police Patrol Work: A Decade in Review." *American Journal of Police* 9:1–79.

Mastrofski, S. (1988). "Community Policing as Reform." Pp. 47–67 in *Community Policing,* edited by J. Greene and S. Mastrofski. New York: Praeger.

Mastrofski, S., and R. Parks (1990). "Improving Observational Studies of Police." *Criminology* 28 (August):475–96.

Mayo, E. (1933). *Human Problems of an Industrial Civilization.* New York: Macmillan.

Mead, G. H. (1934). *Mind, Self and Society.* Chicago: University of Chicago Press.

Meidinger, E. (1987). "A Theory of Regulatory Culture." *Law and Policy* 9 (October):355–86.

Merelman, R. (1969). "The Dramaturgy of Politics." *Sociological Quarterly* 10 (Spring):216–41.

Merelman, R. (1984). *Making Something of Ourselves.* Berkeley: University of California Press.

Meyer, J., and B. Rowan (1977). "Institutionalized Organizations: Formal Structure as Myth and Ceremony." *American Journal of Sociology* 83 (September):340–63.

Michalowski, R. (1985). *Order, Law and Crime.* New York: Random House.

Miller, W. (1977). *Cops and Bobbies.* Chicago: University of Chicago Press.

Mills, C. W. (1951). *White Collar.* New York: Oxford University Press.

Molotch, H., and M. Lester (1974). "News as Purposive Behavior: On the Strategic Use of Routine Events, Accidents and Scandals." *American Sociological Review* 39:101–12.

Molotch, H., and M. Lester (1975). "Accidental News: The Great Oil Spill." *American Journal of Sociology* 81:235–60.

Moore, M., and R. Trojanowicz (1988). "Corporate Strategies for Policing." In *Perspectives on Policing*. U.S. Department of Justice and Harvard University.

Needham, R. (1986). *Exemplars*. Berkeley: University of California Press.

Needham, R. (1983). *The Tranquility of Axioms*. Berkeley: University of California Press.

Norris, C. (1982). *Deconstruction*. London: Methuen.

Nuclear Installations Inspectorate (1982a). *The Work of HM Nuclear Installations Inspectorate*. London: HMSO.

Nuclear Installations Inspectorate (1982b). *Nuclear Safety: HM Nuclear Installations Inspectorate Safety Assessment Principles for Nuclear Power Reactors*. London: HMSO.

O'Donnell, N., and M. Pacanowsky (1983). "The Interpretation of Organizational Cultures." Pp. 225–41 in *Communications in Transition*, edited by M. Mander. New York: Praeger.

O'Riordian, T., R. Kemp, and M. Purdue (1985). "How the Sizewell B Inquiry Is Grappling with the Concept of Acceptable Risk." *Journal of Environmental Psychology* 5:69–85.

O'Riordian, T., R. Kemp, and M. Purdue (1988). *Sizewell B: The Anatomy of the Inquiry*. London: Macmillan.

Orlikowski, W. and D. Robey (1991). "Information Technology and the Structuring of Organizations." *Information Systems Research* 2(2) June:143–169.

Ortega y Gasset (1932). *The Revolt of the Masses*. New York: Norton.

Orton, J. D., and K. Weick (1990). "Loosely Coupled Systems: A Reconceptualization." *Academy of Management Review* 15 (2):203–23.

Ott, J. S. (1989). *The Organizational Culture Perspective*. Pacific Grove: CA: Brooks-Cole.

Pacanowsky, M. (1983). "A Small-Town Cop." Pp. 261–82 in *Communication in Organizations*, edited by L. Putnam and M. Pacanowsky. Beverly Hills, CA: Sage.

Pacanowsky, M., and N. O'Donnell-Trujillo (1984). "Organizational Communication as Cultural Performance." *Communications Monographs* 50 (June):127–48.

Paget, M. A. (1988). *The Unity of Mistakes*. Philadelphia: Temple University Press.

Parsons, T. (1949). *The Structure of Social Action*. Glencoe, IL: Free Press.

Parsons, T. (1951). *The Social System*. Glencoe, IL: Free Press.

Peirce, C. S. (1931). *Collected Papers*. Cambridge, MA: Harvard University Press.

Perinbanayagam, R. (1985). *Signifying Acts*. Carbondale: University of Southern Illinois Press.

Perrow, C. (1984). *Normal Accidents*. New York: Basic Books.

Perrow, C. (1986). *Complex Organizations*. New York: Random House.

Pfeffer, J. (1981). "Management as Symbolic Action." Pp. 1–52 in *Research in Organizational Behavior*, edited by G. Salancik. Greenwich, CT: JAI Press.

Pitt-Rivers, J. (1967). "Contextual Analysis and the Locus of the Model." *Archives of European Sociology* 7 (1):15–34.

Police Foundation (1981). *The Newark Foot Patrol Experiment.* Washington: Police Foundation.

Poole, M. S. (1985). "Communication and Organizational Climates." Pp. 79–108 in *Organizational Communication: Traditional Themes and New Directions,* edited by R. D. McPhee and P. Tompkins. Beverly Hills, CA: Sage.

Potter, J., and M. Wetherell (1987). *Discourse and Social Psychology.* London: Sage.

Power, M. (1985). "Modernism, Postmodernism and Organisation." Unpublished paper presented to conference on organizations, University of Lancaster. February.

Punch, M. (1986). *Conduct Unbecoming.* London: Tavistock.

Putnam, L. (1982). "Paradigms for Organizational Communications Research: An Overview and Synthesis." *Western Journal of Speech Communication* 46 (Spring):192–206.

Putnam, L. (1986). "Contradictions and Paradoxes in Organizations." Pp. 151–67 in *Organization Communication: Emerging Perspectives,* Vol. 1, edited by L. Thayer. Norwood, MA: Ablex.

Quinn, R. E., and K. S. Cameron (eds.) (1988). *Paradox and Transformation: Toward a Theory of Change in Organization and Management.* New York: Ballinger.

Ragin, C., and H. S. Becker (eds.) (forthcoming) *What Is a Case? Issues in the Logic of Social Inquiry.* Berkeley: University of California Press.

Rappaport, R. (1967). "Ritual Regulation of Environmental Relations among a New Guinea People." *Ethnology* 6 (January):17–30.

Rappaport, R. (1968). *Pigs for the Ancestors.* New Haven, CT: Yale University Press.

Rappaport, R. (1971). "Ritual, Sanctity and Cybernetics." *American Anthropologist* 73 (February):59–76.

Rappaport, R. (1984). *Ecology, Meaning and Religion.* Berkeley, CA: North Atlantic Books.

Rawls, A. (1989). "The Interaction Order *sui generis:* Goffman's Contribution to Social Theory." *Sociological Theory* 5:136–49.

Rawls, A. (1990). "Emergent Sociality: A Dialectic of Commitment and Order." *Symbolic Interaction* 13(1):63–82.

Reichers, L. and R. Roberg (1990). "Community Policing: A Critical Review of Underlying Assumptions." *Journal of Police Science and Administration* 17(2):105–14.

Reiss, A. J., Jr. (1971). *The Police and the Public.* New Haven: CT: Yale University Press.

Reiss, A. J., Jr. (1974). "Discretionary Justice." Pp. 679–99 in *The Handbook of Criminal Justice,* edited by Daniel Glaser. Chicago: Rand McNally.

Reiss, A. J., Jr. (1984). "Compliance without Coercion." *University of Michigan Law Review* 83(4):813–19.

Reiss, A. J., Jr., and D. J. Bordua (1967). "Environment and Organization: A Perspective on the Police." Pp. 25–55 in *The Police: Six Sociological Essays,* edited by D. Bordua. New York: Wiley.

Reith, C. (1938). *The Police Idea.* London: Oxford University Press.

Reppetto, T. (1978). *The Blue Parade.* New York: Macmillan.

Richardson, L. (1990). *Writing Strategies*. Newbury Park, CA: Sage.

Roethlisberger, F., and W. J. Dickson (1939). *Management and the Worker*. Cambridge, MA: Harvard University Press.

Rogers, E. (1984). *Silicon Valley Fever*. New York: Basic Books.

Rogers, E., and R. Agarwala Rogers (1976). *Communication in Organizations*. New York: Free Press.

Rorty, R. (1979). *Philosophy and the Mirror of Nature*. Princeton, NJ: Princeton University Press.

Rosaldo, R. (1986). "From the Door of His Tent: The Fieldworker and the Inquisitor." Pp. 77–97 in *Writing Culture: The Poetics and Politics of Ethnography*, edited by J. Clifford and G. Marcus. Berkeley: University of California Press.

Rosaldo, R. (1989). *Culture and Truth*. Boston: Beacon.

Rosch, E., et al. (1976). "Basic Objects in Natural Categories." *Cognitive Psychology* 8:382–439.

Rose, D. (1986). *Patterns of American Culture*. Philadelphia: University of Pennsylvania Press.

Rose, D. (1990). *Living the Ethnographic Life*. Newbury Park, CA: Sage.

Rubinstein, J. (1973). *City Police*. New York: Farrar, Strauss and Giroux.

Ruesch, J., and G. Bateson (1951). *Communication: The Social Matrix of Psychiatry*. New York: Norton.

Rumelhart, D. (1975). "Notes for a Schema for Stories." Pp. 211–36 in *Representation and Understanding: Studies in Cognitive Science*, edited by D. Borow and A. Collins. New York: Academic Press.

Saussure, F. de (1966 [1915]). *Course in General Linguistics*. Edited by C. Bally and A. Sechehaye. Translated by W. Baskin. New York: McGraw-Hill.

Scheppele, Kim Lane (1987). "The Re-Vision of Rape Law: Review of S. Estrich, *Real Rape*." *University of Chicago Law Review* 54 (Summer):1095–16.

Scheppele, Kim Lane (1988). *Legal Secrets*. Chicago: University of Chicago Press.

Scheppele, Kim Lane (1989). "Law without Accidents." Unpublished paper, University of Michigan Law School, Ann Arbor.

Schneiderman, S. (1983). *Lacan: The Death of a Hero*. Cambridge, MA: Harvard University Press.

Schutz, A. (1962). *Collected papers*. Vol. I, *The Problem of Social Reality*, edited by M. Natanson. The Hague: Nijhoff.

Schutz, A. (1964). *Collected Papers*. Vol. II, *Studies in Social Theory*, edited by M. Natanson. The Hague: Nijhoff.

Scott, M., and S. Lyman (1968). "Accounts." *American Sociological Review* 33(2):309–18.

Scott, W. R. (1987). *Organizations: Rational, Natural and Open Systems*. Englewood Cliffs, NJ: Prentice-Hall.

Selznick, P. (1949). *TVA and the Grassroots*. Berkeley: University of California Press.

Selznick, P. (1952). *The Organizational Weapon*. New York: McGraw-Hill.

Shannon, C. E., and W. Weaver (1964 [1949]). *The Mathematical Theory of Communication*. Urbana: University of Illinois Press.

Shapiro, S. (1987). "The Social Organization of Interpersonal Trust." *American Journal of Sociology* 93 (November):623–58.

Sherman, L. W. (forthcoming). "Crack-Ups and Crack-Downs." In *Crime and Justice Annual*, edited by N. Morris and M. Tonry. Chicago: University of Chicago Press.

Siehl, C. and J. Martin (1988). "Measuring Organizational Culture." Pp. 79–103 in *Inside Organizations*, edited by M. Jones, M. Moore, and R. Snyder. Newbury Park, CA: Sage.

Simmel, G. (1954). *The Sociology of Georg Simmel*. Edited by Kurt Wolff. Glencoe, IL: Free Press.

Simon, H. (1969). *The Sciences of the Artificial*. Cambridge, MA: MIT Press.

Slovak, J. (1986). *Styles of Urban Policing*. New York: New York University Press.

Starr, P. (1983). *The Social Transformation of American Medicine*. New York: Basic Books.

Stead, J. (ed.) (1977). *Pioneers in Policing*. Montclair, NJ: Patterson Smith.

Stenning, P., and C. Shearing (eds.) (1987). *Private Policing*. Newbury Park, CA: Sage.

Stinchcombe, A. L. (1964). "Institutions of Privacy in the Determination of Police Administrative Practice." *American Journal of Sociology* 69:150–60.

Stinchcombe, A. L. (1990). *Information and Organizations*. Berkeley: University of California Press.

Stoller, P. (1989). *The Taste of Ethnographic Things*. Philadelphia: University of Pennsylvania Press.

Stone, G. (1962). "Appearance and the Self." Pp. 86–118 in *Human Behaviour and Social Processes*, edited by A. Rose. Boston: Houghton-Mifflin.

Strauss, A. (1987). *Qualitative Analysis for Social Scientists*. New York: Cambridge University Press.

Strine, M. S., and M. E. Pacanowsky (1985). "How to Read Interpretive Accounts of Organizational Life: Narrative Bases of Textual Authority." *Southern Speech Communication Journal* 50 (3):283–97.

Sudnow, D. (1965). "Normal Crimes." *Social Problems* 12 (Winter):255–76.

Suttles, G. (1968). *The Social Order of the Slum*. Chicago: University of Chicago Press.

Swidler, A. (1986). "Culture in Action: Symbols and Strategems." *American Sociological Review* 51 (April):273–86.

Sykes, R. E., and E. E. Brent (1983). *Policing: A Social Behaviorist Perspective*. New Brunswick, NJ: Rutgers University Press.

Sypher, W. (1963). *Loss of the Self in Modern Literature and Art*. New York: Vintage.

Tausky, C., and R. Dubin (1965). "Career Anchorages: Managerial Mobility Orientations." *American Sociological Review* 30:725–35.

Taylor, F. (1911). *Principles of Scientific Management*. New York: Harper.

Thomas, W. I., and F. Znaniecki (1918–20). *The Polish Peasant*. Chicago: University of Chicago Press.

Toulmin, S. (1958). *Uses of Argument*. Cambridge: Cambridge University Press.

Trujillo, N., and G. Dionisopoulos (1987). "Cop Talk, Police Stories, and the Social Construction of the Organizational Drama." *Central States Speech Journal* 38 (Fall/Winter):196–209.

Tyler, S. (1987). *The Unspeakable: Discourse, Dialogue and Rhetoric in the Postmodern World*. Madison: University of Wisconsin Press.

Vandeberg, Ekdom L. H., and N. Trujillo (1989). *Organizational Life on Television*. New York: Ablex.

Van Maanen, J. (1974). "Working the Street. . . ." Pp. 83–130 in *Prospects for Reform in Criminal Justice*, edited by H. Jacob. Newbury Park, CA: Sage.

Van Maanen, J. (1975). "Police Socialization: A Longitudinal Examination of Job Attitudes in an Urban Police Department." *Administrative Science Quarterly* 20 (June):207–28.

Van Maanen, J. (ed.) (1979). *Qualitative Methods*. Beverly Hills, CA: Sage.

Van Maanen, J. (1983). "The Boss: First Line Supervision in an American Police Agency." Pp. 227–50 in *Control in the Police Organization*, edited by M. Punch. Cambridge, MA: MIT Press.

Van Maanen, J. (1988). *Tales of the Field*. Chicago: University of Chicago Press.

Van Maanen, J. (1989). "Review of R. Jackall, *Moral Mazes*." *Administrative Science Quarterly* 34 (June):311–15.

Van Maanen, J. (ed.) (1990). "The Presentation of Ethnographic Research." *Journal of Contemporary Ethnography* (Special issue) 19 (April).

Van Maanen, J. (ed.) (1992). *Trade Secrets*. Newbury Park, CA: Sage.

Van Maanen, J., and S. Barley (1985). "Cultural Organizations: Fragments of a Theory." Pp. 31–53 in *Organizational Culture*, edited by B. Frost et al. Beverly Hills, CA: Sage.

Von Bertalanffy, L. (1968). *General Systems Theory*. New York: Braziller.

Waegel, W. (1981). "Case Routinization in Investigative Police Work." *Social Problems* 28 (February):263–75.

Wagner-Pacifici, R. (1986). *The Moro Morality Play*. Chicago: University of Chicago Press.

Watzlawick, P., J. H. Beavin, and D. Jackson (1967). *The Pragmatics of Human Communication*. New York: Norton.

Weber, M. (1947). *The Theory of Economic and Social Organization*. Translated with an introduction by T. Parsons. Oxford: Oxford University Press.

Weick, K. (1976). "Educational Organizations as Loosely Coupled Systems." *Administrative Science Quarterly* 21:1–19.

Weick, K. (1979). *The Social Psychology of Organizing*. 2d ed. Reading, MA: Addison-Wesley.

Weick, K. and M. Bougon (1980). "Organizations as Cause Maps." Pp. 102–135 in *Social Cognition in Organizations*, edited by H. P. Sims, Jr. and D. A. Gioia. San Francisco: Josey-Bass.

Weick, K. (1988). "Technology as Equivoque: Sense-making in New Technologies." Pp. 1–44 in *Technology and Organizations*, edited by P. S. Goodman and L. Sproull. San Francisco: Josey-Bass.

Weick, K. (1991). "Turning Context into Text: An Academic Life as Data." Unpublished paper, University of Michigan, Ann Arbor. Spring.

Wetheritt, M. (ed.) (1988). *Innovations in Policing*. London: Croom-Helm.

White, H. (1980). *Tropics of Discourse*. Baltimore, MD: Johns Hopkins University Press.

Williams, B. (1981). "Moral Luck." Pp. 20–39 in *Ethics and the Limits of Philosophy*, Cambridge: Cambridge University Press.

Williams, J., L. J. Redlinger, and P. K. Manning (1979). *Police Narcotics Control*. Washington: NIJ/USGPO.

Williamson, O. (1976). *Markets and Hierarchies*. New York: Free Press.

Wilson, J. Q. (1968). *Varieties of Police Behavior*. Cambridge: Harvard University Press.

Wilson, J. Q. (1978). *The Investigators*. New York: Basic Books.

Wittgenstein, L. (1969). *On Certainty*. Edited by G. E. M. Anscombe and G. von Wright. Translated by D. Paul and G. E. M. Anscombe. Oxford: Blackwell.

Wuthnow, R. (1987). *Meaning and Moral Order*. Berkeley: University of California Press.

Wycoff, M. A. (1988). "The Benefits of Community Policing: Evidence and Conjecture." Pp. 101–120 in *Community Policing* edited by J. Greene and S. Mastrofski. New York: Praeger.

Young, R. (1988). "Is Population Ecology a Useful Paradigm for the Study of Organizations?" *American Journal of Sociology* 94:1–24.

Index

Actions, 6
American policing, 136–141 (*See also* Policing)

Bureaucracy, 91

"Cap" example, 211–217
Code analysis (*See* Semiotic analysis)
Code of posed features, 65–66
Communication (*See also* External communication; Internal communication; Organizational communication)
  ambiguity of, 46
  definition of, 4, 12
  modern, 25
  in postmodern societies, 23–26
  in social context, 17–18, 32–33
  in societies, changes in, 18–19
  of risks, 167–170
  studies, 89
Confessional tales, 197
Connotations, 49
Contradictions, 46–48
Coupling (*See* Loose coupling; Tight coupling)
Crisis communication
  definition of, 135
  in policing, 146, 147, 148–150

Culture (*See also* Ethnography)
  definition of, 4
  occupational
    policing and, 125–128
    tight coupling and, 128–131
  organizational, 121–125
  organizational communication and, 199–200

Dallas police killing, 149–150
Decision-making, 40–41, 141
Deconstruction, 202–204
Denotations, 44–45
Discourse analysis
  concepts of, 50–51
  definition of, 50
  focus of discourse and, 165–167
  Nuclear Installations Inspectorate and, 173–174
  postmodernism and, 201–202
  research and, 36, 50–53
  risk communication and, 167–170
Double bind
  concept of, 46–48, 115–119
  organizations and, 118–119
  role of, 46–48
Drama of control, 141–145
Dramaturgy
  definition of, 5
  drama of control and, 141–145

245